Cfine Cooking

ANNUAL

a year of great recipes, tips & techniques

From the Editors and Contributors of *Fine Cooking*

The Taunton Press

The Taunton Press, Inc., 63 South Main Street, PO Box 5506, Newtown, CT 06470-5506
e-mail: tp@taunton.com

EDITORS: Martha Holmberg, Pam Hoenig
JACKET/COVER DESIGN: Alison Wilkes
INTERIOR DESIGN: Alison Wilkes
LAYOUT: David Giammattei
PRINCIPAL PHOTOGRAPHER: Scott Phillips
ADDITIONAL PHOTO CREDITS: Ben Fink, pp. 7, 51, 196, 349; Martha Holmberg, p. 81 top;
Amy Albert, p. 187, 337; Sarah Jay, p. 273 left, p. 291; Mark Ferri, p. 313; Steve Hunter, p. 316

LIBRARY OF CONGRESS CATALOGING-IN-PUBLICATION DATA

Fine Cooking Annual: a year of great recipes, tips & techniques from the editors of Fine cooking /
 photography by Scott Phillips.
      p. cm.
  Includes bibliographical references and index.
  ISBN-13: 978-1-56158-916-6 (alk. paper)
  ISBN-10: 1-56158-916-0 (alk. paper)
  1. Cookery. I. Fine cooking.
  TX651.B4835 2006
  641.5--DC22

                          2006018123

Printed in China
10 9 8 7 6 5 4 3 2 1

The following manufacturer's/names appearing in *Fine Cooking Annual* are trademarks: Anchor Steam Liberty
Ale®; Bundt®; Colman's® mustard powder; Corona® beer; Dos Equis® Amber beer; Lindt® chocolate;
Muir Glen® tomatoes; Pepperidge Farm® Classic white bread; Pyrex®; Shiner Bock® beer; Tabasco® pepper
sauce, Worcestershire® sauce

The Taunton Press publishes *Fine Cooking*, the magazine for people who love to cook.

342

18, 19, 24

182

Contents

55

319

All the good stuff in one place

I'm biased, I realize. But the only thing I can think of that's better than a fresh new hot-off-the-presses issue of *Fine Cooking* magazine is a big, beautiful book full of nearly a year's worth of *Fine Cooking* recipes. For the first time ever, we've gathered the best starters, salads, side dishes, sweets, soups, stews—you name it—from the past year into one volume. And we didn't forget to include the valuable tips, techniques, ingredient profiles, and helpful photos that make *Fine Cooking* recipes work so well.

If you've never tried a *Fine Cooking* recipe, I hope you'll discover the difference after making a few from this book. For instance, every recipe has a "doneness test"—the clues to let you know when a dish looks, smells, or feels done. Every recipe has a realistic but inspiring photo of the finished dish, so you can see what the food will really look like.

But the best part is that our recipes are for the kind of food you love to make—and that your friends love to eat. You might just have to get used to everyone calling you a great cook.

Happy cooking!

Susie Middleton

Susie Middleton, Editor, *Fine Cooking*

P.S. For more great recipes like these, pick up the latest copy of *Fine Cooking* on your nearest newsstand, or check out www.finecooking.com.

1
Starters & Snacks

p33

p30

Apple, Blue Cheese & Hazelnut Salad on Endive Leaves (recipe on page 19)

Roasted Potato Slices with Romesco Sauce (recipe on page 18)

Garlic Roasted Shrimp Cocktail (recipe on page 24)

Olive Oil–Fried Almonds

Yields 2 cups.

2 cups blanched almonds

1 cup extra-virgin olive oil

8 large fresh sage leaves

2 tablespoons fresh rosemary leaves

1 tablespoon fresh thyme leaves

1 teaspoon sea salt

The almonds and herbs are crisp, salty, and sure to whet your appetite. Canned cocktail nuts don't hold a candle to these.

Set a metal strainer over a large heatproof bowl to quickly drain the almonds at the end of cooking. Put the almonds and olive oil in a 3- or 4-quart saucepan with a lid (the nuts and oil should fill no more than one-third of the pot). Set the pot over medium heat, stirring almost constantly until the almonds are lightly golden, 3 to 10 minutes, depending on your stove and pot. Toss in the sage, rosemary, and thyme simultaneously and cover the pot immediately with the lid to prevent the oil from spattering. Remove the pot from the heat. The herbs will make a popping sound as they cook.

After the popping dies down, remove the lid and immediately pour the almonds into the strainer. Spread the drained almonds on a rimmed baking sheet and toss with the salt. When they're thoroughly cooled, store them in an airtight plastic container at room temperature. *—Maria Helm Sinskey*

Spiced Mixed Nuts

Yields 4 cups.

1 pound (4 cups) mixed unsalted whole nuts (such as cashews, macadamias, walnuts, pecans, or almonds)

½ teaspoon ground coriander

½ teaspoon ground cumin

2 tablespoons unsalted butter

2 tablespoons dark brown sugar

2 tablespoons chopped fresh rosemary

¼ teaspoon cayenne

1½ teaspoons kosher salt; more as needed

These sweet-savory nuts are wonderful as a snack or tossed into a salad. Have fun playing with the types of nut you use (but pass on Brazil nuts— their high oil content makes the coating slide off). You can make these up to a week ahead.

Position a rack in the center of the oven and heat the oven to 350°F. Scatter the nuts on a rimmed baking sheet and bake, shaking the sheet a couple of times during baking, until the nuts are nicely toasted, 10 to 15 minutes.

Meanwhile, set a small, heavy skillet over medium-high heat. Sprinkle in the coriander and cumin and toast until aromatic, about 30 seconds. Remove the pan from the heat and add the butter, brown sugar, rosemary, and cayenne. Return the skillet to low heat and stir until the butter melts and the sugar dissolves, 2 to 2½ minutes. Keep warm.

Tip the nuts into a large warmed bowl, pour the warm spiced butter over the nuts, and add the salt. Stir until the nuts are well coated. Taste for seasoning and add more salt if necessary. Let the nuts cool completely.

The nuts can be made up to a week in advance; store in an airtight container. *—Jennifer McLagan*

Zesty Lemon Olives

Lemon and herbs turn ordinary olives into something special. Make a batch or two of these to have on hand for impromptu gatherings; they'll keep in the refrigerator for a few weeks.

If using brine-packed olives, drain them. In a medium bowl, combine the olives, salt, peppercorns, bay leaves, herb sprigs, fennel seeds, garlic, and red pepper flakes, if using. Zest the lemons in whatever size zest you like; a mix of finely grated zest for the brightest flavor and larger strips for color is nice. Add the zest and oil to the olives and mix well. Pour and scrape into a covered jar and refrigerate for at least a half hour (longer is even better) to let the flavors mingle before serving. *—Ruth Lively*

Yields 1 pint.

1 pint oil- or brine-packed olives, green or black or a mix

¼ teaspoon kosher salt

½ teaspoon black peppercorns

3 bay leaves

Several sprigs fresh rosemary or thyme

½ teaspoon fennel seeds, lightly crushed

4 or 5 cloves garlic, halved lengthwise

Big pinch red pepper flakes (optional)

2 medium lemons

3 tablespoons extra-virgin olive oil

Cilantro-Lime Guacamole

Serves four to six as a dip.

2 medium ripe avocados

2 to 3 tablespoons fresh lime juice

¾ teaspoon kosher salt

½ teaspoon ground coriander

Pinch ground cumin

3 to 4 tablespoons chopped fresh cilantro

1 teaspoon minced fresh jalapeño

Tortilla chips for serving

Taste your guacamole as you're making it. Avocados can take a fair amount of lime juice and cilantro, but since both of those ingredients can vary in strength, it's a good idea to taste as you go.

Halve the avocados, pit them, and scoop the flesh with a large spoon into a small mixing bowl. Sprinkle the lime juice over the avocados, add the salt, coriander, and cumin, and use a wooden spoon to break up the avocados, stirring until they're coarsely mashed. Stir in the cilantro and jalapeño. Transfer to a small serving bowl and serve with the tortilla chips. *—Ruth Lively*

Golden Onion & Thyme Dip

One bite of this fresh-flavored dip and you'll forget all about that packaged soup mix you once knew. This dip tastes great the minute it's made but will become more strongly flavored if allowed to sit for a little while before serving.

Heat the oil in a large skillet over medium-high heat. Add the onion, season with the salt, and sauté, stirring often, until the onion softens completely and starts to brown, about 9 minutes. Transfer to a food processor and add the cream cheese, sour cream, thyme, and cayenne. Pulse until the mixture is well combined. Season with salt and pepper to taste. Refrigerate until ready to serve. Offer potato chips, crackers, or toasted pita chips alongside.

—Tony Rosenfeld

Yields about 2¼ cups.

- 2 tablespoons extra-virgin olive oil
- 1 large Spanish or 2 large yellow onions (about 1 pound total), finely diced
- ½ teaspoon kosher salt; more as needed
- One 8-ounce package cream cheese
- 6 tablespoons sour cream
- 1 scant tablespoon fresh thyme leaves, chopped, or 1½ teaspoons dried
- Pinch cayenne
- Freshly ground black pepper
- Potato chips, crackers, or toasted pita chips for serving

Hummus with Mellow Garlic & Cumin

Yields about 3 cups.

⅓ cup plus 1 tablespoon extra-virgin olive oil

4 large cloves garlic, thinly sliced

2 teaspoons ground cumin

Two 15.5-ounce cans chickpeas, drained and rinsed

3 tablespoons tahini

3 tablespoons fresh lemon juice; more to taste

1 tablespoon soy sauce

½ teaspoon kosher salt; more as needed

If you have ever bought the Middle Eastern chickpea dip known as hummus at the supermarket, you will be delighted by how much better this fresh (and quick to make) hummus tastes. Tahini, a paste made of ground sesame seeds, is sold in cans and jars at specialty stores and at many supermarkets, usually in the international aisle. Serve hummus with pita bread or cucumber rounds or other vegetables for dipping.

Combine ⅓ cup of the oil with the garlic and cumin in a small saucepan. Set over medium-low heat and cook until the garlic softens, about 3 minutes from when you can hear the garlic bubbling quickly. Don't let the garlic brown. Take the pan off the heat and let cool completely.

Put the chickpeas, tahini, lemon juice, soy sauce, and salt in a food processor. Use a fork to fish the softened garlic out of the oil and transfer it to the processor (reserve the oil). Turn the machine on, let it run for about 20 seconds, and then start slowly pouring the cumin-flavored oil through the machine's feed tube. Be sure to scrape the pan with a rubber spatula to get all of the cumin and oil. Pour ¼ cup cool water down the tube. Stop the machine, scrape the sides of the bowl, and continue processing until the hummus is creamy and almost smooth. Season to taste with more salt and lemon juice, if you like. For best results, let the hummus sit at room temperature for an hour or two before serving so the flavors can meld. Or better yet, make it a day ahead and refrigerate. Return it to room temperature and adjust the seasonings before serving. To serve, spread the hummus in a shallow dish and drizzle with the remaining 1 tablespoon oil. It keeps for about a week in the refrigerator. *—Jennifer Armentrout*

Crudités with Creamy Roquefort Dip

Serves sixteen.

Kosher salt

1 pound broccoli

1 pound small or medium carrots, preferably with green tops

1 bunch celery

1 medium head radicchio

1 medium fennel bulb, fronds trimmed

8 radishes, preferably with green tops

Creamy Roquefort Dip (recipe follows)

Creamy Roquefort Dip

Yields about 2½ cups dip.

1 medium clove garlic

Kosher salt and freshly ground black pepper

½ pound Roquefort cheese

1½ cups crème fraîche (available in the specialty cheese section of some supermarkets) or sour cream

½ cup heavy cream

Resist the temptation to buy just any blue cheese. Roquefort is softer and creamier than most domestic blue cheeses, and usually milder than Gorgonzola.

Make the dip: In mortar or with the flat side of a chef's knife, mash the garlic to a paste with a pinch of salt. Transfer to a medium bowl, add the Roquefort and roughly mash the cheese with the back of a spoon. Stir in the crème fraîche and several grinds of pepper, then add the cream until the consistency is slightly thinner than sour cream. Taste and add more salt and pepper if needed. Refrigerate until shortly before serving. (The dip will thicken in the refrigerator but will return to its original consistency as it comes to room temperature.) —*Tasha DeSerio*

Rich, tangy Roquefort provides a delicious foil for a variety of fresh, bite-size vegetables. Both the dip and the veggies can be prepared a day ahead.

Prep the vegetables: Combine 4 quarts water and ¼ cup kosher salt in a large pot and bring to a boil over high heat. Meanwhile, trim most of the stem off the broccoli to separate the florets. Using a small, sharp knife, trim the stem of each floret so it's 1½ to 2 inches long. Starting at the top of the stem, cut through the stem lengthwise and divide the floret in half. Repeat the process, dividing each floret into two to four pieces, until the top of each floret is about the size of a quarter. Have ready a bowl of ice water. Boil the florets until they turn bright green, about 1 minute. Drain in a colander and then plunge the florets into the ice water. Drain again.

Trim the carrot tops, but leave about 1½ inches of the green tops intact. Peel the carrots and cut them lengthwise into halves, quarters, or sixths, depending on the size.

Remove the tough outer celery ribs; reserve for another use. Trim the tops of the ribs and about 1½ inches from the root end. Starting with the large ribs, cut each lengthwise into long, thin sticks about ¼ inch wide. Trim the large leaves from the celery heart and cut each rib in the same manner, preserving as much of the tender leaves as possible.

Discard the outer leaves of the radicchio. Trim the root end and cut the radicchio in half through the core. Cut each half into ¼-inch-thick wedges—the core should hold each wedge intact. Trim any stalks from the top of the fennel bulb and cut it in the same manner as the radicchio, but don't discard the outer layers unless they're discolored.

Trim the tops of the radishes, leaving about 1 inch of the green tops. (If the leaves are especially nice, leave a few intact for garnish.) Quarter each radish lengthwise.

Refrigerate the vegetables in separate zip-top bags. When ready to serve, arrange the vegetables on a large platter or in a shallow basket. Mist lightly with water to keep them looking fresh. Serve with the dip on the side. —*Tasha DeSerio*

Mrs. Lenkh's Cheese Sablés

**Yields about 43 two-inch
hexagons, plus scraps.**

2 cups unbleached all-purpose
flour

1 teaspoon table salt

⅛ teaspoon cayenne

⅛ teaspoon baking powder

14 tablespoons cold unsalted
butter, cut into chunks

1½ cups finely grated sharp
Cheddar cheese

½ cup finely grated Parmigiano-
Reggiano cheese

1 large egg, lightly beaten

½ cup finely chopped pecans or
walnuts (optional)

1 large egg yolk mixed with
a pinch of paprika and
½ teaspoon water, as a glaze

Kosher or sea salt for sprinkling

**These are great with drinks and go especially well with dry and off-dry
sparkling wines. The dough keeps for two days in the refrigerator, and for
months in the freezer (thaw it in the fridge before using).**

Put the flour, table salt, cayenne, and baking powder in a food processor.
Pulse to combine. Add the butter and pulse again until the butter is in small
pieces, six to eight 1-second pulses. Add the cheeses, pulse, and, finally, add
the egg and pulse until the mixture just starts to come together.

Dump the dough on an unfloured surface. If you're using nuts, sprinkle
them on the pile of dough. Knead by lightly smearing the ingredients together
as you push them away from you with the heel of your hand until the dough
is cohesive. Shape the dough into a flat disk, wrap in plastic, and chill for an
hour or two to let the butter firm.

Position racks in the top and bottom thirds of the oven. Heat the oven to
400°F. On a lightly floured surface, roll out the dough to about ¼ inch thick.
Stamp out shapes or cut shapes with a knife. Arrange 1 inch apart on two
ungreased baking sheets. Reroll the scraps once and stamp again.

Brush with the glaze and sprinkle lightly with kosher or sea salt. Bake until
golden brown and thoroughly cooked inside, about 14 minutes, rotating the
sheets from front to back and top to bottom about halfway through. To test,
break one in half and look to see if the center still looks doughy. If so, bake
for a few more minutes, but be careful not to overbake. Let cool on a rack and
store only when completely cool. —*Martha Holmberg*

Sesame-Parmesan Twists

If you want to make these more than two hours ahead, store them in an airtight container. But be warned: The twists are so tasty you may not have many left when serving time rolls around.

Heat the oven to 425°F. In a small bowl, mix the Parmigiano, sesame seeds, cayenne, chili powder, thyme, and salt. On a lightly floured surface, roll one of the pastry sheets to a 10x14-inch rectangle. Brush evenly with the egg wash and cut in half lengthwise to make two 5x14-inch strips. Distribute half the cheese filling over one strip and lay the second strip on top, egg wash side down. Press the strips together with the rolling pin to fuse the two sheets. Cut the strip crosswise into 28 strips ½ inch wide. Lift a strip, twist it three times, and lay it on an ungreased baking sheet, pressing each end to keep the twists from unwinding during baking. Repeat with the second pastry sheet and the remaining filling.

Bake the twists until puffed, light brown, and look dry throughout, 12 to 14 minutes. Test one by biting it to make sure it isn't doughy in the center.

Let the twists cool on a rack and serve as soon as they're cool, or within a couple of hours if possible. —Martha Holmberg

Yields 56 five-inch twists.

⅔ cup finely grated Parmigiano-Reggiano cheese

¼ cup sesame seeds, lightly toasted

¼ teaspoon cayenne

¼ teaspoon chili powder

¼ teaspoon dried thyme, crumbled

½ teaspoon kosher salt

2 sheets frozen puff pastry, thawed

1 large egg, beaten with a few drops water and a pinch of salt

Roasted Potato Slices with Romesco Sauce

Yields about 48 hors d'oeuvres.

1 medium plum tomato (about ¼ pound), cored and quartered

16 whole almonds, toasted

1 tablespoon coarsely chopped jarred roasted red pepper

2 small cloves garlic

⅛ teaspoon cayenne

Kosher salt and freshly ground black pepper

1 tablespoon red-wine vinegar

¼ cup extra-virgin olive oil

¾ pound small red potatoes (1 to 2 inches in diameter), rinsed and dried

Finely grated zest of 2 medium lemons

¼ cup fresh flat-leaf parsley leaves

The sauce can be made up to three days ahead and refrigerated. Before using, bring it to room temperature and stir well.

Set a rack in the top third of the oven; heat the oven to 450°F.

Put the tomato, almonds, roasted red pepper, garlic, cayenne, ¼ teaspoon kosher salt, and a few grinds of black pepper in a food processor. Process, scraping the bowl as needed, until the mixture is somewhat smooth, about 1 minute. Add the vinegar and 1 tablespoon of the olive oil and process until well incorporated. Taste and add more salt if needed.

Trim the ends off of each potato and cut the potatoes crosswise into ⅛- to ¼-inch slices. In a bowl, toss the potatoes with the remaining 3 tablespoons olive oil and 1 teaspoon kosher salt to coat well. Lay the slices in a single layer on a baking sheet. Roast the potatoes, turning the slices with a spatula and rotating the baking sheet halfway through roasting, until golden brown, 20 to 30 minutes. Let the potatoes cool slightly.

To serve, arrange the potato slices on a serving platter; blot with a paper towel if they look oily. Top each slice with a generous ¼ teaspoon of the romesco sauce (you may not use all the sauce). Garnish each hors d'oeuvre with a tiny pinch of lemon zest and a parsley leaf. *—Laura Werlin*

Apple, Blue Cheese & Hazelnut Salad on Endive Leaves

To bring this hors d'oeuvre to a party, pack the apple mixture, the endive, and the hazelnuts separately and quickly assemble them once you arrive (don't make the apple mixture more than an hour ahead). Also, you can toast and chop the hazelnuts for up to one month in advance and freeze them in an airtight container.

In a medium bowl, combine the apple, blue cheese, celery, mayonnaise, and lemon juice. Stir gently to combine. Season to taste with salt.

To assemble, mound a small spoonful of the apple mixture in each endive leaf. Sprinkle with the hazelnuts and serve. –*Laura Werlin*

Yields 35 to 40 hors d'oeuvres.

1 large (about 8-ounce) tart-sweet red apple, such as Gala or Braeburn, cored and cut into ⅛-inch dice

3 ounces blue cheese, crumbled (to yield about ¾ cup)

¾ cup finely chopped celery (from about 2 large ribs)

3 tablespoons mayonnaise

1 tablespoon fresh lemon juice

Kosher salt

5 Belgian endives, leaves separated; smallest leaves reserved for another use

½ cup hazelnuts, toasted and coarsely chopped

Spinach & Parmesan Stuffed Mushrooms

Serves six as an appetizer; yields about 24 mushrooms.

1 pound medium white mushrooms (about 24), wiped clean

5 tablespoons extra-virgin olive oil

Kosher salt and freshly ground black pepper

3 slices coarse-grained bread

4 scallions (white and green parts), thinly sliced

¼ cup dry sherry

6 ounces fresh baby spinach, roughly chopped

¼ cup heavy cream

⅓ cup plus 1 tablespoon freshly grated Parmigiano-Reggiano cheese

½ lemon

Fresh breadcrumbs take just seconds to make in a food processor; for best results use coarse-grained bread, not the really soft stuff.

Set an oven rack 6 inches from the top element and heat the broiler to high. Completely remove the mushroom stems; thinly slice the stems. Set the mushroom caps stem side up on a heavy rimmed baking sheet, drizzle with 1½ tablespoons of the oil, and sprinkle with ½ teaspoon kosher salt and a few grinds of pepper. Broil until the mushrooms are brown and completely tender, 6 to 7 minutes.

Pulse the bread in a food processor until it forms uniform crumbs. In a large, heavy sauté pan, heat 2 tablespoons of the oil over medium-high heat. Add the breadcrumbs and ¼ teaspoon kosher salt, and cook, stirring constantly, until the breadcrumbs crisp and turn light brown, 4 to 5 minutes. Transfer to a plate and wipe the pan clean. Return the pan to high heat, add the remaining 1½ tablespoon oil and the scallions, and sauté until browned and softened, about 2 minutes. Add the mushroom stems and ½ teaspoon salt. Cook, stirring, until the stems soften and brown, about 3 minutes. Add the sherry and cook until almost evaporated, 30 to 60 seconds. Add the spinach and stir until it wilts, about 1 minute. Add the cream and ⅓ cup of the Parmigiano, reduce the heat to medium, and cook until the cream reduces slightly, about 2 minutes. Taste for salt and pepper; let cool.

Discard any liquid that may have accumulated in the mushroom caps. Mound the spinach mixture into the caps; top with the breadcrumbs (press them into the filling) and the remaining 1 tablespoon Parmigiano. (The mushrooms can be prepared to this point for up to two days ahead and chilled.)

Heat the broiler to high. Broil the caps until the breadcrumbs brown a little more and the mushrooms heat through, 1 to 3 minutes. Squeeze the lemon over the caps. Serve immediately. *–Tony Rosenfeld*

Prosciutto-Wrapped Greens

Serves eight.

3 tablespoons extra-virgin olive oil

2 teaspoons red-wine vinegar

2 teaspoons fresh lemon juice

½ teaspoon Dijon mustard

¼ pound mesclun or arugula, washed and spun dry

Kosher salt and freshly ground black pepper

2 tablespoons freshly grated Parmigiano-Reggiano cheese

12 thin slices prosciutto

This little bite, with its contrasting flavors and textures (smooth, salty prosciutto versus crisp, peppery greens) will surely stimulate your appetite. If the prosciutto is very long, cut each piece in half crosswise first.

In a small bowl, whisk the olive oil, vinegar, lemon juice, and mustard. Put the mesclun or arugula in a medium bowl and season with a generous pinch of salt and pepper. Add the Parmigiano to the greens and gently toss with just enough of the vinaigrette to coat the greens lightly. Taste for salt and pepper.

Set a slice of prosciutto on a work surface and put a small handful of greens at the narrow end of the meat. Squeeze the greens together and roll the prosciutto into a tight log. Cut the log into 2-inch pieces on the diagonal (two or three pieces, depending on the width of the prosciutto). Repeat with the remaining prosciutto and greens and serve. —*Tasha DeSerio*

Smoked Salmon Rolls

You can mix the cream cheese up to one day ahead and refrigerate it in an airtight container. Bring it to room temperature before using. The rolls can be assembled, covered, and refrigerated up to 4 hours ahead. Let stand at room temperature for about 15 minutes before serving.

In a small bowl, mix the cream cheese, lemon juice, zest, chives, and ⅛ teaspoon kosher salt.

To assemble, lay an 8- or 9-inch-long sheet of plastic wrap on the counter. Slightly overlap slices of salmon on the plastic to create a rectangle measuring about 3½ x 7 inches. The long side of the rectangle should be parallel to the edge of your work surface. Cover with another sheet of plastic and press gently with your hands or a flat spatula to encourage the salmon to stick together. Remove the top sheet of plastic. Using a thin metal offset spatula or a butter knife, spread about 2 tablespoons of the cream cheese mixture on the salmon, leaving a ½-inch border along the long sides. Arrange about a third of the fennel shavings lengthwise on the lower half of the salmon. Sprinkle the fennel lightly with salt. Starting at the long side closest to you and using the plastic wrap as an aid, gently roll up the salmon to enclose the filling. Gently press the roll together at the seams. Transfer the roll to a cutting board and cut into 6 pieces. Repeat with the remaining salmon, cream cheese mixture, and fennel to make 2 more rolls. You may have extra salmon or fennel. Arrange the rolls on a platter, cut side up. Garnish with the chopped fennel fronds. —*Laura Werlin*

Yields 18 hors d'oeuvres.

¼ pound cream cheese, at room temperature

2 teaspoons fresh lemon juice

1 teaspoon finely grated lemon zest

2 tablespoons plus 2 teaspoons thinly sliced fresh chives

Kosher salt

¾ cup shaved fresh fennel

½ pound thinly sliced smoked salmon (not hot-smoked)

1 tablespoon finely chopped fennel fronds

Garlic Roasted Shrimp Cocktail

Serves four to six.

1½ pounds jumbo shrimp (16-20 count), shells peeled, tails left on

2 cloves garlic, finely chopped (about 1 tablespoon)

2 tablespoons extra-virgin olive oil

½ teaspoon kosher salt

¼ teaspoon cracked black pepper

Cocktail Sauce with Red Onion & Jalapeño (recipe follows)

Roasting the shrimp with garlic gives them a punch that stands up to a spicy cocktail sauce. This is a wonderful way to cook shrimp for many other dishes, too. Roast the shrimp with garlic, chill and chop them, and then fold them into a shrimp salad. Or roast and add them at the last minute to a simple pasta dish.

Heat the oven to 450°F. Remove the vein from the shrimp, if necessary. In a large bowl, toss the shrimp with the garlic, olive oil, salt, and pepper. Spread the shrimp on a heavy-duty rimmed baking sheet in a single layer. Roast for 3 minutes, turn the shrimp over with tongs, and continue roasting until the shrimp are opaque and firm, another 2 to 4 minutes. Transfer the shrimp to a shallow dish, cover partially, and refrigerate. When the shrimp are thoroughly chilled (after about 2 hours), serve them with cocktail sauce. *–Rory Trovato*

Cocktail Sauce with Red Onion & Jalapeño

Yields about 1¼ cups.

½ cup tomato ketchup

½ cup chili sauce

¼ cup grated red onion (from about ¼ medium onion; using the large holes on a box grater)

½ teaspoon finely chopped fresh jalapeño

3 tablespoons prepared horseradish

1 tablespoon fresh lemon juice; more to taste

⅛ teaspoon kosher salt; more to taste

Put all the ingredients in a bowl and stir to combine. Chill, covered, until ready to use. This sauce is best made a day in advance and keeps well for up to a week. Just before serving, taste and add more lemon juice and salt as needed.

Seared Tuna with Tropical Salsa

Yields about 48 hors d'oeuvres.

8 to 9 ounces fresh tuna fillet

1 tablespoon vegetable or olive oil

Kosher salt and freshly ground black pepper

¾ cup finely diced fresh pineapple

4 scallions (white and light green parts only), thinly sliced

2½ tablespoons fresh lime juice

1½ tablespoons soy sauce

1 teaspoon minced fresh ginger

1 small ripe avocado (about 6 ounces), finely diced

½ cup coarsely chopped fresh cilantro leaves; plus small whole leaves for garnish

One 3.5-ounce package plain rice crackers

The smaller you can cut the avocado, the easier it will be to top the tuna with the salsa…and for the diner to eat the hors d'oeuvre. While you want the avocado ripe enough to have a full mellow flavor, if it's too ripe, it will be tricky to dice neatly.

Cut the tuna into long, fat, squared-off strips or "logs" 1 to 1½ inches thick. Coat the tuna with the oil and season lightly with salt and pepper. Set a 10-inch heavy-duty skillet over high heat. When the pan is very hot, after 2 to 3 minutes, sear the tuna logs for 20 to 30 seconds on each side—they should be seared outside and rare inside. Transfer to a clean cutting board and slice ¼ inch thick.

In a medium bowl, combine the pineapple, scallions, lime juice, soy sauce, and ginger. Add the avocado and gently stir to combine. Stir in the chopped cilantro.

To assemble, set the tuna slices on rice crackers; top each with a small spoonful of the salsa and a whole cilantro leaf. You may have extra crackers and salsa. —*Laura Werlin*

outstanding

Bacon-Wrapped Ginger Soy Scallops

Ask for "dry" sea scallops—they haven't been treated with a solution to maintain their shelf life, so they brown better, have a nicer texture and flavor, and tend to taste fresher than treated or "wet" scallops.

Set a rack in the upper third of the oven. Line the bottom of a broiler pan with foil, replace the perforated top part of the pan, and put the whole pan on the oven rack. Heat the oven to 450°F.

In a medium bowl, combine the soy sauce, brown sugar, and ginger. If the muscle tabs from the sides of the scallops are still attached, peel them off and discard them. Cut each scallop into quarters. Marinate the scallop pieces in the soy mixture for 15 minutes. Reserve the marinade.

To assemble, stack 2 slices of water chestnut in the center of a piece of the bacon. Put a piece of scallop on top. Wrap each end of the bacon over the scallop and secure with a toothpick. Repeat with the remaining bacon, water chestnuts, and scallops (you may not use all of the water chestnuts).

Remove the broiler pan from the oven and quickly arrange the bacon-wrapped scallops on the hot pan so that an exposed side of each scallop faces up. Drizzle the scallops with the reserved marinade. Bake, turning the scallops over once after 10 minutes, until the bacon is browned around the edges and the scallops are cooked through, about 15 minutes total. —*Laura Werlin*

Yields 2 dozen hors d'oeuvres.

¼ cup soy sauce

1 tablespoon dark brown sugar

1½ teaspoons minced fresh ginger

6 very large "dry" sea scallops (8 to 10 ounces total)

One 8-ounce can sliced water chestnuts, drained

12 slices bacon, cut in half crosswise

Chicken Satays with Spicy Peanut Sauce

*Yields about 32
hors d'oeuvres.*

1 to 1¼ pounds boneless,
    skinless chicken breast halves

2 tablespoons soy sauce

2 tablespoons fresh lemon juice

1 tablespoon vegetable oil

2 medium cloves garlic, minced

½ teaspoon curry powder

Kosher salt and freshly ground
    black pepper

⅓ cup crunchy natural peanut
    butter

⅓ cup unsweetened coconut
    milk

1 teaspoon light brown sugar

Pinch cayenne

About 32 bamboo skewers,
    soaked in water for at least
    20 minutes

Satays make great party food, and this recipe can be easily doubled.

Remove the chicken tenderloins, if still attached, and trim any excess fat from the chicken breasts. With a sharp knife, cut the breasts lengthwise into ½-inch-thick slices (you should have about 6 slices per breast). Cut each slice in half crosswise to make about 32 pieces total. If you have tenderloins, cut those in half, too.

Combine 1 tablespoon of the soy sauce and 1 tablespoon of the lemon juice with the oil, garlic, curry powder, ½ teaspoon kosher salt, and a few grinds of pepper in a medium bowl. Add the chicken and toss well to coat. Let the chicken marinate at room temperature for at least 15 minutes and up to 1 hour. (Or refrigerate the marinated chicken for up to 24 hours.)

Meanwhile, combine the remaining 1 tablespoon soy sauce and 1 table-spoon lemon juice with the peanut butter, coconut milk, brown sugar, cayenne, and ⅛ teaspoon kosher salt in a small saucepan.

Position an oven rack as close to the broiler as possible and heat the broiler to high. Thread one chicken piece onto the end of each skewer. Set the skewered chicken on a broiler pan and broil, turning the skewers once halfway through, until the chicken is lightly browned and cooked through, about 7 minutes total. While the chicken cooks, warm the sauce gently over medium-low or low heat. If the sauce seems very thick, thin it with about 1 tablespoon water. Let the chicken cool slightly and then serve the satays with the peanut sauce for dipping. *—Laura Werlin*

Grilled Chicken Wings

Serves four to six as an appetizer.

2 pounds chicken wings (about 10 whole wings), split at the wing joints (discard the wingtips or save for stock)

Kosher salt and freshly ground black pepper

Oil for the grill

1 sauce recipe (recipes follow)

It's easy enough to double or triple this recipe. Just be sure to do the same with whichever accompanying sauce you choose. For a party, serve more than one sauce for variety.

Heat a gas grill to medium high or prepare a medium-hot charcoal fire. Season the wings with 1 teaspoon kosher salt and ¼ teaspoon pepper.

Rub the grill grate with oil. Grill the wings, covered on a gas grill or uncovered over a charcoal fire, flipping every few minutes, until they're browned, crisp, and completely cooked through, about 20 minutes. If there are flare-ups, move the wings to another part of the grill. If the wings begin to burn, reduce the heat to medium or move the wings to a cooler part of the grill.

As the wings are done, transfer them to a large bowl. Stir the sauce and toss with the wings. Serve immediately on a platter, with plenty of napkins.

—Tony Rosenfeld

Cutting Chicken Wings for Grilling

Using a sharp chef's knife, split the wings at the joints, saving the middle section and drumette for grilling. Discard the wingtips or save them for stock.

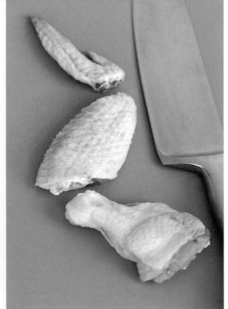

Buffalo-Style Sauce with Rosemary and Lemon

Yields enough for 2 pounds wings.

⅓ cup Frank's Red Hot Original sauce (widely available in supermarkets)

¼ cup unsalted butter, melted

1 teaspoon chopped fresh rosemary

Finely grated zest of 1 lemon

In a small bowl, whisk the hot sauce, butter, rosemary, and lemon zest.

Asian-Style Barbecue Sauce

Yields enough for 2 pounds wings.

¼ cup ketchup

2 tablespoons soy sauce

1 tablespoon light brown sugar

1 tablespoon rice vinegar

4 scallions (white and green parts), trimmed and thinly sliced

Large pinch red pepper flakes

In a small bowl, whisk the ketchup, soy sauce, brown sugar, rice vinegar, half of the scallions, and the red pepper flakes. Reserve the remaining scallions to sprinkle on the wings after tossing.

Honey-Mustard Thyme Sauce

Yields enough for 2 pounds wings.

¼ cup whole-grain mustard

¼ cup honey

2 tablespoons finely diced shallot

½ teaspoon kosher salt

¼ teaspoon freshly ground black pepper

2 teaspoons chopped fresh thyme

In a small bowl, whisk the mustard, honey, shallots, salt, pepper, and half of the thyme. Reserve the remaining thyme to sprinkle on the wings after tossing.

Sweet-and-Sour Orange Glaze

Yields enough for 2 pounds wings

½ cup sweet orange marmalade

2 tablespoons plus 2 teaspoons rice vinegar

1 tablespoon soy sauce

1½ teaspoons Thai chile sauce (like sriracha)

In a small bowl, whisk all the ingredients. Toss with the grilled wings.

Spring Vegetable & Potato Frittata

Serves four.

8 large eggs

¼ cup freshly grated
   Parmigiano-Reggiano cheese

3 tablespoons chopped fresh
   flat-leaf parsley

Kosher salt and freshly ground
   black pepper

⅛ teaspoon cayenne

2 to 3 tablespoons extra-virgin
   olive oil

1 medium Yukon Gold potato,
   scrubbed and cut into
   ½-inch dice

1 medium yellow onion,
   thinly sliced

½ pound medium-thick
   asparagus, trimmed and
   cut on the diagonal into
   1-inch pieces

3 cloves garlic, minced

6 ounces sharp Cheddar cheese,
   shredded

This frittata is a great make-ahead snack, lunch, or light dinner. You don't want to serve it too hot. Let it cool to room temperature and refrigerate until ready to use. The frittata can be warmed briefly in the microwave or served at room temperature.

In a medium bowl, whisk the eggs, Parmigiano, parsley, ½ teaspoon kosher salt, ⅛ teaspoon pepper, and the cayenne.

Heat 2 tablespoons of the oil in a 10-inch ovenproof nonstick skillet over medium-high heat. Add the potato and ¼ teaspoon kosher salt and cook, stirring occasionally, until browned on several sides, 6 to 7 minutes. Transfer to a bowl with a slotted spoon. Reduce the heat to medium. If the pan is dry, add the remaining 1 tablespoon oil. Add the onion and cook, stirring frequently, until it softens and begins to brown, 4 to 5 minutes. Stir in the asparagus, garlic, ¼ teaspoon kosher salt and ⅛ teaspoon pepper. Cook, stirring frequently, until the asparagus is bright green and crisp-tender, 3 to 4 minutes. Lower the heat to medium low and add the eggs and potatoes, stirring until combined, 10 to 15 seconds. Add the Cheddar and stir until well distributed. Cook without stirring until the eggs have almost set, 10 to 12 minutes. (The center may still be loose but should be bubbling a little; the sides should be set.) Meanwhile, position an oven rack 6 inches from the broiler element and heat the broiler to high. Transfer the skillet to the oven and broil until the eggs have set completely and the top is golden brown, 1 to 3 minutes. Let rest for 5 minutes. Transfer to a cutting board and cut into wedges. *—David Bonom*

Smoky Refried Bean Tostadas

Chipotles are dried and smoked jalapeño chiles, so they deliver both heat and intriguing smokiness at the same time. Lots of hot sauces take advantage of chipotle's dual deliciousness, but if you can only find the standard kind of hot sauce, you'll still enjoy these tostadas.

Serves four.

7 tablespoons canola or vegetable oil; more if needed

Eight 5- to 6-inch corn tortillas

Kosher salt

1 medium onion, finely diced

1 teaspoon ground cumin

Two 15-ounce cans pinto beans, rinsed and drained

1 cup water

2 tablespoons chipotle Tabasco® sauce

1 cup crumbled feta cheese

¾ cup finely diced fresh tomato

½ cup thinly sliced red radishes

½ cup loosely packed fresh cilantro leaves

Heat the oven to 200°F (or heat a warming drawer if you have one). Line a baking sheet with paper towels. Heat 5 tablespoons of the oil in an 8-inch nonstick omelet pan over medium-high heat until the oil bubbles right away when the edge of a tortilla is dipped into it. Using tongs and working with one tortilla at a time, fry the tortillas until golden brown on both sides, about 30 seconds per side. As each one finishes frying, briefly dangle the tortilla above the pan to allow some of the excess oil to drip back into the pan, and then transfer the tortilla to the baking sheet lined with paper towels. Sprinkle each tortilla with a little salt while it's still hot. As you fry, adjust the heat to keep the oil from getting too hot or too cool, and if the pan goes dry, add more oil, 1 tablespoon at a time. When all the tortillas are fried, keep them warm in the oven.

Heat the remaining 2 tablespoons oil in a 12-inch skillet over medium-high heat. Add the onion and cook, stirring often, until softened and lightly browned around the edges, about 3 minutes. Stir in the cumin and cook until fragrant, about 30 seconds. Add the beans, 1 teaspoon kosher salt, and the water. Working quickly, mash the beans with the back of a fork until most but not all of them are broken apart, and simmer until the beans look creamy and spreadable and much of the water has been absorbed, about 3 minutes. Stir in the chipotle Tabasco sauce and season to taste with more salt if needed.

To serve, spread each tortilla with about ⅓ cup of the beans, and top with the feta, tomato, radishes, and cilantro leaves. *—Jennifer Armentrout*

Grilled Sausage & Onion Panini

Serves four.

1 large red onion, sliced crosswise ¼ inch thick

5 tablespoons olive oil

1 tablespoon plus 1 teaspoon good-quality balsamic vinegar

Kosher salt and freshly ground black pepper

1 large ripe tomato, thinly sliced

8 slices (about ½-inch-thick) crusty Italian bread

1 clove garlic, smashed

4 links sweet or hot Italian sausage (about 1 pound total)

1 packed cup arugula, washed (if the leaves are large, stem them)

2 to 3 tablespoons freshly grated Parmigiano-Reggiano cheese

Grilling the sausage, onion, and even the bread takes the traditional sausage grinder to a whole new level. Slices of tomato and leaves of peppery arugula add a summery element, too.

Heat a gas grill to high. Drizzle the onions with 1 tablespoon oil and 1 tablespoon vinegar and season well with salt and pepper. Toss gently to keep the disks intact. Season the tomato slices with salt and pepper and drizzle with 1 tablespoon oil. Brush 2 tablespoons of the oil over both sides of the bread, rub with the smashed garlic, and season with salt and pepper.

Put the sausages and onions on the hottest part of the grill. Grill the onions, turning them a few times, until they're browned and have softened to a limp texture, about 8 minutes. Grill the sausages, turning occasionally, until fully cooked (160°F on an instant-read thermometer), 10 to 12 minutes. Remove the sausages and let them rest. Grill the bread for 1 to 2 minutes on each side.

Dress the arugula with the remaining 1 tablespoon oil and 1 teaspoon vinegar; season with salt and pepper. Arrange a small handful of the arugula and 1 or 2 tomato slices over four of the bread slices. Slice the sausages in half lengthwise and lay them flat over the tomatoes. Lay a generous portion of the grilled onion rings and a sprinkling of Parmigiano over the sausages. Top with the remaining four slices of bread. Slice the sandwiches in half and serve immediately. —*Tony Rosenfeld*

Grilled Goat Cheese with Tapenade

Many grocery stores now carry prepared tapenade; to make your own, finely chop or process a handful of pitted Kalamata olives with capers, anchovies, and garlic and then mix with a little olive oil and lemon juice to taste.

Butter all the bread slices on one side only. Put 4 slices, buttered side down, on a cutting board. Spread 1 tablespoon of tapenade on each slice and top with three of the cheese rounds. Top with the remaining bread, buttered side up.

Heat a large nonstick pan or griddle over medium-high heat for 2 minutes. Put as many sandwiches as will fit in the pan or on the griddle without crowding, cover, and cook until the cheese has just begun to melt and the bread is golden brown, about 2 minutes. Remove the lid and turn the sandwiches, pressing each firmly with a spatula to flatten it slightly. Cook uncovered until the bottom is golden brown, about 1 minute. Turn them once more and press with the spatula again to recrisp the bread, about 30 seconds. Cut in half and serve immediately. —*Laura Werlin*

Serves four.

4 teaspoons salted butter, at room temperature

8 slices (¼-inch-thick) Italian country bread or sourdough

¼ cup olive tapenade

One ¼-pound log fresh goat cheese, cut into twelve ¼-inch-thick rounds

2 Salads

p55

p62

Baby Romaine Salad with
Spicy Chicken and Warm
Chipotle Vinaigrette
(recipe on page 66)

Forty Shades of Green Salad

Serves four.

For the vinaigrette:

3 tablespoons extra-virgin olive oil

1 tablespoon plus 1 teaspoon fresh lime juice

1 teaspoon honey

Big pinch kosher salt

1 coarse grind black pepper

For the salad:

1 large head Boston lettuce (largest outer and damaged leaves removed), washed, dried, and torn into bite-size pieces

¾ cup loosely packed fresh parsley leaves (if possible, use a mix of flat and curly)

1 large (or 1½ small) Belgian endive (damaged leaves removed), halved lengthwise, cored, and thinly sliced crosswise

2 to 3 scallions (white and light green parts), very thinly sliced on the diagonal

1 small ripe but firm avocado

The lime vinaigrette and parsley make this salad delightfully refreshing. Serve it at the outset of a big meal or team it with a simple steak or piece of fish for a light, satisfying meal.

In a small bowl, combine the vinaigrette ingredients and whisk until thoroughly emulsified (it will look creamy).

In a large bowl, combine the lettuce, parsley, endive, and scallions. Gently toss the greens thoroughly with about 2 tablespoons of the vinaigrette. Mound the greens onto four salad plates, arranging any endive and parsley pieces that have fallen to the bottom of the bowl on top.

Cut the avocado in half and remove the pit. Slide a large spoon between the skin and flesh to peel each half. Slice the avocado halves crosswise in very thin half-moons (⅛ inch thick).

With the flat side of a chef's knife, transfer the avocado halves to the bowl, fan them out slightly, drizzle over another 1 tablespoon of the vinaigrette, and gently toss just to coat the avocado, keeping the slices somewhat intact.

Arrange a little pile of avocado slices on one quarter of the salad, propped up against the mound of leaves. Drizzle the whole salad with a tiny bit more vinaigrette and serve right away.

—Susie Middleton

Slice Avocados Before Peeling Them

When an avocado is soft and ripe, it's usually easier to slice or dice it before removing its skin. Just before serving, cut the avocado in half lengthwise and remove the pit. Using a paring knife, cut it diagonally into ¼-inch (or wider) slices, without piercing the skin. If dice is your goal, make a second set of diagonal slices perpendicular to the first. To remove the sliced or diced avocado from its skin, hold the avocado in the palm of your hand and, using a large spoon, carefully scoop out the pieces.

Mixed Greens with Goat Cheese & Orange-Fennel Seed Vinaigrette

Serves six.

7 to 8 ounces mixed greens, washed and spun dry

2 large navel oranges, rinsed

1 tablespoon white-wine vinegar

1½ teaspoons fennel seeds, coarsely chopped

Kosher salt and freshly ground black pepper

½ cup extra-virgin olive oil

¼ pound creamy goat cheese

Because salad mixes come in packages, they save time, but be sure they're absolutely fresh: one rotten leaf can spoil a salad. You can also make your own mix of your favorite salad leaves.

Put the greens in a large salad bowl. Finely grate the zest of 1 orange (you should have about 1 tablespoon) and put it into a small bowl.

Slice off the blossom and stem ends of the orange with a small, sharp knife. Stand the orange on one of its cut ends and slice off the skin in strips. Try to get all the white pith. Working over a bowl to catch the juices, cut the orange segments free from the membranes, letting each one fall into the bowl as you go. Remove any seeds from the segments. Squeeze the membranes to extract the juice—you'll need about 3 tablespoons juice. Add the juice to the bowl along with the zest, vinegar, and fennel seeds. Season with ½ teaspoon kosher salt and several grinds of pepper. Whisk in the olive oil in a slow, steady stream. Taste and add more salt and pepper as needed.

Add the orange segments to the bowl of mixed greens. Pour the vinaigrette over the salad and toss. Crumble half of the goat cheese over the top and toss again to mix. Portion the salad among six salad plates and crumble the remaining cheese over the salads. —*Jennifer McLagan*

Grilled Hearts of Romaine with Blue Cheese Dressing

Serves four; yields 2 cups dressing.

For the dressing:

1 cup mayonnaise

½ cup sour cream

¼ cup whole milk; more as needed

6 ounces blue cheese, such as Roquefort or Danish Blue, crumbled; more to taste

1½ tablespoons finely grated shallot

1 clove finely grated garlic

1 tablespoon fresh lemon juice

½ teaspoon kosher salt

⅛ teaspoon freshly ground black pepper; more to taste

For the salad:

2 hearts of romaine lettuce, bases trimmed but left intact, halved lengthwise

Extra-virgin olive oil for brushing

Kosher salt and freshly ground black pepper

4 slices smoked bacon (such as applewood), cooked and crumbled

The dressing recipe makes more than you need for four portions of salad, but it keeps for two weeks in the refrigerator. If you ever come across a smoked blue cheese (such as Oregon's Rogue Creamery's), try it in this salad; it adds one more delicious level of complexity.

In a medium bowl, stir the dressing ingredients. Cover and refrigerate for at least 3 hours to let the flavors develop. Before using, taste and adjust the seasonings if necessary. The dressing will thicken as it sits and may need to be thinned with more milk.

Once the dressing is chilled, heat a gas grill to medium low or prepare a medium-low charcoal fire. (Be sure the grate is hot, too.) Lightly brush olive oil all over the romaine hearts, taking care not to break the leaves. Sprinkle with salt and pepper. Put the lettuce cut side down on the grate, directly over the heat. Grill until the outer leaves are charred and wilted and the lettuce is warm and just barely tender all the way through to the core, 2 to 5 minutes, depending on the heat of your grill. Transfer to a clean platter and let rest for 5 minutes.

To serve, place half a heart of romaine, cut side up, on each plate, top with about 2 tablespoons of the dressing, or more to taste, and sprinkle with the crumbled bacon. Serve immediately. —*Elizabeth Karmel*

Boston Lettuce Wedges with Mimosa Vinaigrette

Serves six.

1 large egg

3 small heads Boston lettuce

2 tablespoons fresh lemon juice

1½ tablespoons Dijon mustard

Kosher salt and freshly ground black pepper

¾ cup extra-virgin olive oil

2 tablespoons chopped fresh flat-leaf parsley

1 tablespoon finely chopped shallot

Be sure not to overcook the eggs; you want the whites set but not rubbery. Something surprising? An older egg will be easier to peel.

Put the egg in a small saucepan and cover with cold water. Bring to a boil, cover the saucepan, and remove it from the heat. Let stand, covered, for 15 minutes.

While the egg cooks, remove any damaged leaves from the lettuce heads and trim their bases. Cut each head through the core into four wedges. Rinse under cold running water, shake gently to get rid of excess water, then set the wedges on a clean dishcloth to drain, cut side down.

In a small bowl, whisk together the lemon juice and mustard. Add ½ teaspoon kosher salt and a few grinds of pepper, then whisk in the oil in a slow, steady stream. Stir in the parsley and shallot.

Drain the egg and cool it under cold running water. Remove the shell and separate the white from the yolk. Using the back of a spoon, press the egg white through a fine sieve. Repeat with the egg yolk. Stir the sieved egg into the dressing and taste for seasoning.

Arrange two lettuce wedges on each of six large salad plates and spoon the dressing over them. Serve immediately. *—Jennifer McLagan*

Grilled Mushroom, Arugula & Comté Salad

Comté and Gruyère are both hard cheeses with a nutty flavor, but Comté's more overt notes of hazelnuts make it a better match for this salad. Mushrooms soak up water like sponges. To clean them, use a soft brush or a moist paper towel instead of rinsing them in water.

Heat a gas grill to medium high or prepare a medium-hot charcoal fire. (Be sure the grate is hot, too.) Wipe the mushrooms clean and trim off the stems. If using portabellas, scrape out the black gills with the side of a spoon. Put the clean whole mushrooms in a large bowl, drizzle with the 5 tablespoons oil, and gently toss. Sprinkle in a pinch of kosher salt and toss again. Grill the mushrooms directly over the heat until tender and well marked, 3 to 5 minutes on each side. If using portabellas, quickly cut the grilled mushrooms into 1-inch-thick slices.

Portion the arugula among four plates and top with the hot mushrooms. Garnish with the nuts and cheese and a generous drizzle of olive oil. Sprinkle lightly with fleur de sel and a grind of pepper. Serve immediately.

—Elizabeth Karmel

Serves four.

1 pound large shiitake or portabella mushrooms, or a mix

5 tablespoons extra-virgin olive oil; more for drizzling

Kosher salt

4 cups baby arugula, washed and dried

¼ cup hazelnuts, toasted and roughly chopped

2 ounces Comté or Gruyère cheese, thinly sliced with a vegetable peeler

Fleur de sel or flaky sea salt

Freshly ground white or black pepper

There's More than One Way to Skin a Hazelnut

Hazelnuts are an unusual but welcome addition to salads, adding crunch as well as flavor. In this salad, the hazelnuts play deliciously off the nutty cheese. If you can buy them already skinned, all the better, but if not, here are two ways to make the task easier. (For both methods: Let the nuts cool completely before using or before storing in a sealed container in the freezer for up to three months.)

The toasting method

Spread the nuts in a single layer on a baking sheet and toast in a 375°F oven until the skins are mostly split and the nuts are light golden brown (the skins will look darker) and fragrant, about 10 minutes. Don't overtoast or the nuts will become bitter. Wrap the hot nuts in a clean dishtowel and let sit for 5 to 10 minutes. Then vigorously rub the nuts against themselves in the towel to remove most of the skins. Try to get at least half of the skins off. This may take a lot of rubbing, so be persistent.

Pros:

The nuts get toasted and skinned all in one step; uses the oven (which might be heating anyway for whatever you'll be making with the nuts) rather than dirtying a saucepan.

Cons:

Almost impossible to get the nuts completely skinned; stains a dishtowel (so don't use one you really care about).

The blanching method

For every ½ cup of hazelnuts, bring 1½ cups water to a boil. Add 2 tablespoons baking soda and the nuts; boil for 3 minutes—expect the water to turn black and watch for boilovers. Run a nut under cold water and see if the skin slips off easily. If not, boil the nuts a little longer until the skins slip off. Cool the nuts under cold running water, slip off the skins, blot dry, and then toast in a 375°F oven.

Pro:

Completely skins the nuts.

Cons:

Each nut must be skinned individually (which is easy but time-consuming if you're skinning a lot of nuts); nuts must be toasted in a separate step; nuts won't be as crisp as with the toasting method.

Bistro Salad with Warm Goat Cheese

Serves four.

½ cup toasted hazelnuts
(skinned, if you like; see p. 43)

One ¼-pound log fresh
goat cheese

1 tablespoon sherry vinegar

3 tablespoons hazelnut oil

Kosher salt

Freshly ground black pepper

4 generous, loose handfuls of
small lettuce leaves (or large
ones torn up) from a variety
(three is nice) of butter and
loose-leaf lettuces, washed
and thoroughly dried

A combination of butter lettuce and a few different-colored loose-leaf lettuces make a pretty and tasty salad. You can substitute walnuts for the hazelnuts and walnut oil (or even olive oil) for the hazelnut oil, if you can't easily find it.

Heat the oven to 400°F and lightly coat a baking sheet with cooking spray. Roughly chop half of the hazelnuts and finely chop the other half. Slice the goat cheese into four equal portions (if the slices crumble a bit, pat the cheese back together into a sort of patty). Press the finely chopped hazelnuts into the cheese rounds to coat them on all sides. Set the rounds on the baking sheet and bake until heated, 6 to 8 minutes.

Meanwhile, make the dressing. In a small bowl, whisk together the vinegar, oil, a big pinch of salt, and a few grinds of pepper. Taste and adjust the seasonings. When the cheese is ready, toss the lettuce with the dressing in a large bowl until evenly coated. Mound the lettuce on individual plates, top with a round of warm goat cheese, and scatter the rest of the hazelnuts over all.

—Ruth Lively

tip: To make your salad look great on the plate, shape salad greens into tall stacks, lightly dress the greens and pack them loosely in a clean plastic container; pints work well. Invert the container onto a salad plate, lift it away, and voilà— a statuesque salad.

Spinach & Basil Salad with Tomatoes, Candied Walnuts & Warm Bacon Dressing

Serves four.

½ pound baby spinach leaves, washed and dried

1 cup lightly packed fresh basil leaves, washed and dried

6 slices bacon

2 tablespoons white-wine vinegar

1 tablespoon Dijon mustard

⅓ cup plus 2 teaspoons olive oil

Sea salt and freshly ground black pepper

1 pint grape tomatoes

1½ teaspoons dried herbes de Provence

½ teaspoon dehydrated minced or granulated garlic

½ teaspoon kosher salt

Candied Walnuts (recipe follows)

Adding herbs, both fresh and dried, gives a classic wilted spinach salad a Mediterranean twist. Herbes de Provence usually includes dried fennel seed, lavender, rosemary, thyme, marjoram, sage, and summer savory. If you don't have it, use any of those herbs to make your own mix. Broiling the tiny tomatoes brings out their sweetness and adds another warm element to the salad. If you can't find tiny grape tomatoes, use cherry tomatoes.

In a large salad bowl, toss the spinach and basil together.

Cut each slice of bacon into thirds. Cook in a medium skillet over medium to medium-high heat, stirring occasionally, until crisp; drain on paper towels. Reserve 1 tablespoon of the bacon fat. Crumble the bacon into pieces.

In a medium metal bowl, whisk the vinegar with the mustard. Slowly whisk in ⅓ cup of the olive oil, then whisk in the 1 tablespoon bacon fat. Season to taste with sea salt and pepper. Set aside in a warm place.

Position an oven rack as close as possible to the broiler element. Put a heavy-duty rimmed baking sheet on the rack and heat the broiler to high. Toss the tomatoes with the remaining 2 teaspoons olive oil, the herbes de Provence, garlic, and kosher salt. Pour the tomatoes onto the hot pan and broil, stirring occasionally, until the skins are cracked and blistered and the flesh is warmed through, 4 to 5 minutes. Turn off the broiler. Transfer the tomatoes with a slotted spoon to the bowl with the salad dressing. Stir to coat and mix the seasonings into the dressing. Put the bowl in the oven to keep warm until ready to serve.

Just before serving, transfer the tomatoes from the dressing to another bowl with a slotted spoon. Whisk the dressing to recombine. Add half the bacon to the greens. Drizzle with 3 tablespoons of the dressing and toss lightly to coat. Add more dressing only if needed; don't overdress the salad. Mound the greens on four salad plates. Garnish with the tomatoes, the remaining bacon, and some of the candied walnuts (you'll have leftovers for snacking). Serve immediately. —*Elizabeth Karmel*

Candied Walnuts

Yields about 3 cups.

⅓ cup granulated sugar

2½ tablespoons brown sugar

½ teaspoon kosher salt

½ teaspoon ground cinnamon

Pinch cayenne

1 large egg white, at room temperature

1 tablespoon water

½ pound walnut halves

These nuts are as versatile as they are addictive. In addition to salads, you can add them to toppings for fruit crisps, sprinkle on top of roasted sweet potatoes, or just devour them as is.

Heat the oven to 300°F. In a small bowl, mix together the sugars, salt, cinnamon, and cayenne. In a large bowl, whisk the egg white until frothy; whisk in the water until combined. Add the walnuts and stir to coat. Sprinkle on the sugar mixture and stir to evenly distribute.

Line a rimmed baking sheet with parchment. Spread the sugared nuts in a single layer on the sheet. Bake for 15 minutes, stir the nuts, and continue baking until they smell toasted and the sugar coating has caramelized, about another 15 minutes.

Let the nuts cool on the pan, separating them as they cool. When completely cool, transfer to an airtight container. They'll keep for two weeks.

Chopped Vegetable & Couscous Salad with Black Olive Vinaigrette

Serves ten to twelve.

For the vinaigrette:

⅓ cup red-wine vinegar or sherry vinegar

¼ cup finely chopped black olives, such as Kalamatas

1 teaspoon Dijon mustard

⅔ cup extra-virgin olive oil

Freshly ground black pepper

For the salad:

Extra-virgin olive oil for brushing

Kosher salt

1 yellow bell pepper

3 small carrots, peeled and left whole

3 medium zucchini, trimmed, and cut lengthwise into ½-inch-thick slices

1 small radicchio, core left in and cut lengthwise into quarters

1 medium eggplant, cut into ½-inch-thick rounds

1 small bunch scallions, trimmed

For the couscous:

2 cups water

1 tablespoon extra-virgin olive oil

½ teaspoon sea salt; more to taste

1¾ cups couscous

2 tablespoons finely chopped fresh mint, basil, or flat-leaf parsley, or a mix

Freshly ground black pepper

Fresh lemon juice to taste

This salad is very accommodating—you can use just about any combination of grilled vegetables (though try to pick a colorful mix), and you can grill them in advance, or make the whole thing up to three days ahead. The salad is delicious warm or at room temperature.

Heat a gas grill to medium high or prepare a medium-hot charcoal fire. (Be sure the grate is hot, too.)

Make the vinaigrette: In a small bowl, whisk the vinegar, 1 tablespoon of the olives, and the mustard. Whisk in the olive oil in a slow, steady stream, making sure it's emulsified before adding more oil. Whisk in the remaining olives. Season to taste with pepper.

Grill the vegetables: Brush a light coating of oil onto the vegetables and sprinkle lightly with salt. Lay the whole bell pepper, the carrots, and as many of the remaining vegetables as will fit on the cooking grate, directly over the heat. Grill, turning every few minutes as needed, until the pepper is charred all over and the rest of the vegetables are well marked and tender. Grilling time will vary: The zucchini, radicchio, and scallions cook fastest, the eggplant will take a little longer, and the carrots and pepper may take up to 15 minutes more. As they finish cooking, transfer them to a large platter and add more raw vegetables to the grill. Continue until everything is cooked. Let cool slightly.

Prepare the couscous: While the vegetables cool, combine the water, oil, and salt in a medium saucepan and bring to a boil. Add the couscous. Stir well, remove from the heat, cover, and let sit for 5 minutes.

When the pepper is cool enough to handle, peel and seed it. Coarsely chop all the vegetables. Transfer them to a large serving bowl and toss them with ½ cup of the vinaigrette.

When the couscous is done, fluff it with a fork and add it to the vegetables. Add the remaining vinaigrette and herbs. Toss to distribute evenly. Season with salt, pepper, and lemon juice to taste. Serve warm or at room temperature. This salad can be covered and refrigerated for up to three days.
—Elizabeth Karmel

Baby Greens with Mango & Marinated Onion

Serves six to eight.

½ cup very thinly sliced
 red onion

⅓ cup red-wine vinegar

Kosher salt and freshly ground
 black pepper

2 tablespoons seasoned
 rice vinegar

2 tablespoons canola or
 grapeseed oil

2 tablespoons extra-virgin
 olive oil

8 to 10 ounces baby greens or
 mesclun, washed and dried

2 medium ripe mangos, peeled,
 pitted, and finely diced

The marinated onions in this salad are tasty on sandwiches, so make a double batch; they'll keep for a few days in the refrigerator.

In a small bowl, combine the onion and red-wine vinegar with a little salt and pepper. Set aside for at least 20 and up to 90 minutes. In a small bowl, combine the rice vinegar and the oils.

Just before serving, generously season the greens with salt and pepper, whisk the dressing, and toss the greens with just enough of the dressing to lightly coat. Portion onto salad plates. Drain the onion. Arrange the onion and mangos over the greens. Serve immediately. *—Joanne McAllister Smart*

For Even Onion Slices, Use a Radial Cut

Start cutting thin slices at a low angle and follow the natural curve of the onion.

Adjust the angle of your knife as you slice; it should be at 90 degrees when you reach the middle.

Flip the onion over and repeat.

Sun-Ripened Tomato & Olive Salad

Capture the flavor of ripe, just-picked tomatoes at their peak with this salad. If your tomatoes are very sweet and need more acid, adjust the flavor by adding another tablespoon of sherry vinegar. For variation, try substituting 2 tablespoons of torn basil or a mix of chopped fresh herbs for the parsley.

Quarter the olives. Core the tomatoes and slice into large bite-size wedges or large cubes. Put the olives, tomatoes, and shallot in a large bowl and season with salt and pepper to taste. Add the vinegar and parsley. Season again with salt and pepper to taste; then add the olive oil and toss. (The salad may be prepared up to 2 hours ahead, covered, and left at room temperature. Toss again before serving.) —*Maria Helm Sinskey*

Serves six.

1 cup pitted Niçoise or Kalamata olives

2 pounds heirloom tomatoes, assorted colors and sizes

1 medium shallot, minced

Sea salt and freshly ground black pepper

1 tablespoon sherry vinegar

1 tablespoon coarsely chopped fresh flat-leaf parsley

3 tablespoons extra-virgin olive oil

Summer Squash Salad with Lemon, Capers & Parmesan

Serves six to eight.

1 clove garlic

Kosher salt

¼ cup fresh lemon juice

½ cup extra-virgin olive oil

1 pound summer squash (yellow squash, zucchini, or a mix)

Freshly ground black pepper

4 cups loosely packed baby arugula

½ cup fresh flat-leaf parsley leaves

½ cup chopped fresh chives, cut into ½-inch lengths

2 tablespoons capers, rinsed well

¼ cup finely grated Parmigiano-Reggiano cheese; plus a chunk to shave for garnish

Try adding other tender herbs like marjoram or basil, if you'd like. And above all, use tender, slender squash, not the overgrown club-like zucchini that your neighbor may offer from his garden.

In a mortar or using the flat side of a chef's knife, mash the garlic to a paste with a pinch of salt. Put the paste in a small bowl (or keep it in the mortar) and whisk in the lemon juice. Let sit for 5 to 10 minutes, then whisk in the olive oil.

Using a mandoline or a sharp chef's knife, cut the squash diagonally into very thin (1/16- to 1/8-inch) ovals. Put them in a medium bowl, season with salt and pepper, and gently toss with about two-thirds of the vinaigrette.

Combine the arugula, parsley, chives, and capers in a separate bowl, season with salt and pepper, and toss with just enough vinaigrette to lightly coat. Taste both the squash and herbs and adjust the seasoning with salt or pepper if necessary. Layer about a third of the squash in a shallow bowl or platter, scatter about a third of the arugula mixture on top, and sprinkle with a third of the grated Parmigiano. Repeat the process with the remaining squash and arugula mixture, sprinkling each layer with Parmigiano. For garnish, use a vegetable peeler to shave long strips from the chunk of Parmigiano onto the salad. Serve immediately. —*Tasha DeSerio*

The Secrets of a Successful Salad

- Clean your greens with a brief soak. Gently swirl the leaves in cool water to dislodge any grit, then lift the greens out with loosely splayed fingers. The grit will stay behind in the bottom of the bowl. Rinse out the bowl and repeat until there's no grit left.

- Get the greens good and dry with a salad spinner. After a couple of spins, drain the bowl, rearrange the leaves, and spin again. Repeat until there's no more water in the bowl.

- Make the vinaigrette in a separate container until you get an eye for the amount needed. Pour in just enough to lightly coat the greens; you can always add a little more.

- Toss until the greens are well-coated. Use two large spoons or your hands for gentle tossing. Taste a leaf, adjust the seasonings, and serve right away.

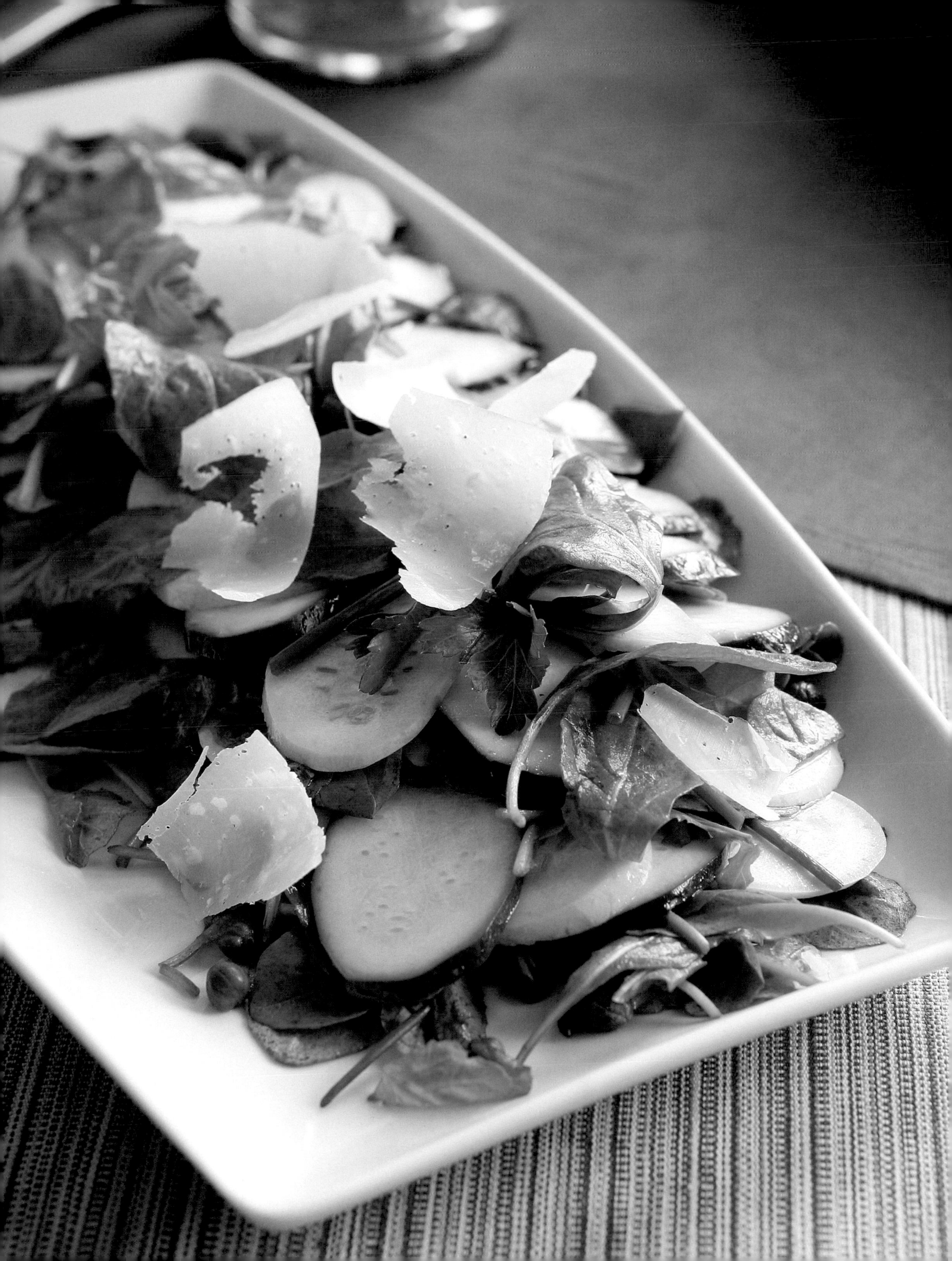

Wilted Arugula Salad with Crisp Potatoes, Feta & Warm Black Olive Vinaigrette

Serves four as a light main course or six as a starter.

½ pound baby arugula, washed and spun dry

3 tablespoons red-wine vinegar

⅓ cup pitted Kalamata olives, drained and finely chopped

1 teaspoon Dijon mustard

2 teaspoons chopped fresh thyme

½ cup plus 2 tablespoons extra-virgin olive oil

3 tablespoons water

1 large russet potato, peeled and cut into ½-inch dice

Kosher salt and freshly ground black pepper

¾ cup finely diced red onion

¼ pound feta cheese, crumbled

½ pound cherry or grape tomatoes, halved (1 heaping cup)

The diced potatoes in this salad are a lovely surprise, and they make the dish more substantial that a typical green salad. To make it even more of a main dish, top it with a seared chicken breast.

Put the arugula in a large bowl. In a food processor, pulse together the vinegar, olives, mustard, and 1 teaspoon of the thyme. Processing continuously, slowly pour in ½ cup of the olive oil and the water to make a loose dressing. Transfer to a measuring cup.

Heat the remaining 2 tablespoons oil in a 12-inch nonstick skillet over medium-high heat for 30 seconds. Add the diced potatoes, sprinkle with 1 teaspoon kosher salt and ½ teaspoon pepper, and cook, stirring occasionally, until they begin to brown all over, 5 to 8 minutes. Reduce the heat to medium and cook until just tender, another 4 to 5 minutes. Add the onion and cook, stirring, until it's soft and lightly browned, 3 to 5 minutes. Stir in the remaining 1 teaspoon thyme. Transfer to a bowl or plate.

Reduce the heat to low and pour the vinaigrette into the pan. Cook, stirring with a wooden spoon or spatula until the vinaigrette is warmed through, about 1 minute. Return the vinaigrette to the measuring cup and whisk to recombine.

Toss the arugula with about half the vinaigrette or enough to lightly coat, then portion it among four (or six) plates. Top with the potato and onion mixture, then the feta and tomatoes. Drizzle with some of the remaining vinaigrette (you may not need it all) and serve. —*Tony Rosenfeld*

Green Bean Salad with Corn, Cherry Tomatoes & Basil

If you can't find juicy cherry tomatoes, substitute small wedges of ripe beefsteak tomatoes. Crunchy sugar snap peas would make a sweet swap for the green beans.

Bring a medium pot of water to a boil. Add the corn and blanch for 1 minute. Scoop out the corn with a strainer; set aside. Season the water with a generous amount of salt, let it return to a boil, add the beans, and cook until just tender, about 3 minutes. Drain and spread the beans on a baking sheet to cool.

Meanwhile, put the onion in a small bowl filled with ice water (this will crisp it and mellow its flavor). Using a mortar and pestle or the flat side of a chef's knife, mash the garlic to a paste with a pinch of salt. Put the paste in a small bowl (or keep it in the mortar) and whisk in the vinegar. Let sit for 5 to 10 minutes, then whisk in the olive oil.

Just before serving, drain the onion. Put the beans, corn, onion, tomatoes, and basil in a large bowl. Season with salt and pepper and toss with the vinaigrette. Taste again and add more salt, pepper, or vinegar if needed. Serve right away. *–Tasha DeSerio*

Serves six to eight.

3 cups fresh corn kernels (from 3 to 4 ears)

Kosher salt

1 pound fresh green beans, trimmed and halved diagonally

1 small red onion, cut in half through the root end and cut lengthwise into very thin slices

1 clove garlic

¼ cup red-wine vinegar; more to taste

⅓ cup extra-virgin olive oil

1 pint cherry tomatoes, halved

1 cup roughly chopped fresh basil

Freshly ground black pepper

Keep Fresh Kernels at the Ready

Here's a simple way to preserve the sweetness of fresh corn and to keep corn kernels on hand for tossing into salads, side dishes, sautés, or other weeknight dishes. Cut the kernels off the cobs and blanch them in boiling water for 1 or 2 minutes. Drain, let cool, and store in a covered container in the fridge for up to five days. Or freeze the kernels in a single layer on a baking sheet until hard, then store in an airtight container in the freezer, where they'll keep for up to three months.

Ruby Salad with Crumbled Feta & Spicy Pepitas

Serves eight.

For the beets:

1 bunch small beets (4 to 5), trimmed and scrubbed

2 to 3 sprigs fresh thyme or rosemary, or 3 fresh bay leaves

½ teaspoon kosher or sea salt

1 tablespoon olive oil

For the vinaigrette:

1 tablespoon Dijon mustard

2 tablespoons sherry vinegar

2 tablespoons fresh lemon juice

Kosher salt and freshly ground black pepper

¼ cup extra-virgin olive oil

For the salad:

4 cups very thinly sliced red cabbage (from 1 very small head)

1 medium red onion, very thinly sliced

¼ pound mixed baby greens

6 ounces feta cheese, crumbled

Spicy Pepitas (recipe follows)

A trio of garnet-hued vegetables set off by tender greens and crumbled feta makes this salad a knockout. Roasting the beets with fresh woodsy herbs adds a welcome layer of complexity. The roasting takes a bit of time, but you can do it days in advance. Make the spicy pepitas ahead of time too, and this salad can be on the dinner table even on the busiest nights.

Roast the beets: Heat the oven to 400°F. Line a rimmed baking sheet with aluminum foil. Put the beets, herbs, salt, and a drizzle of olive oil in the center; toss the beets to coat. Fold the foil into a loose-fitting but tightly sealed packet around the beets. Roast on the baking sheet until the beets are tender, about 1 hour and 20 minutes. Let the beets cool completely in the foil. When cool, use a paring knife to peel and slice them into wedges (6 to 8 per beet). They can be roasted up to two days ahead and refrigerated.

Make the vinaigrette: In a small bowl, combine the mustard, vinegar, lemon juice, ¼ teaspoon kosher salt, and a few grinds of pepper. Slowly whisk in the oil.

Make the salad: Combine the cabbage and onion in a medium bowl and set aside. Up to an hour before serving, add the beet wedges; toss gently with half the vinaigrette.

Just before serving, add the baby greens, half of the feta, and half of the pepitas; toss with the remaining vinaigrette. Arrange on a big serving platter and garnish with the remaining feta and pepitas. *—Paula Disbrowe and David Norman*

Spicy Pepitas

Toss 6 ounces pepitas (available in natural-foods or specialty stores) with 1 teaspoon corn or peanut oil, 1 teaspoon pure chile powder (such as New Mexico or ancho), and ¾ teaspoon kosher salt. Spread evenly on a rimmed baking sheet and roast at 375°F until golden and fragrant, 6 to 8 minutes (you'll hear them popping). Let cool completely on the baking sheet. If making ahead, store in an airtight container.

Slivered Red Pepper, Carrot & Snap Pea Salad

Serves six to eight.

1 red bell pepper

2 medium carrots, peeled

½ pound snap peas, trimmed

4 scallions (white and light green parts), trimmed

1 jalapeño

1 clove garlic

Kosher salt

1 teaspoon peeled and minced fresh ginger

2 tablespoons fresh lime juice; more to taste

1 tablespoon Champagne vinegar or white-wine vinegar

1 teaspoon granulated sugar

¼ cup extra-virgin olive oil

½ cup fresh flat-leaf parsley leaves

½ cup fresh cilantro leaves, coarsely chopped

½ cup small fresh basil leaves

¼ cup small fresh mint leaves

The confetti colors of this salad can perk up a plate of simply grilled chicken, pork, or beef. Briefly marinating the vegetables softens their texture and allows them to soak up the flavor of the vinaigrette. Be sure to add the herbs just before serving to keep them from wilting. To make this into a light meal, add grilled shrimp or squid or thinly sliced grilled chicken or beef.

Halve and seed the red pepper. Cut the pepper halves in half lengthwise and cut each quarter diagonally into very thin slices. Cut the carrots into thin matchsticks about 3 inches long. Cut the snap peas diagonally into ¾-inch pieces. Slice the scallions thinly on the diagonal. Halve and seed the jalapeño; cut the halves diagonally into thin slices. Combine the red pepper, carrots, snap peas, scallions, and jalapeño in a large bowl.

To make the vinaigrette, mash the garlic and a pinch of salt to a smooth paste with a mortar and pestle or with the flat side of a chef's knife. Combine the garlic, ginger, lime juice, vinegar, and sugar in a small bowl (or in the mortar) and whisk to combine. Let the mixture sit for 5 to 10 minutes, then whisk in the olive oil. Add about half the vinaigrette to the vegetables, toss well, and let sit for 15 to 20 minutes.

Just before serving, add the parsley, cilantro, basil, and mint and season with salt. Drizzle in the remaining vinaigrette and toss well. Taste and season with more salt or lime juice if necessary. Serve immediately. *—Tasha DeSerio*

The Julienne Cut

Knowing how to cut fruits and vegetables into thin little matchsticks is a basic but important skill for every cook to master. The matchstick cut, known in culinary lingo as julienne, is either used on its own or as the first step in dicing. Technically, the julienne cut is about ⅛ inch thick and 2 inches long. Cutting across a julienne results in a very fine dice, known in French as brunoise. When a larger stick or dice is needed, the same steps shown below apply—just space the cuts wider.

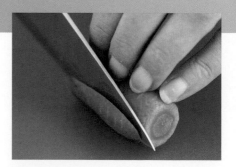

1 If the vegetable or fruit is rounded, cut a thin slice off one side to make a flat, stabilizing base. Turn it onto this new flat side.

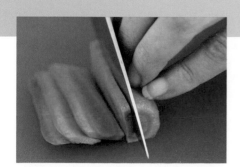

2 Now slice into ⅛-inch-thick slabs (or thicker for wider sticks or dice). Stack some of the slabs flat on the board—but don't try to do too many at once, or they may slide apart during the next step.

3 Slice the slabs lengthwise in the same thickness. For a shorter length, you could also slice crosswise or diagonally. If julienne is your goal, you're done.

4 To cut a dice, simply slice across the sticks.

Arugula & Fried Mozzarella Salad with Tomato-Basil Vinaigrette

Serves four as a light lunch.

1 large (about 7 ounces) smoked mozzarella

1 large egg

Kosher salt and freshly ground black pepper

1 cup fresh breadcrumbs

1½ cups medium diced fresh tomatoes

⅓ cup loosely packed fresh basil leaves, roughly chopped

1 medium clove garlic, minced

¼ cup plus 3 tablespoons extra-virgin olive oil

2 teaspoons balsamic vinegar

5 ounces baby arugula, washed and dried

In this satisfying salad, cheese is battered with egg and breadcrumbs before being fried into warm, crispy-gooey slices. The slight bitterness of the arugula is the perfect foil for the melty, rich fried mozzarella. Smoked mozzarella is divine and adds depth to the salad, but regular mozzarella will make a delicious salad, too. Be sure to coat the cheese slices thoroughly so they don't ooze during cooking.

Slice the mozzarella into eight slices, then again in half crosswise, so you have 16 pieces of cheese. Whisk the egg in a medium bowl with a pinch of salt and pepper. Put the breadcrumbs in another medium bowl. Working with a few pieces at a time, dip the cheese in the egg, turning to coat all sides of the cheese. Dredge the cheese in the breadcrumbs, pressing to help the crumbs adhere and cover the cheese as much as possible. Transfer the breaded cheese slices to a plate and refrigerate until ready to cook. You can prepare the cheese up to 1 hour ahead. Discard any leftover egg and crumbs.

In a small bowl, combine the tomatoes, basil, and garlic and season with ½ teaspoon kosher salt and a few grinds of pepper. Let this sit for 5 minutes, then add ¼ cup of the oil and the vinegar.

Heat 1½ tablespoons of the oil in a 10-inch nonstick skillet over medium-high heat. Put half the cheese in the pan and cook until the breadcrumbs turn golden, 30 to 60 seconds. Use two forks to turn the cheese and cook until the second side is golden, another 30 to 60 seconds. Transfer to a plate. Using the remaining 1½ tablespoons oil, repeat with the second batch of cheese.

Put the arugula in a large bowl. Stir the tomato mixture and toss it with the arugula. Taste and add salt and pepper as needed. Portion the salad among four plates. Arrange four pieces of cheese on top of each salad and serve immediately. *—Eva Katz*

Bibb & Cilantro Salad
with Shrimp & Toasted Corn

*Serves four as a light
main course.*

2 heads bibb or Boston lettuce,
washed, dried, and torn into
bite-size pieces

2 cups packed fresh cilantro
leaves, washed and dried

¼ cup finely diced red onion

3 tablespoons fresh lime juice

2 teaspoons honey

½ teaspoon Asian fish sauce

¼ cup plus 2 tablespoons extra-
virgin olive oil

Kosher salt and freshly ground
black pepper

2 cups fresh corn kernels

1 jalapeño, cored, seeded, and
finely diced

1½ pounds large shrimp, peeled
and deveined

**This salad makes a great wrapped sandwich; divvy it up among warm
tortillas and you're ready to roll. You can substitute frozen corn for fresh.
Let it thaw almost all the way and expect it to take a little longer to turn
golden as you toast it.**

Put the lettuce and cilantro in a large bowl, cover with a damp paper towel,
and refrigerate. In a small bowl, combine the onion, lime juice, honey, and fish
sauce. Whisk in ¼ cup of the oil. Season with ¼ teaspoon kosher salt and
several grinds of pepper.

Heat the remaining 2 tablespoons oil in a large nonstick skillet over medium
heat until shimmering. Add the corn and jalapeño and cook, stirring frequently,
until the corn is golden, 4 to 5 minutes. Add the shrimp and cook until pink
and cooked through, about 4 minutes. Remove from the heat, add
2 tablespoons of the dressing, and toss well.

Toss the lettuce and cilantro with the remaining dressing. Portion the
greens onto four plates. Spoon the corn and shrimp evenly onto the greens.
Serve immediately. *–Eva Katz*

Tuna & White Bean Salad with Arugula, Yellow Tomatoes & Olives

You can, of course, use red tomatoes instead of yellow in this salad, but using yellow allows the pink of the tuna to stand out against the greens. Spinach makes a fine substitute for arugula, if need be.

Put the arugula in a large bowl, cover with a damp paper towel, and refrigerate. In a small bowl, whisk together the vinegar, lemon juice, garlic, and ½ cup oil. Season with salt and pepper.

Heat a 12-inch heavy skillet over medium-high heat. Brush the tuna generously with the remaining 1 to 2 tablespoons oil and season with salt and pepper. Cook until the first side is browned, about 3 minutes. Flip and cook until the second side is browned and the tuna is cooked to your liking, about 3 minutes more for medium rare. Transfer to a plate and keep warm.

In a medium bowl, combine the beans, tomatoes, olives, and lemon zest and toss with just enough of the dressing to coat, about 3 tablespoons Season generously with salt and pepper. Toss the arugula with just enough dressing to coat lightly, about 5 tablespoons, and season with salt and pepper. Portion it onto four plates and top with a mound of the bean mixture. Cut the tuna into ¼-inch-thick slices and arrange on the arugula around the beans. Drizzle with a little of the remaining dressing and serve. *—Eva Katz*

Serves four as a main course.

5 ounces baby arugula leaves, washed and dried

1½ tablespoons balsamic vinegar

1½ tablespoons fresh lemon juice

1 clove garlic, finely chopped

½ cup plus 1 to 2 tablespoons extra-virgin olive oil

Kosher salt and freshly ground black pepper

4 tuna steaks (about 1½ inches thick), 4 to 6 ounces each

One 15.5-ounce can Great Northern or cannellini beans, drained and rinsed

½ pint yellow teardrop or grape tomatoes, halved

½ cup pitted green olives, drained and roughly chopped

1 teaspoon finely grated lemon zest

Crab & Avocado Salad

Serves four as a first course; serves two for lunch.

3 tablespoons mayonnaise

2 tablespoons buttermilk

½ teaspoon grated lemon zest

2 teaspoons fresh lemon juice; more for sprinkling

½ teaspoon Dijon mustard

Kosher salt and freshly ground black or white pepper

½ pound crabmeat, preferably lump, picked over to remove bits of shell

½ cup finely chopped celery from the inner ribs and leaves

3 tablespoons fresh chives cut into ½-inch pieces

1 ripe avocado, peeled, pitted, and cut into ¾-inch pieces

1 head Boston or bibb lettuce (for lining the plates), washed

For the best flavor, use fresh, unpasteurized crabmeat. You can also substitute thinly sliced cooked shrimp or lobster for the crabmeat. If you don't have buttermilk, use sour cream and add a teaspoon of water or so to thin the dressing, or use heavy cream and add an extra few drops of lemon juice.

In a small bowl, whisk the mayonnaise, buttermilk, lemon zest, lemon juice, and mustard. Season with salt and pepper to taste. In a medium bowl, mix the crabmeat, celery, and 2 tablespoons of the chives. Fold in the dressing gently so as not to break up the crabmeat. Gently fold in the avocado. Taste for salt and pepper. Line four salad plates with lettuce leaves, heap a scoop of the crab salad on each, and garnish with the remaining chives. Sprinkle each serving with ½ teaspoon lemon juice and serve. *—Molly Stevens*

Turkish Bread & Olive Salad

This salad is a great way to use up old bread. If you only have fresh bread on hand, tear it into pieces, spread them in a single layer on a baking sheet, and dry them out for about 10 minutes in a 375°F oven.

In a large bowl, combine the tomatoes, their seeds and juice, the onion, olives, lemon juice, olive oil, and salt and pepper to taste. Mix well and let stand at room temperature until the flavors meld, half hour to an hour.

Tear the bread into rough 1-inch pieces. Just before serving, add the bread to the tomato mixture, toss well, and sprinkle with the mint. —*Joanne Weir*

Serves six to eight.

1 pound ripe tomatoes, cored and cut into ½-inch dice, reserving as much of the juice and seeds as possible

1 medium red onion, cut into ½-inch dice

1 cup pitted dry-cured black olives, drained and coarsely chopped

¼ cup fresh lemon juice

⅓ cup extra-virgin olive oil

Kosher salt and freshly ground black pepper

½ pound coarse-textured sourdough bread, 1 to 2 days old

¼ cup coarsely chopped fresh mint

Baby Romaine Salad with Spicy Chicken & Warm Chipotle Vinaigrette

Serves four.

6 ounces baby romaine, washed and spun dry

¼ pound iceberg lettuce, thinly sliced (about 2 cups), washed, and spun dry

½ cup loosely packed fresh cilantro leaves

1 canned chipotle chile in adobo, chopped, plus 2 tablespoons of the sauce

3 oil-packed sun-dried tomatoes, chopped

2 tablespoons balsamic vinegar

2 teaspoons light brown sugar

1 teaspoon Dijon mustard

½ cup plus 3 tablespoons extra-virgin olive oil

Kosher salt and freshly ground black pepper

2 tablespoons unbleached all-purpose flour

2 tablespoons fine cornmeal (preferably white)

1 tablespoon chili powder

1 teaspoon ground cumin

1¼ pounds boneless, skinless chicken breast halves, cut crosswise into 1-inch-thick strips

½ small red onion, thinly sliced into half moons

1 ripe avocado, peeled, pitted and cut into ¾-inch dice

1½ cups cooked fresh (from about 2 ears) or thawed frozen corn kernels

1 lime, quartered

Smoky chipotle chiles canned in a rich adobo sauce are one of those incredibly versatile condiments no pantry should be without. Once you buy them for this salad, you'll find you can add them to soups, tacos, quesadillas, even eggs. Refrigerate the remaining chiles and sauce in an airtight container for a few weeks, or freeze them individually in ice cube trays.

Toss the romaine, iceberg, and half the cilantro in a large bowl. In a blender or food processor, purée the chipotle and adobo sauce, sun-dried tomatoes, vinegar, brown sugar, and mustard. With the machine running, slowly pour in ½ cup of the oil. Transfer to a measuring cup; season to taste with salt and pepper.

In a shallow dish, combine the flour, cornmeal, chili powder, and cumin with 1½ teaspoons kosher salt and ½ teaspoon black pepper. Season the chicken with 1 teaspoon kosher salt, then dredge in the flour mixture.

Heat 2 tablespoons of the remaining oil in a large heavy nonstick skillet over medium-high heat until it's shimmering, about 1 minute. Add half the chicken strips, evenly spaced, and cook without touching for 2 minutes. Flip and cook until the strips are just cooked through and firm to the touch, 1 to 2 minutes. Transfer to a large plate lined with paper towels and sprinkle with salt. Reduce the heat to medium, add the remaining 1 tablespoon oil, and cook the remaining strips in the same manner.

Discard the fat from the pan and wipe it clean with paper towels. Set it over low heat, add the vinaigrette, and cook, stirring with a wooden spoon or spatula, until warmed through, about 1 minute. Return the vinaigrette to the measuring cup and whisk to recombine.

Gently toss the greens with about ¼ cup of the vinaigrette or enough to lightly coat. Portion among four plates and top with the chicken, onion, avocado, corn, and the remaining ¼ cup cilantro. Drizzle with some of the remaining vinaigrette (you may not need it all) and serve with lime wedges on the side for squeezing over the salads. —*Tony Rosenfeld*

Spinach Salad with Stir-Fried Pork & Warm Ginger Vinaigrette

Serves four.

½ pound baby spinach, washed and spun dry

3 tablespoons rice vinegar

2½ tablespoons soy sauce

1 teaspoon granulated sugar

3 tablespoons water

1 pound ¼- to ½-inch-thick boneless pork chops, trimmed of excess fat and sliced crosswise ¼ inch thick

Kosher salt

1 tablespoon dry sherry

1 teaspoon cornstarch

½ cup canola or peanut oil

2 teaspoons Asian sesame oil

6 scallions, cut into 2-inch pieces

3½ ounces fresh shiitake mushrooms, stemmed and caps thinly sliced

½ red bell pepper, cored, seeded, and thinly sliced

2 tablespoons peeled and minced fresh ginger

For a splash of heat, drizzle this salad with some Asian hot sauce, such as sriracha (available in many grocery stores and in Asian markets). You can set a bottle of this hot sauce on the table for guests to add as they like.

Put the spinach in a large bowl. In a small bowl, whisk the vinegar with 1½ tablespoons of the soy sauce, the sugar, and water. Put the pork in a medium bowl and season with ½ teaspoon kosher salt. Toss with the remaining 1 tablespoon soy sauce, the sherry, and cornstarch. Let sit for 10 minutes.

Heat 1½ tablespoons of the canola oil in a heavy 12-inch skillet over medium-high heat until hot. Add the pork and cook, stirring, until it loses its raw color and is just firm, about 2 minutes. Transfer to a clean medium bowl.

To the skillet, add 1½ tablespoons of the canola oil, the sesame oil, the scallions, mushrooms, and bell pepper. Sprinkle with salt and cook, stirring, until the mushrooms and scallions soften and brown in places, about 3 minutes. Transfer to the bowl with the pork and toss.

Still over medium-high heat, add 1 tablespoon of the canola oil and the ginger and cook, stirring until very fragrant, about 30 seconds. Remove the skillet from the heat, add the vinegar-soy mixture, and stir well with a wooden spoon or spatula, scraping the pan to incorporate the browned bits. Whisk in the remaining ¼ cup canola oil; the mixture will remain largely separated. Transfer the vinaigrette to a measuring cup and whisk to emulsify thoroughly (the cornstarch from the browned bits will help).

Toss the spinach with half the vinaigrette (or enough to lightly coat). Portion among four plates, top with the pork and vegetables, and drizzle with some of the remaining vinaigrette (you may not need it all). Serve immediately.

–Tony Rosenfeld

Key Steps to Vibrant Warm Salads

1 First, sauté the toppings. The cooking moves quickly, so be sure to prep all your ingredients in advance.

2 Use the same skillet to warm the vinaigrette, which will pick up flavors left in the bottom of the pan.

3 Wilt the greens with about half of the warm vinaigrette, tossing to coat the greens evenly.

4 Arrange the greens on plates and add the toppings; then drizzle the remaining dressing on the finished salads.

Grilled Lamb Kebab Salad with Cucumber, Tomatoes & Pita

Serves four as a main course.

6 tablespoons fresh lemon juice

2 large cloves garlic, mashed or crushed through a garlic press

1¼ teaspoons ground allspice

¾ teaspoon kosher salt; more as needed

¾ teaspoon freshly ground black pepper

½ cup plus 2 tablespoons extra-virgin olive oil

2 pounds boneless lamb leg or shoulder meat, trimmed well and cut into 1½-inch cubes

1 small head romaine lettuce, washed, dried, and torn or cut into large bite-size pieces

1 large cucumber, peeled, seeded, and cut into large dice

2 ripe tomatoes, cored and cut into large dice

1 cup packed fresh mint leaves, roughly chopped

2 pita breads, 5 to 6 inches in diameter

Instead of tucking lamb and vegetables into a pita, tear up your bread and toss it with the lamb and fresh vegetables and herbs to create a main course salad with Middle Eastern flavor. (If you're not a lamb fan, this salad is delicious with chunks of tender beef, such as sirloin or rib-eye.) You can make the vinaigrette in advance to speed things up at dinner time.

Heat a gas grill to medium. In a small bowl, whisk the lemon juice, garlic, allspice, salt, and pepper. Whisking constantly, drizzle in ½ cup of the oil. Toss the lamb pieces in a medium bowl with 2 tablespoons of the vinaigrette, then thread onto three or four metal skewers; sprinkle with salt.

Combine the lettuce, cucumber, tomatoes, and all but about 2 tablespoons of the mint in a large bowl. Using a knife, split the pitas and pull the sides apart. Brush the pita halves with the remaining 2 tablespoons oil. Grill until crisp and charred in places, 30 to 60 seconds per side, and transfer to a plate.

Grill the lamb, turning the skewers every 90 seconds or so, until cooked to medium, 6 to 8 minutes. Remove from the grill and let rest for 5 minutes. Meanwhile, rip the pitas into large bite-size pieces, add to the bowl with the vegetables, and toss. Slide the lamb off the skewers and cut each cube in half. In a medium bowl, toss it with 3 tablespoons of the vinaigrette (whisk to recombine first).

Toss the vegetables with the remaining dressing and season to taste with salt and pepper. Portion onto four plates. Top the salads with the lamb and sprinkle with the remaining mint. Serve immediately. *—Eva Katz*

Asian Steak, Watercress & Spinach Salad with Hoisin Vinaigrette

Strip steak, also called top loin steak or New York steak, is a flavorful and readily available cut of beef that stays tender and juicy when quickly seared. Letting the meat rest for a few minutes before carving allows it to reabsorb its juices so they end up in the meat, not all over the cutting board. The sweet and spicy hoisin sauce can be found on the international foods aisle at most supermarkets.

Put the watercress and spinach in a large bowl, cover with a damp paper towel, and refrigerate.

In a small bowl, whisk the scallions, vinegar, hoisin, soy sauce, and ginger. Whisk in the sesame oil and vegetable oil. Season to taste with salt and pepper.

Heat a large, heavy pan (preferably cast iron) over medium-high heat for at least 1 minute. Use paper towels to pat the steaks dry. Season them generously with salt and pepper, rub with oil, put them in the pan, and cook until well browned, about 4 minutes. Flip and continue to cook, about another 3 minutes for medium rare. Transfer the steaks to a cutting board, let rest for 5 minutes, then slice them thinly.

Add the water chestnuts to the bowl of greens. Whisk the vinaigrette and toss the greens and water chestnuts with just enough of it to coat (there should be a few tablespoons vinaigrette left over). Taste and add salt and pepper as needed. Portion among four plates. Arrange the beef over the greens, drizzle with any remaining dressing, and serve. *—Eva Katz*

Serves four as a main course.

2 bunches watercress (6 to 7 ounces each), thick stems trimmed, tender stems and leaves separated into bite-size sprigs, washed and dried

¼ pound baby spinach, washed and dried

4 scallions (white and light green parts), minced

1 tablespoon rice vinegar

2 teaspoons hoisin sauce

2 teaspoons soy sauce

1 teaspoon peeled and finely grated fresh ginger

2 tablespoons Asian sesame oil

2 tablespoons vegetable or peanut oil; more for cooking the steak

Kosher salt and freshly ground black pepper

1½ pounds beef strip steaks (about 1 inch thick)

One 8-ounce can sliced water chestnuts, drained

3 Soups

p98

p92

**Butternut Squash Soup
with Apple & Bacon
(recipe on page 110)**

Yellow Tomato Gazpacho with Avocado Salsa

Yields about 10 cups.

For the soup:

5 pounds ripe yellow heirloom tomatoes, cored and cut into chunks

3 cloves garlic, peeled

1 cucumber (about ¾ pound), peeled, seeded if necessary, and cut into large pieces

1 medium yellow bell pepper, cored, seeded, and cut into large pieces

1 small red onion, cut into large pieces

½ small hot red chile (or to taste), seeded and cut into large pieces

½ cup red-wine vinegar

¾ cup extra-virgin olive oil

Kosher salt and ground white pepper

For the garnish:

Avocado Salsa (recipe follows)

6 each red and yellow cherry tomatoes, halved

Avocado Salsa

Yields about 3 cups.

You can use the salsa as a dip on its own or as a topping for grilled fish or chicken.

2 small ripe Hass avocados, peeled, pitted, and cut into small dice

1 small hot red chile, seeded and minced

1 small red onion, cut into small dice

1 red heirloom slicing tomato, cored, seeded, and diced

1 tablespoon finely chopped fresh cilantro

Juice of 1 lime

¼ cup extra-virgin olive oil

Kosher salt and freshly cracked black pepper to taste

So many yellow tomatoes are available in late summer, especially at farmers' markets. Yellow Taxis have great flavor, but if you can't find them, substitute any truly ripe, in-season tomato.

Make the soup: Working in batches, purée the tomatoes, garlic, cucumber, yellow pepper, onion, chile, vinegar, and olive oil in a blender until smooth. Strain through a fine sieve into a bowl. Press on the solids with a wooden spoon in order to extract as much liquid as possible; discard the solids. Season to taste with salt and pepper. Refrigerate in an airtight container for at least 2 hours or up to two days.

Make the salsa: In a medium bowl, stir all the ingredients. Refrigerate, covered, for at least 20 minutes and up to 3 hours before serving.

To serve, taste the soup and adjust the seasonings. Spoon 2 generous tablespoons of the avocado salsa in the center of each soup bowl. Pour or ladle the gazpacho over the salsa and garnish with the cherry tomato halves.

–Stu Stein

Summer Corn Soup

When corn is in season, you want to eat it as much as possible; here's a lovely soup that highlights its sweetness. If you don't have marjoram, fresh thyme is delicious. Or you can skip those herbs and just let the basil garnish do the talking.

Cut the kernels off the ears of corn by starting to cut halfway down the ear and slicing to the bottom, rotating the ear as you go; don't try to cut too close to the base of the kernels. Turn the ear over and repeat to remove all the kernels. You'll need 3½ to 4 cups of kernels for the soup.

Stand one cob on end in a pie plate or other shallow dish and use the back edge of the knife to scrape the cobs and extract as much "milk" and solids as you can. Set this raw corn purée aside.

Break the cobs in half and put them in a heavy 4-quart pot. Add the water and 1 teaspoon kosher salt and bring to a boil. Reduce the heat to medium low, cover, and simmer for 30 minutes. Discard the cobs. Pour the liquid into a bowl and set aside.

Set the pot back over medium-high heat and add the oil. When it's hot, add the onion and sauté until translucent, about 3 minutes. Add the garlic and cook for 1 minute. Reduce the heat to medium, add the celery, sprinkle with salt, and stir. Cover the pot and cook, stirring occasionally, until the vegetables start to soften, 5 to 6 minutes; don't let them color. (If they start to brown before softening, reduce the heat.) Add the potatoes, marjoram, black pepper (about 6 turns of the grinder), and cayenne and stir to distribute the seasonings. Add the corn stock. Bring to a boil over medium-high heat, cover, reduce the heat to medium low, and simmer until the vegetables are tender enough to purée, 20 to 30 minutes. Add most of the corn kernels, reserving about 1 cup. Simmer gently for another 10 minutes.

Purée the soup in batches in a blender (be careful to fill the blender no more than one-third full and hold a towel over the lid while you turn it on). Return the puréed soup to the pot. Taste for seasoning and add more salt or pepper if necessary. Add the reserved corn kernels and corn "milk," and simmer just long enough to take the raw edge off the corn, about 5 minutes. Serve hot, warm, or at room temperature, garnished with a small dollop of sour cream and the tomatoes and basil. –*Ruth Lively*

Serves six.

5 to 6 large ears corn, shucked and silks removed

6 cups water

Kosher salt

3 tablespoons olive oil or unsalted butter, or a combination

1 large onion, diced

4 cloves garlic, roughly chopped

½ cup diced celery

1 medium red potato, peeled and cut into 1-inch cubes

Leaves from 3 to 4 sprigs fresh marjoram, chopped

Freshly ground black pepper

Pinch cayenne

¼ cup sour cream, for garnish

½ cup finely diced fresh tomatoes, for garnish

¼ cup thinly sliced fresh basil, for garnish

Creamy Roasted Garlic Soup with Sautéed Cauliflower & Fresh Herbs

Serves four.

For the soup:

4 heads garlic, loose, papery skins removed

5 tablespoons extra-virgin olive oil

Kosher salt

½ cup chopped onion

1 leek (white and light green parts), chopped and well rinsed

2 large boiling potatoes, peeled and chopped

1 tablespoon fresh thyme leaves, chopped

½ cup dry white wine

1 quart low-salt chicken or vegetable broth

Freshly ground black pepper

¼ cup chopped fresh sorrel or chives, or a combination

For the cauliflower:

2 tablespoons olive oil

1 small head cauliflower, cut into small florets (about ½ inch at the widest point)

In this rich, deeply flavored soup, the cauliflower acts almost as a garnish. It adds a nutty toastiness to the soup's sweet garlic flavor.

Make the soup: Heat the oven to 375°F. Cut off the top ¼ inch from each garlic head to expose the cloves. Put the heads in a small baking pan, drizzle on 2 tablespoons of the oil, and sprinkle with ½ teaspoon kosher salt. Add 2 tablespoons water to the pan, cover with foil, and roast until a squeezed clove yields a soft purée, 30 to 45 minutes. When cool, squeeze the pulp from each clove.

In a soup pot over low heat, sauté the onion and leek in 1 tablespoon of the oil until very soft but not brown, about 10 minutes. Add the potatoes and thyme, cook 1 minute. Turn the heat to medium high, add the wine, and let it reduce to just a few teaspoons, about 4 minutes. Add the broth; bring to a boil. Reduce the heat and simmer for 10 minutes. Add the garlic pulp and simmer until the potatoes are very soft, 15 to 20 minutes. Strain the soup, saving both the liquid and solids. In a blender or food processor, purée the solids in batches, using some liquid to help it blend. Pour the purée back in the pot and add as much of the remaining liquid as necessary to get a consistency like heavy cream. Season to taste with salt and pepper.

Sauté the cauliflower: Heat the oil in a large sauté pan over medium heat. Add the cauliflower and sauté. Once it begins to soften, after about 5 minutes, season with salt and pepper. Continue to sauté until deep golden brown and tender but still firm, another 7 to 10 minutes. Reheat the soup. Ladle it into individual bowls, add the cauliflower, and garnish with the sorrel or chives.

—Peter Hoffman

Roasted Carrot Soup

A tablespoon of ginger gives a nice, throat-warming heat to this soup, which tastes best if it sits in the fridge for several hours or overnight.

Heat the oven to 375°F. Put the carrots in a medium baking dish (11x7-inch is a good size, or any dish that will hold the carrots in a single layer without touching) and drizzle with the olive oil. Toss to coat well and roast, stirring once halfway through roasting, until they're tender, blistered, and lightly browned in a few places, about 1 hour.

Melt the butter in a medium, heavy saucepan set over medium heat. Add the onion and cook until translucent and fragrant, 2 to 3 minutes. Stir in the celery and ginger and cook until the celery softens a bit and the onion starts to brown, 4 to 5 minutes. Add the roasted carrots, broth, salt, pepper, and water. Bring to a boil, reduce the heat to medium low, and cover. Cook at a lively simmer until the carrots are very tender, about 45 minutes. Turn off the heat and let the liquid cool somewhat (or completely).

Purée the soup in a blender in batches, never filling the blender more than a third full. Cover the lid with a towel and bear down firmly so the soup doesn't come flying out. If serving immediately, return the soup to the pot and reheat; garnish with the chives if you like. Otherwise, refrigerate for up to five days; reheat gently and taste for salt before serving. –*Ruth Lively*

Serves four.

- 1 pound carrots, peeled and cut into 3-inch lengths
- 1 tablespoon olive oil
- 1 tablespoon unsalted butter
- ½ medium onion, cut into medium dice
- 1 large rib celery, cut into medium dice
- 1 tablespoon peeled and minced fresh ginger
- 2 cups low-salt chicken broth
- 1 teaspoon kosher salt
- ⅛ teaspoon ground white pepper
- 2 cups water
- Chopped fresh chives or chervil for garnish (optional)

Summer Vegetable Soup with Shrimp & Lemon

Serves six to eight.

2 tablespoons olive oil

1 medium-large onion, finely diced

1 large clove garlic, finely chopped

1 quart low-salt chicken broth

1 cup diced fresh tomato

1 medium-large red bell pepper, cored, seeded, and cut into medium dice

2 small zucchini, cut into medium dice

1 2/3 cups fresh or frozen corn kernels

1 pound red potatoes, cut into medium dice

Kosher salt and freshly ground black pepper

1/2 pound shrimp, peeled, deveined, and cut crosswise into 1/2-inch pieces if large; left whole if small

2 tablespoons chopped fresh herbs, such as basil, cilantro, parsley, or a mix

2 teaspoons fresh lemon juice; more to taste

To save time as you cook, get the onion going while you prep the other vegetables. If you're not finished with the dicing and chopping, add just the chicken broth to stop the onion's sautéing while you finish up.

Heat the olive oil in a 4-quart or larger Dutch oven or soup pot. Add the onion and cook over medium heat, stirring occasionally, until softened, about 8 minutes. Add the garlic and cook, stirring, another minute or two, being careful not to let it brown. Add the broth, tomato, bell pepper, zucchini, corn, potatoes, and 1/2 teaspoon kosher salt. Simmer until the vegetables are tender, about 10 minutes. Add the shrimp and simmer until it just begins to turn pink, 1 to 2 minutes. Let the soup rest for 5 minutes (the shrimp will continue to cook off the heat), then add the herbs and the lemon juice. Taste and season with salt and pepper and additional lemon juice if needed. Serve immediately. *—Pam Anderson*

Roasted Red Bell Pepper Soup with Star Anise

Serves three to four.

2 tablespoons olive oil

2 onions (about ¾ pound total), chopped

2 cloves garlic, chopped

½ cubic inch fresh ginger, peeled and chopped

1 medium carrot, peeled and chopped

1 quart low-salt chicken broth

3 large red bell peppers, roasted, peeled, and seeded; juices reserved

1 whole star anise (or ¾ teaspoon broken pieces)

½ teaspoon kosher salt; more to taste

¼ teaspoon freshly ground black pepper; more to taste

Small pinch cayenne

6 fresh basil leaves

Extra-virgin olive oil and sherry vinegar, for garnish (optional)

This vibrant soup is also delicious served cold, and it can be garnished with a few cooked shrimp, a mound of crabmeat, or a bit of goat cheese.

Heat the olive oil in a 6-quart soup pot over medium heat. Add the onions, garlic, ginger, and carrot and sauté until very soft but not browned, 15 to 20 minutes. Add the broth and turn the heat to high. Add the roasted peppers and any reserved juices, along with the star anise, salt, pepper, and cayenne. As soon as the mixture comes to a boil, reduce the heat and simmer, uncovered, for 30 minutes. Stir occasionally.

Purée the soup in batches in a blender, with all the basil leaves going in the blender along with the first batch. Purée each batch of soup for at least 1 minute. Combine all the puréed soup in one container, taste, and add more salt and pepper to bring all the flavors into balance. (For a thinner soup, strain through a wide-mesh sieve.) Serve with a drizzle of extra-virgin olive oil and a splash of sherry vinegar, if you like. *—Brian Patterson*

How to Roast a Red Pepper

1 Coat each pepper in a little oil. If you have gas burners, you can roast a pepper directly on the grate over high heat, turning the pepper with tongs occasionally until it's charred all over.

To char a batch of peppers, a hot charcoal or gas grill is best, but the broiler works, too. Put the oiled peppers on a foil-lined baking sheet and broil as close to the element as possible, turning them so they char evenly.

2 Put the charred peppers in a bowl while they're still hot and cover with plastic. Let them rest until they're cool enough to handle. Pull on the stem; the seed core will pop out. Cut the pepper open, flick off any seeds, and turn skin side up.

3 Use a paring knife to scrape away the charred skin. Don't rinse the peppers with water or you'll dilute their flavor.

tip: If you have an electric stove, get a stovetop pepper roaster. It turns your electric burner into a little grill, and it's also handy for heating tortillas.

Tomato Bisque & Cheese Toasts

Serves two.

For the bisque:

2 tablespoons olive oil

1 small onion, diced

1 clove garlic, minced

3 large sprigs fresh thyme

One 28-ounce can crushed
tomatoes in purée

1½ cups low-salt chicken broth

3 tablespoons honey

1½ teaspoons kosher salt; more
to taste

¼ teaspoon finely ground black
pepper; more to taste

⅓ cup heavy cream

2 tablespoons chopped fresh
flat-leaf parsley (optional)

For the toasts:

4 slices country-style bread,
about ½ inch thick

1 tablespoon Dijon mustard

4 to 6 slices Gruyère cheese

1 tablespoon freshly grated
Parmigiano-Reggiano cheese

Honey is the unexpected ingredient in this simple soup, adding a sweet, mellow undertone. The cheese toasts add even more flavor as well as a welcome crunch; they make the soup feel more like a meal. You should feel free to dip an edge of the toast right into the soup.

Make the bisque: In a medium pot, heat the oil. Add the onion and cook over medium heat, stirring frequently, until tender and lightly browned on the edges, about 7 minutes. Add the garlic and thyme; stir until fragrant, about 1 minute. Add the tomatoes, broth, honey, salt, and pepper. Bring to a boil, then reduce the heat and simmer, stirring frequently, until reduced by a quarter and thickened, about 15 minutes. Using a stand or immersion blender, purée about half the soup; it will still be chunky and thick. Return all the soup to the pot and stir in the cream. Heat gently and adjust the seasonings.

Make the toasts: Arrange an oven rack to the highest rung and heat the broiler on high. Line a baking sheet with aluminum foil. Put the bread on the foil and toast each side until golden brown. Spread the mustard evenly on one side of each toast, cover with the Gruyère, and sprinkle with the Parmigiano. Slide the toasts back under the broiler and cook until bubbling and lightly browned on top, about 2 minutes. Cut each toast in half.

Ladle the soup into bowls, sprinkle with the parsley if using, and serve the soup and toasts immediately. *—Abigail Johnson Dodge*

Fresh Zucchini Soup with Cilantro, Lime & Spiced Yogurt

Serves four.

For the soup:

12 sprigs fresh cilantro; more
   leaves for garnish

1 small head garlic, cut
   across the equator; plus
   1 tablespoon minced garlic

5 cups water

3 tablespoons unsalted butter

1 large onion, sliced

2 teaspoons kosher salt; more
   to taste

1 tablespoon peeled and
   minced fresh ginger

2 tablespoons minced jalapeño

½ teaspoon cumin seeds

½ teaspoon coriander seeds

⅛ teaspoon cardamom seeds
   or 1 green cardamom pod
   (optional)

1 pound zucchini, sliced into
   ½-inch-thick rounds

¼ teaspoon fresh lime juice;
   more to taste

For the raita:

½ cup whole-milk yogurt

¼ teaspoon kosher salt;
   more to taste

1 teaspoon vegetable oil

½ teaspoon brown mustard
   seeds

¼ teaspoon cumin seeds

This soup looks like a lot of work, but many of the ingredients are spices that come right from the jar. (And you don't even have to peel the squash!) For the most satiny texture, purée the soup through a fine sieve.

Make the soup: Put the cilantro, halved garlic head, and water in a large saucepan or stockpot. Bring to a boil, reduce the heat to a simmer, and cook, uncovered, for 15 minutes. Strain the broth.

Melt the butter in a large, heavy saucepan over medium heat. Add the onion, salt, ginger, jalapeño, cumin, coriander, and cardamom, if using. Cover and cook, stirring occasionally, until the onion is translucent, about 10 minutes; don't let it brown. Stir in the 1 tablespoon minced garlic and the zucchini, cover, and cook, stirring occasionally, until the squash is softened, about 5 minutes. Add 4 cups of the broth, bring to a simmer, and cook until the zucchini is tender, about another 3 minutes.

Meanwhile, make the raita: In a small bowl, combine the yogurt and salt. Heat the oil in a small skillet. When hot, add the mustard and cumin seeds. When they start to pop, add the oil and seeds to the yogurt and stir. Set aside.

Purée the soup in a blender and strain through a fine sieve. Add the lime juice; taste and add salt if needed. Serve warm, garnished with 1 to 2 tablespoons raita and the cilantro leaves. *—Eve Felder*

Weeknight Chicken Noodle Soup with Ginger & Watercress

Serves two to three.

One 1-inch piece fresh ginger

1 tablespoon vegetable oil

2 skinless, boneless chicken thighs

Kosher salt and freshly ground black pepper

2 medium shallots, thinly sliced

1 quart low-salt chicken broth

¼ pound fresh Chinese egg noodles

2 cups tender watercress sprigs

1 teaspoon ponzu sauce (or a mix of soy sauce and lemon juice)

Here's a soup so easy and so soothing, you'll find yourself turning to it again and again. Look for fresh Chinese egg noodles in the supermarket produce section and ponzu sauce in the soy sauce aisle.

Peel the ginger and slice it thickly. Lay the slices on a cutting board, cover with plastic wrap, and smash with a meat mallet or heavy pan.

Heat the vegetable oil in a 5- to 6-quart soup pot over medium-high heat. Season the chicken with salt and pepper and brown each side for about 2 minutes. Transfer to a plate (it won't be fully cooked). Reduce the heat slightly, add the shallots and ginger, and sauté until browned, stirring to break up the ginger, about 2 minutes. Add the broth and scrape the bottom of the pot to loosen any browned bits. Return the chicken to the pot and bring the broth to a simmer. Cook, partially covered, for 3 minutes, skimming off any foam that forms on the surface. Add the noodles (cut into shorter lengths if you like) and simmer 3 minutes longer (more or less if the package instructions differ). Remove the pan from the heat and transfer the chicken to a cutting board. Add the watercress and ponzu to the soup and stir well. Roughly shred or chop the chicken and return it to the pot. Serve right away. —*Susie Middleton*

Tortellini in Broth with Roasted Vegetables

This is a great way to use up extra winter vegetables. Carrots, parsnips, sweet potatoes, and cauliflower make a delicious mix. Don't bother to peel most of these, as the skins are perfectly tender when roasted.

Heat the oven to 450°F. Put a large pot of water on to boil. In a 9x13-inch Pyrex® baking dish, toss the vegetables with 2 tablespoons of the oil and ¼ teaspoon kosher salt and spread out in one layer. Roast until well browned and shrunken, 28 to 30 minutes, stirring occasionally with a flat metal spatula.

After the vegetables have roasted for about 15 minutes, add 2 teaspoons kosher salt and the tortellini to the boiling water; cook the pasta until tender. Save some of the water to pour into two large shallow soup bowls to warm them. Drain the tortellini in a colander. In a small saucepan, heat the remaining 1 tablespoon oil over medium heat. Add the shallot; sauté until softened and browned, about 2½ minutes. Stir in the red pepper flakes and add the broth. Bring to a simmer, cover, and simmer for 4 to 5 minutes. Turn off the heat and keep covered.

Pour the water out of the soup bowls. Divide the tortellini between the warmed bowls. Spoon the roasted vegetables over the pasta. Pour the broth over the vegetables and garnish with the Parmigiano and parsley. Season with salt and pepper to taste. Serve with a lemon wedge. *–Susie Middleton*

Serves two.

3 cups ¾-inch-diced winter vegetables (carrots, parsnips, turnips, cauliflower, broccoflower, winter squash, sweet potatoes)

3 tablespoons extra-virgin olive oil

Kosher salt and freshly ground black pepper

6 ounces frozen small cheese tortellini

1 small shallot, sliced into rings

Pinch red pepper flakes

1½ cups low-salt chicken broth

¼ cup freshly grated Parmigiano-Reggiano cheese

2 teaspoons coarsely chopped fresh flat-leaf parsley

½ small lemon, cut into two wedges

Chicken Coconut Soup (Tom Kha Gai)

Serves four as a starter or two as a light meal.

2 stalks fresh lemongrass

2 tablespoons fresh lime juice

2 tablespoons Asian fish sauce

2 scallions (white and green parts), sliced very thinly crosswise

6 fresh or frozen wild lime leaves, torn or quartered (or substitute the peel from 1 lime; use a vegetable peeler to peel wide strips, then slightly bruise them)

10 to 12 thin slices galangal, fresh, frozen, or dried (or 10 to 12 thin slices fresh unpeeled ginger)

8 to 10 fresh hot red and green Thai chiles, stemmed and lightly pressed with the side of a knife (or 3 or 4 serranos, thinly sliced) for garnish (optional)

2 tablespoons coarsely chopped fresh cilantro

1 boneless, skinless chicken breast half, cut into bite-size chunks or sliced across the grain into strips

¼ pound white mushrooms, stems trimmed, and thinly sliced

One 14-ounce can unsweetened coconut milk (shake the can before opening it)

One 14-ounce can low-salt chicken broth or 1¾ cups water

This soup is a treasure: a quintessentially Thai dish that you can make at home simply, quickly, and with great success. To easily get all of the ingredients, your best bet is an Asian market. Many supermarkets, however, now carry stalks of lemongrass (look for it in the produce section) and fish sauce, which is usually in the international foods aisle.

Trim away and discard the root end and the top 3 inches of each stalk of lemongrass, along with any brittle leaves. Pound each stalk lightly with the spine of a cleaver or an unopened can. Cut crosswise into 2-inch lengths and set aside.

In a large serving bowl, combine the lime juice, fish sauce, scallions, and half the lime leaves. Set the bowl by the stove, along with small dishes containing the galangal, lemongrass, the remaining lime leaves, the chiles (if using), cilantro, chicken, and mushrooms.

In a medium saucepan, combine the coconut milk and broth. Bring to a gentle boil over medium-high heat. Stir in the galangal, lemongrass, and lime leaves. Add the chicken and mushrooms. Return to a gentle boil, reduce the heat, and simmer for 10 minutes to infuse the flavors and cook the chicken.

Remove the pan from the heat, pour the hot soup over the seasonings in the serving bowl, and stir well. Sprinkle with the cilantro and serve hot. Pass around the chiles for those who want them. —*Nancie McDermott*

Miso Mushroom Soup

Serves two.

2 dried shiitake mushrooms, rinsed

3 cups cold water

½ cup baby spinach leaves

½ cup medium-diced silken tofu

2½ tablespoons miso (preferably red or brown)

2 tablespoons thinly sliced scallion greens

½ teaspoon Asian sesame oil

This quick-to-make soup is a perfect way to introduce yourself to the savory flavor of miso. You can make it with any type of miso, but the darker types will have a richer, deeper flavor.

In a medium saucepan, combine the mushrooms and water. Bring to a boil over medium heat. Remove from the heat and use a fork or tongs to transfer the mushrooms to a cutting board. As soon as they are cool enough to handle, trim off and discard the stems and slice the caps very thinly. Return the sliced mushrooms to the water, bring back to a simmer, then reduce the heat to low. Let the mushrooms steep for 15 minutes (the water needn't be simmering, but it's fine if it does). Taste one of the mushroom slices. If you like the texture, leave the mushrooms in; otherwise, fish them out and discard them.

Bring the mushroom broth to a simmer over medium heat. Add the spinach and tofu and simmer for 1 minute. Remove from the heat. In a small bowl, combine the miso with 2 tablespoons of the broth and mix well. Stir the thinned miso into the soup. Sprinkle each serving with 1 tablespoon of the scallion greens and ¼ teaspoon of the sesame oil. Serve immediately.

—Jennifer Armentrout

All About Miso

Types of miso

For flavor-pairing purposes, think of miso in terms of two broad categories: Light miso—typically called white, yellow, or sweet miso—and dark miso—red, brown, barley, and soybean miso.

Generally, the lighter the miso, the sweeter and more delicate its flavor. Light miso is good in salads and dressings, and with lighter foods like fish, chicken, and vegetables.

Dark miso, which is fermented longer, will be saltier and "meatier." Its rich, robust flavor is good for adding depth to soups and sauces. Try it with root vegetables, beans, or winter squash.

Cooking with miso

Always add miso toward the end of cooking and never boil it, as high heat will destroy both its flavor and nutrients. For the smoothest sauces and soups, whisk miso into an equal amount of slightly warm broth until smooth, then gradually stir the thinned miso back into the pot. Use about 1 to 1½ tablespoons of miso for every cup of liquid. Miso is a good substitute for salt or soy sauce or in place of anchovy paste for vegetarian recipes. Just remember, miso is quite concentrated in flavor, so a little goes a long way.

Buying and storing miso

Look for miso in plastic tubs or bags in the refrigerated section of Asian markets or health-food stores. Miso keeps for up to a year if sealed well and refrigerated.

Golden Chicken, Corn & Orzo Soup

Serves five to six.

Kosher salt

2 tablespoons olive oil

2 large ribs celery, finely diced

1 medium onion, finely diced

Pinch saffron threads

½ teaspoon dried thyme

2 quarts low-salt chicken broth

2 cups finely diced or shredded
  cooked chicken

½ cup orzo

1 cup frozen corn

¼ cup chopped fresh flat-leaf
  parsley

3 tablespoons fresh lemon
  juice; more to taste

Freshly ground black pepper

This soup is deliciously restorative after a long day of work. If saffron isn't in your pantry, go ahead and make the soup without it, but buy some for next time because it adds such an intriguing flavor.

Bring a medium saucepan of generously salted water to a boil. Meanwhile, heat the oil in a large soup pot over medium heat. Add the celery, onion, saffron, and thyme and cook, stirring occasionally, until the vegetables soften, 5 to 6 minutes. Add the broth and bring to a boil over medium-high heat. Reduce the heat to a simmer, add the chicken, and cook until the vegetables are tender, about 15 minutes.

While the soup simmers, cook the orzo in the boiling salted water until tender, 8 to 10 minutes. Drain. Add the orzo, corn, and parsley to the soup and cook just until the corn is heated through, about 2 minutes. Stir in the lemon juice and season to taste with salt, pepper, and more lemon juice, if needed. Serve immediately. —*Jennifer Armentrout*

Serves eight to ten.

For the soup:

½ tablespoon coriander seeds

¾ teaspoon black peppercorns

1½ cups pink lentils (also known as red lentils or masoor dal), picked over and washed well

1 medium white onion, cut into ½-inch dice

2 ribs celery, cut into ½-inch dice

1 medium carrot, peeled and cut into ½-inch dice

3 cloves garlic, thinly sliced

One 1-inch piece fresh ginger, peeled and coarsely chopped

½ fresh serrano chile, thinly sliced (don't remove seeds)

15 sprigs fresh cilantro, tied in a cheesecloth pouch

Kosher or sea salt

10 cups water

1 cup plain yogurt, whisked until smooth, for garnish

2 tablespoons sliced fresh chives, for garnish

For the tarka:

2 tablespoons canola oil

1 teaspoon mustard seeds

1 teaspoon cumin seeds

Peppery Pink Lentil Soup

This fragrant, Indian-inspired soup gets a final flourish of flavor from a tarka, whole spices cooked in oil and swirled into the soup.

Make the soup: Heat a small, dry sauté pan over medium-high heat. When hot, add the coriander seeds and toast—stir constantly (or shake the pan gently) to keep them from burning—until they darken slightly and become very fragrant, 1 to 2 minutes. Immediately transfer to a dish and set aside. Return the sauté pan to the heat; add the peppercorns and toast, shaking the pan, for about 2 minutes. Pour onto the plate with the coriander. Put the toasted spices in a spice grinder or mortar and pestle and grind to a fine powder.

In a large saucepan, combine the lentils, onion, celery, carrot, garlic, ginger, chile, cheesecloth-wrapped cilantro sprigs, and 2 teaspoons kosher salt with the water. Bring to a boil over medium-high heat. Reduce the heat to medium low and simmer for 30 minutes. Remove the cilantro sprigs. Add the ground spices to the soup and simmer for another 10 minutes. Purée the soup using an immersion blender or a regular blender until the soup is very smooth. Strain the purée through a medium sieve into a large serving bowl. The soup can be made to this point one day ahead; reheat it gently before continuing.

Make the tarka and garnish the soup: Set a small deep saucepan over medium heat and add the oil. When it's shimmering, add the mustard seeds and cook, uncovered, until they pop, 30 to 60 seconds. Add the cumin seeds and cook for another 1 minute. Quickly but carefully, pour the hot tarka over the soup and mix well. Season with salt to taste. Ladle the soup into individual serving bowls and garnish with a dollop of yogurt and a sprinkling of the chives. *—Floyd Cardoz*

Helping Spices Release Their Flavor

Spices are naturally fragrant, but to reach their full flavor potential, they need your help. Cracking and grinding spices is part of the equation. But it's heat that really wakes up those aromatic oils. Toasting (dry heat) and blooming in oil (moist heat) are classic techniques. A flat metal or silicone spatula is best for cooking with spices; wooden spoons absorb spices' flavors.

Grinding spices

Grinding releases a spice's flavorful aromatic oils. A coarser grind adds textural interest and a mosaic of flavors to a dish. (But not all spices should be left coarse: cinnamon, cloves, mace, nutmeg, and green and black cardamom are so strongly flavored that biting into a big piece is not pleasant.) Finer grinds tend to be more subtle, with the flavors more evenly blended.

A small electric coffee grinder lets you grind a few tablespoons of spice at a time. If you use a mortar and pestle, grind in a circular motion and hold a piece of plastic wrap over the bowl while you grind to keep the spices from sneaking out. Before grinding whole dried chiles or bay leaves, put them in a low oven for about 5 minutes to evaporate moisture and make them brittle.

Toasting whole spices

When you toast spices, moisture cooks off and the spice takes on a warm, smoky, earthy flavor that can be totally different from the character of the raw spice. Raw coriander, for example, has a very citrusy aroma, but when toasted it becomes almost nutty.

Raw ground spices are quick to burn, so always toast spices whole, then grind them. And only toast one kind of spice at a time: If you toast a mixture of whole spices, some will burn before the others are even close to being done.

To toast whole spices, heat a dry sauté pan over medium heat. When the pan is very warm, add the whole spice. Shake the pan to keep the spice moving and to control browning. After toasting, immediately remove the spice from the pan to stop the cooking. When cool, grind the spice and add it to your dish toward the end of cooking or right before serving.

Blooming whole spices

Blooming a spice in oil is a bit like sautéing a vegetable: It's quick, and the resulting flavor is bright. The combination of heat and oil quickly extracts aromatic compounds from a spice.

To bloom whole spices, heat the oil over medium heat until it's hot but not smoking. Add the whole spices and cook until very fragrant and little bubbles form around the spices. Don't let them brown. You can then add other ingredients to the hot pan and proceed with your recipe. (If you bloom large spices like cardamom pods, cloves, or cinnamon sticks, be sure to remove them from the finished dish before serving because you don't want people to bite into them.)

What is a tarka? Small, whole, edible spices bloomed in hot oil and added to a dish at the end of cooking.

Frying a paste of ground raw spices

Toasting ground spices in a dry pan isn't a great idea because they're very quick to burn. Instead, you can bloom them in oil—but even then, hot oil can scorch ground spices, so you must take care.

To bloom ground spices, you need to first mix them with a little of the liquid from your recipe—vinegar, water, stock, wine, whatever—to make a thick paste. The moisture in the spice paste helps keep the ground spices from burning when you put the paste in the hot oil. Then you cook the paste until all the liquid evaporates. You can tell it's time to stop cooking when the oil starts to separate from the spices.

Silky Leek & Celery Root Soup

Yields about 24 two-ounce appetizer portions, or serves four to six as a first course.

3 tablespoons unsalted butter

2 medium leeks (white and light green parts), trimmed, halved lengthwise, cut crosswise into thin half-moon slices, rinsed well, and drained

1 medium yellow onion, thinly sliced

Kosher salt

1½ pounds celery root

¾ cup crème fraîche

¼ cup heavy cream; more as needed

Freshly ground black pepper

¼ cup thinly sliced fresh chives

For the best flavor, make this soup a day in advance, and take your time with the leeks. Wash them thoroughly to remove any grit (which is common with leeks) and cook them slowly to coax out their sweetness.

In a 4-quart or larger heavy pot, melt the butter over medium-low heat. Add the leeks, onion, and a generous pinch of salt and cook, stirring occasionally, until very soft and lightly golden but not brown, 15 to 20 minutes. Reduce the heat to low if you see signs of browning.

Meanwhile, peel the celery root with a sharp knife (expect to slice quite a bit off the exterior as you trim). Halve the root lengthwise and cut each half into 1-inch-thick wedges. Cut each wedge crosswise into ¼-inch-thick slices. You should have about 5 cups. Add the celery root, 1 teaspoon kosher salt, and ½ cup water to the leeks. Cover and cook until the celery root is tender, 10 to 15 minutes. (Check occasionally; if all the water cooks off and the vegetables start to brown, add another ½ cup water.) Add 4½ cups water, bring to a simmer, and continue to cook another 20 minutes. Let cool slightly.

Purée the soup (with an immersion blender or in small batches in a stand blender) to a very smooth, creamy consistency. Let cool completely, then store in the refrigerator at least overnight or for up to two days.

About an hour before serving, put the crème fraîche in a small bowl and stir in enough of the heavy cream so the mixture reaches the consistency of yogurt. Leave this at room temperature until you are ready to serve the soup. (If the cream is too cold, it will cool the soup.)

Reheat the soup. (If it's too thick, gradually thin it with as much as 1 cup water.) Taste and add more salt as needed. Ladle the soup into small espresso cups or shot glasses. Top each portion with a small spoonful of crème fraîche (it should float on top of the soup). Finish each cup with a pinch of black pepper and a sprinkle of chives. *—Tasha DeSerio*

Wild Rice & Mushroom Soup with Almonds

If you can't find a ham hock, just leave it out. Even a vegetarian version will be lovely and full of flavor; leave out the bacon and just use vegetable broth. You can prepare the soup up to three days ahead (to just before you add the cream), or you can freeze it for up to a month. When ready to serve, heat the soup and add the heavy cream and garnishes.

Heat the oil in a heavy soup pot over medium-high heat. Add the bacon and cook, stirring occasionally, until the fat is rendered and the bacon is crisp, about 5 minutes. Add the mushrooms, stir well to coat in the fat, then spread out in an even layer. Brown on one side without disturbing them, 4 to 6 minutes. Stir in the onion, celery, and carrot; let cook until the onion is soft, about 5 minutes. Add the rice, stirring to coat. Stir in the broth, ham hock (if using) and herb bundle. Bring to a boil, then reduce the heat to maintain a gentle simmer. Cook, uncovered, until the rice is tender but still toothsome, 30 to 40 minutes.

Meanwhile, melt the butter in a small heavy saucepan over medium-high heat. Add the flour and whisk constantly until the mixture, called a roux, darkens to a caramel color, 2 to 3 minutes. Set aside.

Once the rice is cooked, discard the herbs. If you've used a ham hock, fish it out and, when it's cool enough to handle, take the meat off and return the shredded meat to the soup. Discard the bone. Return the soup to a boil and thoroughly whisk in the roux a little at a time. This amount of roux should thicken the soup perfectly. You can adjust the amount to your taste if it's too thick or thin, but keep in mind that the cream you'll add later will thin the soup. Season to taste with salt and pepper.

When ready to serve, heat the soup first, then add the cream. (If you like a lighter soup, you may not want to add all the cream.) Taste for seasoning and adjust if needed, and thin with broth, if you like. Garnish each serving with the toasted almonds and sliced chives. —*Ris Lacoste*

Serves six generously.

1 tablespoon olive oil

6 ounces sliced applewood-smoked bacon (about 7 slices), thinly sliced crosswise

1 pound button mushrooms, stems trimmed and quartered

1 large yellow onion, cut into medium dice

3 medium ribs celery, cut into medium dice

1 large carrot, cut into medium dice

½ cup wild rice

6 cups low-salt chicken broth; more if needed

1 smoked ham hock (optional)

15 sprigs fresh thyme, 10 sprigs fresh flat-leaf parsley, 6 sprigs fresh sage, and 1 bay leaf, tied together with kitchen twine

5 tablespoons unsalted butter

½ cup unbleached all-purpose flour

Kosher salt and freshly ground black pepper

1½ cups heavy cream

For the garnish:

½ cup slivered almonds, toasted

¼ cup thinly sliced fresh chives

Barley Minestrone

Yields about 3 quarts.

2 tablespoons extra-virgin olive oil

¼ cup finely diced pancetta (about 1 ounce)

2 cups large-diced Savoy cabbage

1 cup medium-diced yellow onion

1 cup carrot sliced ¼ inch thick

¼ cup medium-diced celery

2 cloves garlic, minced

2 quarts low-salt chicken broth

One 14.5-ounce can diced tomatoes, with their juices

½ cup pearl barley, rinsed

2 large sprigs fresh rosemary

One 2-inch square Parmigiano-Reggiano cheese rind (optional)

Kosher salt

1 cup water

1 cup canned kidney beans, rinsed and drained

Freshly ground black pepper

Freshly grated Parmigiano-Reggiano cheese for serving

This rendition of the classic Italian vegetable and bean soup uses barley instead of pasta. Simmering a piece of the rind from Parmigiano-Reggiano in the soup is a traditional way of adding flavor. When you finish off a wedge of Parmigiano, just stash the rind in the freezer so you always have it on hand when you need it.

Heat the oil in a heavy 6-quart or larger pot over medium heat. Add the pancetta and cook, stirring frequently, until it becomes ever so slightly golden, 2 to 3 minutes. Add the cabbage, onion, carrot, celery, and garlic. Cook, stirring frequently, until the vegetables begin to soften, about 6 minutes. Add the broth, the tomatoes with their juices, the barley, rosemary, Parmigiano rind (if using), ½ teaspoon kosher salt, and water. Bring to a boil, then reduce the heat to a simmer and cook until the barley and vegetables are tender, about 20 minutes. Discard the rosemary sprigs and Parmigiano rind. Stir in the beans and season to taste with salt and pepper. Serve sprinkled with the grated Parmigiano. *–Jennifer Armentrout*

Cooking with Barley

Barley has a mild flavor that's not as nutty as many other grains, but it has an unusually chewy texture—it pops softly as you bite it. It can be used in just about every way that rice is used—in pilafs, soups, and even risottos. Rolled barley is often eaten as a hot cereal.

It's usually a good idea to rinse barley before cooking. Hulled whole barley takes about an hour to cook (though a pressure cooker can speed things along). Pearl barley and rolled barley need about 20 minutes to get tender. Quick-cooking barley is usually done in 12 to 15 minutes.

Types of barley

Like most grains, barley is processed into a number of different forms. Hulled barley (barley groats) has had its inedible husk removed but still has its nutritious, fiber-rich bran layer. Pearl barley has been refined to strip it of its bran and germ. It's still nutritious, though not so much as hulled barley; it's to hulled barley as white rice is to brown rice. Pot or scotch barley is a less refined type of pearl barley. Rolled or flaked barley is hulled barley that's been flattened, like rolled oats. Quick-cooking barley is flattened and parcooked, so it cooks faster; nutritionally, it's similar to pearl barley.

Where to find barley

Look in health-food stores for whole hulled barley, pot barley, and rolled barley. In supermarkets, you'll find pearl barley near the dried beans, and quick-cooking barley in the hot cereal section.

Pearl barley

Quick-cooking barley

Rolled barley

Hulled barley

Wild Mushroom Soup with Sherry & Thyme

Serves six.

2 tablespoons unsalted butter

2 tablespoons olive oil

1 medium onion, cut into medium dice

4 cloves garlic, minced

¾ pound fresh wild mushrooms, trimmed (stems removed from shiitakes), and thinly sliced

2 tablespoons plus 1 teaspoon fresh thyme leaves

½ teaspoon kosher salt; more to taste

½ teaspoon freshly ground black pepper; more to taste

1 quart low-salt chicken or vegetable broth

¼ cup half-and-half

3 tablespoons dry sherry

1 tablespoon soy sauce

If you like, a drizzle of white truffle oil just before serving makes this soup especially fragrant and luxurious. For the mushrooms, a mix of half chanterelles or cremini and half shiitakes makes a fine blend, but if other interesting wild varieties are available, feel free to experiment.

Melt the butter with the olive oil in a 5-quart or larger pot over medium-high heat. Add the onion and cook until it begins to brown (resist the urge to stir too often), about 4 minutes. Stir in the garlic and cook for 1 minute. Add the mushrooms, 2 tablespoons of the thyme, and the salt and pepper; cook until the mushrooms become limp, 2 to 4 minutes. Add the broth, scraping up any browned bits in the pot with a wooden spoon. Bring to a boil, reduce the heat to maintain a simmer, and cook until the mushrooms are tender, 7 to 10 minutes. Remove from the heat and let cool slightly.

Transfer about half the soup to a blender and process until smooth. Return the mixture to the pot and stir in the half-and-half, sherry, and soy sauce. Add more salt and pepper to taste, if needed, and reheat. Garnish each serving with a small pinch of the remaining 1 teaspoon thyme. *—Jill Silverman Hough*

Smoky Black Bean Soup

Serves four to six.

1 pound dried black beans, picked over for debris

3 tablespoons olive oil

1 small onion, cut into ¼-inch dice

2 leeks (white and light green parts), chopped and rinsed well

2 medium ribs celery, cut into ¼-inch dice

1 large carrot, peeled and cut into ¼-inch dice

1 smoked ham hock, rinsed

3 cups low-salt chicken broth

3 cups water

2 large bay leaves

3 large sprigs fresh thyme

1 teaspoon kosher salt

One 14-ounce can crushed tomatoes (use Muir Glen® fire-roasted for a smoky flavor, if you can find it)

5 to 6 drops hot sauce

2 tablespoons olive oil, to finish (optional)

Sour cream, for garnish (optional)

Giving the beans a jump-start with the "quick-soak" method will help them cook faster, and is said to make them a bit easier to digest. But you can skip the quick soak and just cook the beans a bit longer. Do pay attention to the water level, however, and add a bit more if the soup is getting too thick.

For the quick-soak method: Put the beans in a large pot, cover with cold water, and bring to a hard boil. Take the pot from the heat, cover, and let the beans soak for at least an hour. When it's time to cook the soup, drain and rinse the beans.

In a large, heavy soup pot or Dutch oven, heat the oil over medium-high heat and add the onion, leeks, celery, and carrot. Cook, stirring frequently, until the vegetables are soft and beginning to brown lightly, about 10 minutes. Add the beans, ham hock, broth, water, bay leaves, thyme, and salt; bring to a boil. Reduce the heat to a low simmer, cover, and cook until the beans are very soft, 2 to 2½ hours (taste a few to be sure of their texture; if the level of liquid drops below the beans during cooking, add a little more broth or water).

Remove the ham hock, bay leaves, and thyme and add the tomatoes and their juices and the hot sauce. Cook for another 15 minutes or so to blend the flavors.

Meanwhile, if you like, pick the meat off the ham hock, mince it, and add it to the soup. Purée about half of the soup in a blender until very smooth, then stir it back into the rest of the soup. Taste and adjust the salt and hot sauce. To give the soup a more satiny texture, you can stir in the additional 2 tablespoons olive oil. Serve hot, with a dollop of sour cream if you like.

—Martha Holmberg

Parsnip & Parmesan Soup

Serves five to six.

¼ cup unsalted butter

1½ pounds parsnips, peeled and cut into ½-inch dice

6 ounces shallots, cut into ¼-inch dice

8 cloves garlic, minced

1 tablespoon finely chopped fresh oregano; plus tiny sprigs for garnish

1½ teaspoons kosher salt; more to taste

½ teaspoon freshly ground black pepper; more to taste

4½ cups low-salt chicken or vegetable broth

½ cup freshly grated Parmigiano-Reggiano cheese

2 teaspoons soy sauce

2 teaspoons fresh lemon juice

Salty and savory Parmigiano-Reggiano marries well with sweet parsnips, and the fresh oregano pulls it all together.

Melt the butter in a 5-quart or larger pot set over medium heat. While the butter is still foaming, add the parsnips and cook until lightly browned, 7 to 10 minutes (resist the urge to stir too often or they won't brown). Stir in the shallots, garlic, chopped oregano, salt, and pepper and cook until the shallots are very limp and the entire mixture is beginning to brown, 8 to 10 minutes. Add the broth, using a wooden spoon to scrape up any browned bits in the pot. Bring to a boil, reduce the heat to maintain a low simmer, and cook until the parsnips are very soft, 6 to 8 minutes. Remove from the heat and let cool somewhat.

Purée the soup using an immersion or stand blender (you'll need to work in batches if using a stand blender). Return the soup to the pot and stir in the Parmigiano, soy sauce, and lemon juice. Taste and add more salt and pepper if needed. Reheat the soup and garnish each serving with an oregano sprig, if you like. —*Jill Silverman Hough*

Potato & Cheddar Soup with Smoked Ham & Chives

This soup is smooth, soothing and satisfying as a meal in itself when paired with a salad. The better the cheese you use, the better the soup.

In a large soup pot or Dutch oven, heat the butter over medium-high heat, add the onion and celery, and cook, stirring frequently, until very soft but not browned, 5 to 8 minutes. Add the potatoes, broth, thyme, and salt. Adjust the heat to a simmer, cover partially, and simmer until the potatoes are completely soft and falling apart, 25 to 30 minutes. Remove as many of the herb stems as possible.

Working carefully in batches, purée the soup in a blender until it's completely smooth and return it to the pot. Add the cream and let the soup simmer gently for another minute or two. Take off the heat and add the cheese, stirring until it's completely melted. Season generously to taste with the black pepper. Taste and adjust the salt, if necessary. The soup will be fairly thick, so if you'd like a thinner consistency, add a little more broth or some water.

Serve the soup hot with some of the diced ham and a spoonful of the chives. —*Martha Holmberg*

Serves four to six.

2 tablespoons unsalted butter

1 large onion, chopped

1 rib celery, chopped

2½ pounds russet potatoes, peeled and cut into 1-inch chunks

1 quart low-salt chicken broth

4 large sprigs fresh thyme

1½ teaspoons kosher salt

½ cup heavy cream

½ pound aged, extra-sharp Cheddar cheese, grated

Freshly ground black pepper

One ¼-inch-thick slice good-quality smoked ham, cut into ¼-inch dice

¼ cup snipped fresh chives

Tips for the Best Puréed Soups

- Cut your vegetables small for faster cooking. A ½-inch dice needs no more than 10 minutes of simmering before it's soft enough to purée.

- Don't stir the vegetables too often during the sauté; once every two minutes or so is good. This helps them brown, and that, in turn, will flavor your soup, giving it nuance beyond simply simmered vegetables.

- Use a blender to get the smoothest soup. If you use a stand blender, be sure to let the liquid cool slightly, work in batches, and hold a towel over the lid to avoid overflowing. An immersion blender works well, too, and is even more convenient.

- Don't be afraid of salt—it can make all the difference. Taste your soup before serving and add salt to taste. The flavors will get brighter and more pronounced.

- Add an attractive garnish: It can really give the soup pizzazz. Use a sprig of an herb that's in your soup, a drizzle of a flavored oil, or a sprinkle of shredded cheese. A dollop of sour cream or crème fraîche can also enhance a simple puréed soup, making it party-fancy in both flavor and appearance.

Colombian Chicken Soup

Serves eight.

For the soup:

3 pounds cut-up chicken, skin removed and rinsed well

1 large white onion, quartered

1 leek (white and light green parts), cut into 1-inch rings and rinsed well

1 green bell pepper, seeded and cut into 1-inch pieces

2 ears corn, shucked and cut crosswise into quarters

2 ribs celery, cut into 1-inch pieces

2 large carrots, peeled and cut into 1-inch pieces

2½ pounds potatoes (Yukon Gold, Idaho, or red, or a mix), peeled and cut into 1-inch cubes

6 cloves garlic, peeled

½ cup fresh cilantro leaves

2 chicken bouillon cubes

Kosher salt and freshly ground black pepper

For the aji:

4 scallions (white and light green parts)

1 medium ripe tomato, peeled and seeded

1 small white onion, peeled

2 fresh Scotch bonnet or habanero chiles, or 2 fresh hot red chiles, cored and seeded

3 tablespoons chopped fresh cilantro

3 tablespoons white vinegar

¼ teaspoon kosher salt

For the garnishes:

2 ripe avocados, peeled, pitted, and cut into ½-inch cubes

1 cup sour cream or crème fraîche

½ cup nonpareil or other small capers (if using large capers, chop them coarsely), rinsed and drained

½ cup chopped fresh cilantro

Once you try this soup (called *ajiaco*, ah-hee-ah-koh), you'll be hard pressed to find another chicken soup that matches its earthy aromas, hearty textures, and bright flavors. Aji is traditionally made with chiles that haven't been seeded, but is plenty spicy without the seeds. Leftover aji is delicious on roasted or grilled meats. Both the soup and the aji can be made a day ahead.

Make the soup: Put the chicken in a large (at least 8-quart) stockpot and add 8 cups water. Bring to a boil, then reduce the heat to a vigorous simmer. Simmer for 10 minutes, frequently skimming off the foam that floats to the surface.

Add all the vegetables, the garlic, cilantro, bouillon cubes, 1 tablespoon kosher salt, and ½ teaspoon pepper. Stir a few times to distribute the vegetables and submerge as many of the solids as possible. When the broth returns to a gentle boil, partially cover the pot and simmer, stirring once or twice, for 1½ hours. Taste for salt and add more if needed.

Using tongs or a slotted spoon, pick out the chicken pieces and put them on a large plate. Stir the soup with a large spoon, breaking up some of the potatoes to thicken it slightly. Keep hot if serving soon or let cool and refrigerate.

When the chicken is cool enough to handle, pull the meat off the bones and shred it by hand. Discard the bones and tendons, and put the shredded chicken in a serving bowl.

Make the aji: In a food processor, pulse the aji ingredients together until finely minced. Transfer to a serving bowl.

To serve, put the avocados, sour cream, capers, and cilantro in small bowls and set them on the table along with the bowls of shredded chicken and the aji. Reheat the soup, if necessary, and ladle it into large soup bowls, putting a quarter ear of corn in each bowl. Let your guests add the garnishes and the aji to their own servings. —*Tania Segal*

Don't Throw Out Cilantro Stems

When preparing cilantro for chopping, you don't necessarily have to remove all of the stems. Cilantro stems are quite flavorful, so if they're thin and tender-crisp (bite one to check), just chop them up along with the leaves.

Cioppino

Serves six to eight.

For the garlic oil and garlic chips:

4 large cloves garlic

½ cup extra-virgin olive oil

Kosher salt and freshly ground
black pepper

For the shellfish stock:

1 pound large shrimp
(16-20 count)

6½ cups low-salt chicken broth

For the cioppino broth:

¼ cup olive oil

3 cups coarsely chopped yellow
onions

1 cup coarsely chopped carrots

⅔ cup coarsely chopped celery
or fennel

3 tablespoons coarsely chopped
garlic

Two 28-ounce cans peeled
whole tomatoes, broken up,
with their juices

2½ cups medium-bodied red
wine, such as Zinfandel or
Pinot Noir

3 large bay leaves

¼ cup coarsely chopped fresh
basil (or 1 tablespoon dried)

1 tablespoon coarsely chopped
fresh oregano (or 1 teaspoon
dried)

2 teaspoons fennel seeds

½ teaspoon red pepper flakes

For finishing the stew:

Eight ¾-inch-thick slices
sourdough bread

1 to 1½ pounds small hardshell
clams, scrubbed, or 1 whole
Dungeness crab, cleaned and
cut into sections (have the
fishmonger do this)

1 to 1½ pounds mussels,
scrubbed and debearded

2½ pounds halibut, monkfish, or
other firm-fleshed white fish
fillets, cut into 1-inch cubes

¼ cup chopped fresh flat-leaf
parsley

Make the garlic oil and chips: Cut the garlic cloves into ⅛-inch slices, put them in a small saucepan with the oil, and season with salt and pepper. Cook over low to medium-low heat until the garlic turns light golden brown, 15 to 20 minutes, adjusting the heat as needed to keep the garlic bubbling gently as it cooks. Remove from the heat and let cool to room temperature. Strain, reserving both the oil and the garlic chips separately. Reserve the garlic chips for garnish. Refrigerate the oil in a clean, sealed container. (You'll use the oil for the sourdough croutons; use any leftover oil for vinaigrettes, roasted vegetables, pasta, or roast chicken.)

Make the shellfish stock: Peel the shrimp, reserving the shells. (Refrigerate the shelled shrimp to use later in the stew.) Simmer the shells in the broth for 5 minutes, covered. Strain and refrigerate until ready to use.

Make the cioppino broth: Heat the olive oil in an 8-quart or larger pot over medium heat. Add the onions, carrots, celery, and chopped garlic. Cook, stirring occasionally, until lightly browned, 15 to 20 minutes. Add the tomatoes with their juices, the wine, 6 cups of the shellfish stock, the bay leaves, basil, oregano, fennel seeds, red pepper flakes, 1 teaspoon kosher salt, and several grinds of pepper. Bring to a boil, then reduce the heat to a simmer and cook for about 20 minutes. Strain through a medium sieve, pressing on the solids. Discard the contents of the sieve. Rinse the pot and return the broth to it. Boil the broth until reduced to 8 cups. (If you overreduce the broth, just add water to compensate.) Taste and add more salt and pepper if needed, remembering that the fish will add some saltiness. Refrigerate until ready to use.

To finish the stew: Position a rack directly under the broiler and heat the broiler. Brush the bread on both sides with the reserved garlic oil. Put the bread on a baking sheet (or directly on the rack) and toast on both sides. While you toast the bread, return the broth to a simmer over medium-high to high heat.

When each batch of seafood is added, it will cause the temperature of the broth to plunge, so you might need to raise and lower the heat to maintain a simmer. If using clams, start by adding them to the broth and simmer until open, 3 to 5 minutes. Add the mussels and crab, if using, and simmer until the mussels have opened, 2 to 3 minutes. Add the fish and reserved shrimp. Stir carefully with a slotted spoon to get it all into the broth, but try not to break up the pieces. Cover and cook until the fish is just barely cooked through, another 3 to 5 minutes, keeping in mind it will continue to cook a little in the time it takes to dish out the servings.

Set a piece of toasted sourdough in the bottom of each warm bowl and evenly portion the seafood into the bowls (be sure to discard any unopened clams or mussels). Ladle the broth on top. Sprinkle the chopped parsley and garlic chips over all and serve immediately. —*John Ash*

Butternut Squash Soup with Apple & Bacon

Serves six to seven.

8 slices bacon, cut crosswise into ¼-inch-wide strips

2½ pounds butternut squash, peeled, seeded, and cut into ½-inch dice

1 small Granny Smith or other tart-sweet apple, peeled, cored, and cut into ½-inch dice

1½ tablespoons finely chopped fresh sage

1 teaspoon kosher salt

½ teaspoon freshly ground black pepper

1 quart low-salt chicken or vegetable broth

Smoky bacon, herby sage, and sweet apple give this squash soup layers of flavor. Need a shortcut? Many markets sell peeled, chunked butternut squash in bags.

In a 5-quart or larger pot set over medium heat, cook the bacon, stirring occasionally, until crisp and golden, 8 to 10 minutes. Use a slotted spoon to transfer the bacon to a plate lined with paper towels.

Increase the heat to medium high. Add the squash and cook until lightly browned, 4 to 6 minutes (resist the urge to stir it too often or it won't brown). Stir in the apple, sage, salt, and pepper and cook for about 4 minutes (you'll see more browning occur on the bottom of the pot than on the vegetables). Add the broth, scraping up any browned bits in the pot with a wooden spoon. Bring to a boil, reduce the heat to maintain a simmer, and cook until the squash and apples are very soft, 6 to 8 minutes. Remove from the heat and let cool somewhat.

Add about half the bacon to the soup and purée, using a stand or immersion blender (you'll need to work in batches if using a stand blender). Taste and add more salt and pepper if needed. Reheat the soup and garnish each serving with the remaining bacon. —*Jill Silverman Hough*

White Bean Soup with Sautéed Shrimp & Garlic Croutons

All of the various elements in this refreshing twist on bean soup—the puréed beans, the seared shrimp, the crisp croutons, even the dash of cayenne—come together in the bowl in a wonderful assortment of flavors and textures. Puréeing most but not all of the white beans gives the soup a more interesting texture.

In a large saucepan, heat 2 tablespoons of the olive oil over medium-high heat. Add the onion, carrot, and celery. Season with a little salt and cook, stirring occasionally, until the vegetables soften and start to brown, about 7 minutes. Reserve 1 teaspoon of the chopped garlic; add the rest to the pot, along with the bay leaves and rosemary. Cook, stirring, for about a minute. Add the beans and broth. Season well with salt and pepper. Bring to a boil, reduce the heat to a gentle simmer, and cook for 20 minutes. Let cool a bit. Discard the bay leaves. Scoop out 1 cup of the beans and set aside.

Working in batches, purée the remaining beans and all of the broth in a blender or food processor or in the pot with an immersion blender. Transfer the puréed soup and the reserved beans back to the saucepan and keep warm over low heat. Add the lemon juice and season with more salt and pepper to taste. (This can be made up to a day ahead; cover and refrigerate and reheat before serving.)

Make the croutons: Set a large skillet over medium-high heat for 1 minute. Add 2 tablespoons of the olive oil and the bread cubes and season well with salt and pepper. Cook, tossing frequently, until the bread starts to brown around the edges, 2 to 3 minutes. Toss in the reserved 1 teaspoon garlic and continue cooking for a few seconds, tossing well, taking care not to burn the garlic. Transfer to a large plate.

Sear the shrimp: Season the shrimp well with salt and pepper. Add the remaining 2 tablespoons olive oil and the shrimp to the skillet and sauté, stirring often, until the shrimp is firm, opaque, and browned slightly, 3 to 4 minutes.

To serve, ladle the soup into large, shallow bowls and dust with a pinch of cayenne. Garnish with a few of the croutons, a portion of the shrimp, and a drizzle of olive oil. —*Tony Rosenfeld*

Serves four as a first course.

- 6 tablespoons extra-virgin olive oil; more for drizzling
- 1 large yellow onion, cut into ¼-inch dice
- 1 carrot, peeled and cut into ¼-inch dice
- 1 inner rib celery, cut into ¼-inch dice
- Kosher salt and freshly ground black pepper
- 5 to 6 cloves garlic, finely chopped
- 2 bay leaves
- 1 tablespoon chopped fresh rosemary
- Two 15.5-ounce cans cannellini beans, drained and rinsed
- 1 quart low-salt chicken or vegetable broth
- 4 teaspoons fresh lemon juice; more to taste
- 2½ cups ¾-inch-diced country bread or baguette
- ¾ pound large (21-25 count) shrimp, peeled, deveined, rinsed, and patted dry
- Pinch cayenne

Beef & Wild Rice Soup with Winter Vegetables

Serves eight.

2 tablespoons unsalted butter or bacon fat

1 pound boneless beef chuck, cut into ¾-inch pieces

Kosher salt and freshly ground black pepper

1 medium yellow onion, cut into ⅓-inch dice

2 cloves garlic, minced

1 cup full-bodied red wine

2 quarts low-salt chicken broth

2 cups ½-inch-diced butternut squash

1 cup ½-inch-diced medium purple turnip

1 cup wild rice, rinsed

2 tablespoons tomato paste

1 teaspoon dried thyme

1 bay leaf

Give yourself some leeway time-wise when making this comforting, full-flavored winter soup, as the cooking time for wild rice can vary. The best method for testing its doneness is to wait until most of the grains have "popped," meaning they've split open to reveal a creamy interior, and then tasting the grains, which should be a little toothy but also tender.

In a Dutch oven or heavy soup pot, melt the butter over medium-high heat. Season the beef generously with salt and pepper and place in a single layer in the pot. Don't stir for about 1½ minutes, then stir occasionally until the meat is well browned on all sides, about 5 minutes. With a slotted spoon, transfer the meat to a plate. Reduce the heat to medium low, add the onion and garlic to the pot, and cook—stirring and scraping the bottom of the pot occasionally with a wooden spoon—until they're softened, about 5 minutes. Add the wine, bring to a boil, and cook until it's reduced by about half, about 5 minutes. Add the broth, squash, turnip, wild rice, tomato paste, thyme, and bay leaf and bring to a boil. Add the beef and any accumulated juices, reduce the heat to medium low, cover, and simmer until the wild rice is soft and most of the grains have popped open and are tender, 40 to 60 minutes. (Check occasionally to be sure the soup isn't simmering too quickly or too slowly; it should be a moderate simmer.) Discard the bay leaf. Season the soup with salt and pepper to taste and serve garnished with the parsley.

—Beth Dooley and Lucia Watson

4 Pasta & Grains

p130

p140

Campanelle with Broccoli
Raab, Sausage & Olives
(recipe on page 121)

Bow-Tie Pasta in Fresh Tomato & Basil Sauce

Serves four to five.

3 tablespoons extra-virgin
   olive oil

3 large cloves garlic, sliced as
   thinly as possible

2 pounds cherry tomatoes,
   halved

1 teaspoon kosher salt; more
   to taste

Freshly ground black pepper

1 cup loosely packed fresh basil
   leaves, very thinly sliced

1 pound farfalle or other pasta
   shape

This simple sauce is the essence of summer. You can make it in the time it takes to boil the water. And it's incredibly versatile. Serve it with pasta or spoon it over grilled shrimp, scallops, or whitefish. You can even spread it on thick slices of grilled bread. For another variation, try stirring in 1 cup of diced ricotta salata cheese.

In a 10- or 11-inch sauté pan, heat the oil and garlic over medium-low heat, stirring occasionally, until the garlic is softened but not browned, about 5 minutes. Add the tomatoes, salt, and pepper to taste. Toss gently to coat, then raise the heat to medium. Cook, stirring occasionally and adjusting the heat to maintain a lively but not too vigorous simmer, until the tomatoes have been reduced to a thick, pulpy sauce, 15 to 20 minutes. Remove from the heat. Sprinkle on the basil and stir to combine thoroughly.

While the sauce is cooking, bring a large pot of generously salted water to a vigorous boil and cook the pasta until al dente. Drain it well. Taste the sauce and adjust the seasonings if needed. Toss the pasta with three-quarters of the sauce and divide among individual serving bowls. Spoon a little of the remaining sauce over each serving and sprinkle on some grated cheese, if you like.

—*Domenica Marchetti*

Fusilli with Sausage, Olives, Sun-Dried Tomatoes & Cream

Cream tempers the bold flavors of this sauce. To save some of the cooking water and drain the pasta at the same time, set the colander in a large bowl in the sink. It will naturally collect more than enough of the starchy water.

Bring a large pot of generously salted water to a boil over high heat.

Meanwhile, in a large sauté pan, heat the olive oil over medium heat. Add the onion and cook until softened, stirring a few times, about 5 minutes. Add the garlic and cook for 1 minute. Add the sausage and cook, breaking it into bite-size pieces with a spoon, until just cooked through, 6 to 8 minutes. Spoon off the fat if it's excessive. Add the wine, increase the heat to medium high, and cook, scraping up any browned bits in the pan, until most of the wine is evaporated, 3 to 5 minutes. Stir in the olives and tomatoes and cook for 2 minutes. Add the cream, increase the heat to high, bring to a boil, and cook, stirring a few times, until the cream thickens slightly, 2 to 5 minutes. Stir in 2 tablespoons of the parsley and 2 tablespoons of the Parmigiano. Keep the sauce warm over low heat.

Cook the pasta in the boiling water until al dente. Reserve ¼ cup of the cooking water, then drain the pasta. Return the pasta to its pot, add the sauce and the reserved cooking water, and set the pot over high heat. Gently toss the pasta for 30 to 60 seconds and season to taste with salt and pepper. Divide among warm bowls and sprinkle with the remaining 2 tablespoons parsley and Parmigiano. *—Joanne McAllister Smart*

Serves six to eight.

- 2 tablespoons extra-virgin olive oil
- 1 medium yellow onion, finely diced
- 1 medium clove garlic, finely chopped
- 1¼ pounds hot Italian sausage, casings removed
- ½ cup dry white wine
- 1 cup pitted Kalamata olives, drained and coarsely chopped
- 1 cup oil-packed sun-dried tomatoes, drained and coarsely chopped
- 1 cup heavy cream
- ¼ cup chopped fresh flat-leaf parsley
- ¼ cup freshly grated Parmigiano-Reggiano cheese
- 1 pound farfalle or fusilli pasta
- Kosher salt and freshly ground black pepper

Spaghetti & Meatballs

Serves four to six; yields twelve beautiful meatballs.

For the marinara sauce:

Three 28-ounce cans crushed Italian plum tomatoes, whole or crushed (San Marzanos, if possible)

½ cup olive oil

6 cloves garlic, lightly smashed

1 tablespoon kosher salt; more as needed

¼ cup chopped fresh basil

1 teaspoon freshly ground black pepper

¼ teaspoon dried oregano

For the meatballs and spaghetti:

½ pound ground beef

½ pound ground pork

½ pound ground veal

1 tablespoon kosher salt

½ teaspoon freshly ground black pepper

1 clove garlic, minced, plus 1 clove garlic, lightly smashed

2 large eggs, lightly beaten

1 cup finely grated imported Locatelli Romano or Parmigiano-Reggiano cheese (or half and half); more for serving

1½ cups plain dry breadcrumbs

1½ cups water

1 tablespoon chopped fresh flat-leaf parsley

1 cup olive or vegetable oil; more as needed

1 pound spaghetti

¼ cup chopped fresh basil

No jarred sauce can beat the flavor of homemade marinara sauce, particularly if it's made with imported San Marzano tomatoes, which are known for their sweetness. You can find them at gourmet grocery stores and Italian delis. If you can't buy the ground meats individually, use 1½ pounds of meatloaf mix, which is often available in supermarkets.

Make the marinara sauce: If you are using whole tomatoes, put them in a large bowl and crush them with your hands. Discard the cores.

In a 7-quart or larger saucepot, heat the oil over medium heat. Add the garlic and sauté until lightly golden brown, about 2 minutes. Add the tomatoes and salt. Bring to a boil, reduce the heat to a simmer, and cook, stirring occasionally, for 45 minutes to 1 hour; the sauce will reduce and thicken slightly but shouldn't get too thick. Stir in the basil, pepper, and oregano. Taste and add more salt as needed. Proceed with the meatball recipe, or let cool and refrigerate for up to four days.

Make the meatballs: Break up the ground meat into a large bowl. Sprinkle on the salt, pepper, minced garlic, eggs, cheese, breadcrumbs, water, and parsley. Mix with your hands until everything is nicely distributed, but don't overmix. Shape into 12 meatballs by gently scooping up a handful of meat and rolling it into a nice even ball; each should weigh about 4 ounces and be about 2½ inches in diameter.

In a 10-inch nonstick skillet, heat the olive oil and the lightly smashed garlic clove over medium heat. (If your skillet is larger than 10 inches, you'll need to add more oil; there should be enough to come about halfway up the sides of the meatballs.) When the garlic is lightly browned, the oil should be hot enough to start frying. (Remove the garlic from the oil once it becomes fully browned.) Gently set six of the meatballs in the oil and fry until lightly browned on the bottom half, 5 to 6 minutes. Carefully turn them over using a slotted spatula and brown the other side. Drain the meatballs on a few paper towels to soak up excess oil. Fry the remaining six meatballs the same way.

When the marinara has finished its initial simmer and you've seasoned it, add the meatballs to the sauce and cover the pot. Simmer together for 30 minutes to let the sauce permeate the meatballs and the meat flavor infuse the sauce.

Meanwhile, bring a large pot of salted water to a boil. When the meatballs and sauce have been simmering for about 20 minutes, add the spaghetti to the boiling water and boil until it's just about al dente. When the spaghetti is done, drain and return it to the pot; add the basil and a couple of ladlefuls of the sauce. Put the pot over high heat and, with a wooden spoon or tongs, toss the pasta until each piece is coated with sauce, about 1 minute. Transfer to serving bowls and ladle more sauce over the spaghetti, along with two to three meatballs. Serve with grated cheese. —*Frank Pellegrino*

The Secret to Perfect Saucing

Ladle some sauce onto the drained pasta and cook over high heat so the pasta absorbs the sauce.

tip: Pat, don't pack. Scoop up a handful of meat and gently roll it in your palms to make a large, smooth meatball.

Cavatappi in Tomato Sauce alla Siciliana

Serves four to five.

3 tablespoons extra-virgin olive oil

½ cup chopped yellow onion

1 clove garlic, minced

½ pound baby eggplants, cut into ½-inch cubes

1½ pounds cherry tomatoes, halved

1 teaspoon kosher salt; more to taste

Freshly ground black pepper

1 tablespoon aged balsamic vinegar

2 tablespoons chopped fresh mint

1 pound cavatappi or other short pasta

Eggplant, mint, and balsamic vinegar come together beautifully in this chunky tomato sauce. A short sturdy pasta will catch all the juicy bits. The sauce would also go well with hearty meats such as grilled lamb chops or sausages, or add grilled or roasted peppers, squash, or onions to make a ratatouille-style dish.

In a 10- or 11-inch sauté pan, heat the oil, onion, and garlic over medium heat, stirring frequently, until the onion is softened but not browned, 3 to 5 minutes. Stir in the eggplant and cook, stirring frequently, until it softens and begins to brown, 5 to 7 minutes. Add the tomatoes, salt, and pepper to taste and cook, stirring occasionally and adjusting the heat to maintain a lively but not too vigorous simmer, until the tomatoes reduce to a thick, pulpy sauce, 15 to 20 minutes. Sprinkle the vinegar over the sauce, stir, and simmer for another 5 minutes. Stir in the mint and more salt and pepper to taste.

While the sauce is cooking, bring a large pot of generously salted water to a vigorous boil and cook the pasta until al dente. Drain it well. Taste the sauce and adjust the seasonings if needed. Toss the pasta with three-quarters of the sauce and divide among individual serving bowls. Spoon a little of the remaining sauce over each serving and serve immediately.

—*Domenica Marchetti*

Campanelle with Broccoli Raab, Sausage & Olives

Campanelle, Italian for "bellflowers," is an elegant pasta shape perfect for catching this intensely flavored sauce.

Bring a large pot of generously salted water to a boil over high heat. Have a bowl of ice water ready. Add the broccoli raab and cook until bright green and tender, 2 minutes (the water doesn't have to come back to a full boil). With tongs or a slotted spoon, transfer the broccoli raab to the bowl of ice water to stop the cooking. Drain it well and gently squeeze to remove excess water.

Return the pot of water to a boil, add the pasta, cook until al dente, and drain.

While the campanelle cooks, heat the oil in a 12-inch skillet over medium-high heat. Add the sausage and cook, stirring and breaking it into smaller pieces with a wooden spoon until it's browned and almost cooked through, 4 to 6 minutes. Add the garlic and red pepper flakes and cook until the garlic is lightly golden, about 1 minute. Pour in the broth and bring to a boil; cook, scraping the pan with a wooden spoon a few times, until the broth is reduced by about half, 3 to 4 minutes. Add the broccoli raab, olives, and lemon zest and cook, stirring, until hot, 1 to 2 minutes. Add the pasta and cheese and toss well. Season to taste with salt and serve immediately. *—David Bonom*

Serves three to four.

- 1 pound broccoli raab, thick stems trimmed off, leaves and florets rinsed well
- 6 ounces campanelle pasta (2 cups)
- 3 tablespoons extra-virgin olive oil
- ¾ pound sweet Italian sausage, casings removed
- 3 cloves garlic, minced
- ¼ teaspoon red pepper flakes
- ¾ cup low-salt chicken broth
- ½ cup pitted Kalamata olives, drained and quartered
- 2 teaspoons lightly packed finely grated lemon zest
- ⅓ cup freshly grated Pecorino Romano cheese
- Kosher salt

Broccoli Raab, a Better Bitter

Broccoli raab, rapini, broccoli rabe, broccoli rape, brocoletti di rape, brocoletto—all are names for a vegetable that looks like turnip greens topped with small broccoli florets. Native to the Mediterranean and related to both turnips and broccoli, this may be the plant from which the more familiar broccoli was cultivated. For some people, broccoli raab's bitter, peppery flavor takes getting used to, but for those who like bitter flavors, it can be addictive.

Look for bunches that show no signs of wilting or yellowing. Rinse well and trim off the lower, thicker stalks. Broccoli raab cooks quickly—it gets tender in about 3 minutes. Steaming, sautéing, braising, and stir-frying are all good ways to cook it, but to cut some of the bitterness, blanch it first in boiling water for a minute or two.

Gemelli with Asparagus & Caramelized Onions

Serves four.

3 tablespoons extra-virgin olive oil

One ¼-pound slice pancetta, cut into ¼-inch dice

1 pound asparagus, trimmed, peeled if thick, and cut on the diagonal into 2-inch pieces

Kosher salt and freshly ground black pepper

¾ cup Caramelized Onions (recipe follows)

¾ cup low-salt chicken broth

¾ pound gemelli or penne pasta

¾ cup freshly grated Parmigiano-Reggiano cheese

1 teaspoon sherry vinegar or balsamic vinegar

The rich flavor of caramelized onions can boost a wide variety of dishes, but they can be time consuming to make. Keep a stockpile on hand by making a large batch in advance and freezing portions for use in soups, sandwiches, pastas, pizzas—you name it.

Bring a large pot of generously salted water to a boil.

Meanwhile, heat 2 tablespoons of the oil and the pancetta in a 12-inch skillet or sauté pan over medium heat, stirring, until the pancetta begins to brown and renders much of its fat, 5 to 7 minutes. Using a slotted spoon, transfer it to a plate lined with paper towels. Raise the heat to medium high, add the asparagus, and season with ¼ teaspoon kosher salt. Stir often until the asparagus starts to brown, about 3 minutes. Add the caramelized onions and broth, reduce the heat to medium-low, cover, and cook until the asparagus is tender, about 4 minutes. Stir in ¼ teaspoon pepper and set aside in a warm spot.

Cook the pasta in the boiling water, stirring often, until it's just tender, about 11 minutes. Reserve ¼ cup of the pasta water. Drain the pasta and add it to the pan with the asparagus. Set the pan over medium-high heat and toss well. Add ½ cup of the Parmigiano, the vinegar, and pancetta and cook, stirring, for 1 minute to meld all the flavors. If the pasta begins to dry, add the reserved pasta water. Serve with a drizzle of the remaining 1 tablespoon olive oil and a sprinkling of the remaining Parmigiano. —*Tony Rosenfeld*

Caramelized Onions

Yields about 1½ cups.

2 tablespoons extra-virgin olive oil

2½ pounds Spanish or large yellow onions, halved and thinly sliced lengthwise

1 teaspoon kosher salt

This recipe for caramelized onions has been developed for a 12-inch skillet. If you use a 10-inch skillet, reduce the recipe proportionally by about one quarter.

Heat the oil in a 12-inch skillet over medium-high heat until it immediately bubbles when an onion touches it, about 1 minute. Add the onions, sprinkle with the salt, and cook, stirring frequently, until they wilt completely and begin to stick to the bottom of the pan, 10 to 20 minutes (much of the onions' moisture will evaporate and the pan will begin to brown; the cooking time varies with the onions' moisture content). Reduce the heat to medium low and cook, stirring and scraping the pan with a wooden spoon every few minutes. (If the pan begins to look like it's burning, add 2 tablespoons water, stir, and lower the heat a bit.) Cook, stirring, scraping, and adding water as needed, until the onions are a uniform caramel brown, another 30 to 45 minutes. (If they haven't begun to brown much after 20 minutes, raise the heat to medium.) Add a couple of tablespoons of water and scrape the pan well. Use right away or spread the onions on a baking sheet, let cool to room temperature, and store, tightly covered, in the refrigerator for up to one week.

—*Tony Rosenfeld*

The Road to Caramelized Onions is Long but Sweet

Slice the onions thinly and pile them into the skillet. They will shrink considerably as they cook.

The onions will darken and sweeten into a marmalade-like consistency after about an hour; no need to add any additional sugar. If the bottom of the pan begins to burn, add a few spoonfuls of water.

A container of caramelized onions in the fridge is like culinary gold; use them to top pizzas, bruschetta, sandwiches, stir them into soups and dips, or use them as a bed for roasted meats and poultry.

Egg Noodles with Lemon & Fresh Herbs

Serves four.

½ pound egg noodles

2 tablespoons unsalted butter

2 tablespoons fresh lemon juice

Kosher salt and freshly ground
black pepper

¼ cup lightly packed fresh,
tender herbs (choose from
parsley, dill, chervil, tarragon,
or a mix)

1 teaspoon lightly packed finely
grated lemon zest

2 scallions (optional), thinly
sliced

**This recipe is a quick way to turn a package of noodles into a vibrant,
colorful side dish to serve with pot roast or a chop.**

Boil the noodles in generously salted water according to package
directions. Just before draining, scoop out about ¼ cup of the cooking water.
Drain the noodles; set aside.

Put the pan you used to cook the noodles over medium heat, add the
butter, lemon juice, and about 2 tablespoons of the reserved cooking water,
and swirl to combine. Add the noodles and toss gently but thoroughly to coat,
adding a touch more of the cooking water if necessary. Remove from the heat.
Season generously to taste with salt and pepper, add the herbs, zest, and
scallions (if using), and toss once more to mix. Serve immediately.

—Martha Holmberg

Pappardelle with Shrimp & Zucchini

This dish, in which the thinly sliced zucchini takes on the same shape as the pasta, is gorgeous as well as delicious. You could dress it up even more by tossing in some sauteed scallops or a few chunks of fresh crabmeat.

Put a large pot of generously salted water on to boil.

Using a vegetable peeler (preferably a sharp, Y-shaped one), gently peel and discard the dark green skin of the zucchini. Pressing as hard as you can, continue to "peel" each zucchini lengthwise to make wide strips about 1/8 inch thick, rotating the zucchini as you go. Discard the squared-off seed cores.

Heat 1 1/2 tablespoons of the oil in a large skillet over high heat. Add the shrimp, season with salt and pepper, and sauté until firm and pink, 2 to 3 minutes. Transfer the shrimp to a plate. Lower the heat to medium, add the remaining 4 1/2 tablespoons oil and the garlic, and cook, swirling the pan, until the garlic browns and the oil is fragrant, 2 to 3 minutes.

Put the pasta in the boiling water.

Transfer all but 1 tablespoon of the oil from the skillet to a small bowl. Raise the heat under the skillet to high, add the red pepper flakes, and pile in the zucchini strips. Season with salt and pepper and sauté until the strips begin to soften (but don't let them turn mushy), 1 to 2 minutes. Discard the garlic cloves.

Finish cooking the pappardelle until it's just tender, about 5 minutes total. Drain and add to the shrimp, along with the zucchini, lemon juice, and reserved garlic oil. Toss gently. Stir in the basil and prosciutto, taste for salt and pepper, and serve immediately. —*Tony Rosenfeld*

Serves two to three.

2 medium zucchini, trimmed

6 tablespoons extra-virgin olive oil

3/4 pound large shrimp, peeled and deveined

Kosher salt and freshly ground black pepper

2 cloves garlic, smashed and peeled

1/2 pound pappardelle

1/4 teaspoon red pepper flakes

2 teaspoons fresh lemon juice; more to taste

15 fresh basil leaves, torn into large pieces

2 1/2 ounces thinly sliced prosciutto, cut crosswise into 1/2-inch-wide strips

Peppery Egg Noodle, Farmer's Cheese & Cauliflower Gratin

Serves eight.

¾ pound (about 1½ cups) farmer's cheese

¾ cup heavy cream

3 tablespoons unsalted butter; more for the dish

¼ cup plain dry breadcrumbs

1 tablespoon chopped fresh thyme

Kosher salt and freshly ground black pepper

1 small head cauliflower, cut into 1-inch-long florets

1 cup low-salt chicken or vegetable broth

9 ounces fresh egg fettuccine

To make this dish several hours in advance, prepare the recipe (but don't add the breadcrumb topping), cover, and refrigerate. When ready to bake, top with the crumbs and pop into the oven.

Heat the oven to 400°F. Set a large pot of generously salted water over high heat and bring to a boil. Butter a 9x13-inch baking dish.

In a food processor, combine the cheese and cream and process until well blended. (You can also mix them in a bowl; it will just take some elbow grease.)

Melt 1 tablespoon of the butter in a 12-inch skillet over high heat. Stir in the breadcrumbs, thyme, a pinch of salt, and a few grinds of black pepper. Sauté, stirring, until the crumbs are light golden brown and crisp, 1 to 2 minutes. Immediately scrape them into a small bowl and set aside. Wipe the skillet clean.

Melt 1 tablespoon of the butter in the same skillet over high heat, until it begins to bubble and brown. Add half the cauliflower and cook until well browned, 2 to 3 minutes, stirring only once about halfway through, then transfer to a bowl. Lower the heat to medium high, add the remaining 1 tablespoon butter, and repeat with the remaining cauliflower. When it's well browned, return the first batch of cauliflower to the pan, add the broth, and cook until the cauliflower begins to get tender but is still a little crunchy, about 3 minutes. Remove from the heat and stir in 1 teaspoon pepper.

Cut the fettuccine into about 3-inch lengths and cook in the boiling water until tender, 2 to 3 minutes. Drain. Put the cauliflower with its cooking liquid and the cheese mixture in the empty pasta pot. Stir to combine. Return the fettuccine to the pot and stir it all together. Season to taste with about ½ teaspoon kosher salt. Spread the mixture in the buttered baking dish. Sprinkle the breadcrumbs evenly over the top. Bake until the top is lightly golden brown and the cheese is bubbling, 20 to 30 minutes. Let cool briefly before serving. —*Bill Telepan*

Double-Cheese Penne with Sausage & Hot Cherry Peppers

Contrary to what many people think, a baked pasta does not require hours and hours to make and bake. The sauce for this dish cooks on the stovetop in minutes and gets its full flavor not from long cooking but from the judicious addition of pickled hot peppers.

In a large covered pot, bring 4 quarts of generously salted water to a boil. Lightly grease an 8x11-inch baking dish or 6 individual (1½-cup) gratin dishes with 1 teaspoon of the olive oil.

Add the penne or ziti to the boiling water and cook until al dente, about 11 minutes. Drain well and return it to its cooking pot.

Meanwhile, heat the remaining 2 tablespoons oil in a large straight-sided skillet over medium-high heat. When the oil is hot, add the sausage, let it sit for a minute, then start stirring and breaking it into bite-size pieces with the side of a slotted metal spoon. Cook until lightly browned, another 2 to 3 minutes. Transfer to a plate using the slotted spoon.

Add the garlic to the pan, season with salt, and cook, stirring constantly, until it colors slightly, about 30 seconds. Add the tomatoes and their juices and cook at a rapid simmer, stirring occasionally and breaking up the tomatoes with the spoon, for 5 minutes so the sauce thickens slightly.

Meanwhile, position an oven rack about 6 inches from the broiler element and heat the broiler on high.

Stir the sausage and its juices, the diced peppers, and ⅓ cup of the Parmigiano into the sauce. Cook, stirring, until the sausage is cooked through, 3 to 5 minutes. Taste for salt and pepper. Pour the sauce over the cooked pasta in the pot and stir well. Spread the pasta and sauce evenly in the baking dish or gratin dishes. Sprinkle with the mozzarella and the remaining ⅓ cup Parmigiano. Place on a baking sheet and broil until the cheese melts and browns in places, 2 to 4 minutes (check often to be sure it doesn't burn). Serve immediately with more Parmigiano, if you like. —*Tony Rosenfeld*

Serves four to six.

2 tablespoons plus 1 teaspoon extra-virgin olive oil

¾ pound penne or ziti

1 pound sweet Italian sausage, casings removed

2 large cloves garlic, minced

Kosher salt

One 28-ounce can peeled whole tomatoes

2 or 3 pickled Italian hot cherry peppers, cored, seeded, and diced

⅔ cup freshly grated Parmigiano-Reggiano cheese; more for serving

Freshly ground black pepper

½ pound low-moisture part-skim mozzarella cheese, shredded

Singapore Noodles (Sing Jau Chow Mai)

Serves four to six as a side dish; three to four as a main course.

4 dried or fresh shiitake
  mushrooms

6 ounces fine rice vermicelli

3 tablespoons vegetable oil

1½ tablespoons Madras (hot)
  curry powder

2 cloves garlic, minced

½ cup low-salt chicken or
  vegetable broth

2 tablespoons low-salt
  soy sauce

2 teaspoons granulated sugar

1 teaspoon hot chile paste

½ teaspoon kosher salt

1 tablespoon peeled and
  minced fresh ginger

½ cup very thinly sliced celery
  sticks (2 inches long)

½ cup thinly sliced yellow onion

½ cup very thinly sliced green
  bell pepper

½ cup bean sprouts, rinsed and
  well drained

4 scallions (white and green
  parts), cut into 2-inch pieces

½ pound small shrimp, peeled
  and deveined

6 ounces honey-cured ham, cut
  into 2-inch-long matchsticks
  (about 1 cup)

1½ tablespoons oyster sauce

If you can't find small shrimp at the market, cut medium or large ones into smaller pieces. For the best flavor, choose shrimp that are still frozen, preferably with their shells on.

If using dried shiitakes, soak them in hot water until softened, about 30 minutes, and drain well. For dried and fresh mushrooms, remove and discard the woody stems. Slice the caps thinly.

Put the vermicelli in a heatproof bowl with enough very hot water to cover. Soak until softened, 8 to 10 minutes. Drain well. If you like, cut the noodles into shorter lengths (4 or 5 inches). Loosen the noodles and spread them on a dishtowel to dry while you proceed.

Put 1 tablespoon of the oil in a small saucepan and heat over medium heat. Add the curry powder and half the minced garlic and sauté for 20 seconds. Add the broth, soy sauce, sugar, chile paste, and salt, cover, and cook for 5 minutes. Remove from the heat and set aside.

Heat a large wok or sauté pan over high heat, add 1 tablespoon of the oil, and tilt the pan to coat. When hot, add the remaining garlic and the ginger. Stir-fry until the garlic is golden, 10 to 20 seconds. Add the celery, onion, green pepper, bean sprouts, scallions, and mushrooms. Stir-fry until crisp-tender, 2 to 3 minutes. Transfer to a plate and set aside.

Heat the remaining 1 tablespoon oil in the pan over high heat. When hot, add the shrimp and stir-fry until just cooked through, 1 to 2 minutes. Add the ham; toss well. Add the noodles, vegetables, soy-curry mixture, and oyster sauce. Toss to mix thoroughly and coat the noodles with the sauce. Serve immediately.—*Nathan Fong*

Shells with Arugula, Feta & Sun-Dried Tomatoes

Serves four as a light main dish or eight to ten as a side dish.

¼ pound arugula, well washed and dried (stem and rip the leaves into smaller pieces if they're large)

6 ounces feta cheese, crumbled

½ cup pitted Kalamata olives, drained and quartered

2 heaping tablespoons drained, thinly sliced oil-packed sun-dried tomatoes

1 pound small or medium shells or orecchiette

1 tablespoons red-wine vinegar

3 tablespoons olive oil

Kosher salt and freshly ground black pepper

10 fresh basil leaves, cut into thin strips

If you can't find high-quality arugula (smallish leaves with no brown spots or large holes), use baby spinach instead.

Bring a large pot of generously salted water to a boil. Combine the arugula, feta, olives, and tomatoes in a large bowl.

Cook the pasta in the boiling water until just tender. Meanwhile, add the vinegar and oil to the arugula salad, season liberally with salt and pepper, and toss well. Drain the pasta, add it to the salad, and toss. Check the seasonings and serve hot, warm, or at room temperature, adding the basil just before serving.

Creamy Goat Cheese Polenta

When you're in the mood for polenta but don't want to wait, look to instant polenta; punch up its flavor with a little goat cheese and create a luxurious texture with the addition of a bit of heavy cream. You can use this polenta as a bed for grilled meats and poultry or pasta sauces, or just serve a bowl as a simple warming supper.

Serves six.

1 quart whole milk

Kosher salt

1 cup instant polenta

½ pound fresh goat cheese, crumbled

Pinch cayenne

½ cup heavy cream

½ to 1 cup water

Freshly ground black pepper

Bring the milk to a boil in a 4-quart saucepan over medium-high heat. Season with 2 teaspoons kosher salt. Slowly whisk in the polenta and cook, stirring constantly, for 5 minutes until the polenta thickens and begins to pull away from the sides of the pan.

Add the goat cheese and cayenne. Whisk until well combined. Whisk in the cream and the water to thin the polenta to a porridge-like consistency. Season with salt and pepper to taste and serve immediately. —*Arlene Jacobs*

Butternut Squash Risotto with Bacon & Sage

Serves four as a main course, or six as a starter.

1 quart low-salt chicken broth; more as needed

½ cup dry white wine

2 tablespoons olive oil

10 large fresh sage leaves

4 slices bacon, cut crosswise into thirds

2 medium shallots, minced (about ¼ cup)

2 cups ¼-inch-diced butternut squash

1½ cups arborio or carnaroli rice

½ cup freshly grated Parmigiano-Reggiano cheese

Kosher salt and freshly ground black pepper

Sage and butternut squash are a classic Italian combination perfectly suited to creamy risotto. Bacon adds a savory flavor. You can also try using thick-cut pancetta instead. It's more flavorful without being smoky.

Combine the broth and wine in a small saucepan set over medium heat.

In a 3-quart saucepan, heat the oil over medium heat. Add the sage leaves and fry, turning once, until they've turned dark green in most places, about 1 minute total. Don't brown. With a fork, transfer to a plate lined with paper towels to drain. Put the bacon in the saucepan and cook, stirring occasionally, until nicely browned, 5 to 7 minutes. Transfer the bacon to the plate with the sage. Add the shallots to the saucepan and cook, stirring with a wooden spoon, until softened, about 1 minute. Add the squash and rice and cook, stirring, for 1 minute.

Ladle in enough of the hot broth mixture to just cover the rice. Cook, stirring frequently, until the broth is mostly absorbed. Add another ladleful of broth and continue cooking, stirring, and adding more ladlefuls of broth as the previous additions are absorbed, until the rice is tender with just a slightly toothsome quality, about 25 minutes. As the risotto cooks, adjust the heat so that it bubbles gently. The broth mixture needn't be boiling; it should just be hot. If you use all the broth and wine before the rice gets tender, use more broth but not more wine.

Set aside the nicest looking sage leaves as a garnish (1 leaf per serving). Crumble half of the bacon and the remaining sage into the risotto. Stir in the Parmigiano. Season to taste with salt and pepper. Crumble the remaining bacon over each serving and garnish with a sage leaf.

—*Jennifer Armentrout*

Risotto with Peas & Porcini

Porcini are among of the most flavorful mushrooms around. Fresh or dried, they can add a rich, savory note to many dishes. Dried porcini are easy to reconstitute, just be sure to strain out any fine grit. You can also grind dried porcini into a powder that can be sprinkled into soups, pan sauces, and pastas.

Soak the mushrooms in hot water to cover until softened, then drain. Remove the woody stems from the shiitakes and chop the mushrooms. Strain the soaking liquid.

In a 3-quart saucepan over medium heat, heat the broth with the mushroom soaking liquid. In another medium saucepan over medium heat, melt the butter. Add the onion and a sprinkling of salt, and cook, stirring occasionally, until soft and lightly browned, 5 to 7 minutes. Add the rice and cook, stirring, for 1 minute. Add the mushrooms and cook, stirring, for 1 minute. Add the wine and cook, stirring, until almost completely reduced, about 1 minute. Add 1 cup of the hot broth and cook, stirring frequently, until it is almost completely absorbed. Adjust the heat as needed to maintain a gentle simmer. Continue adding the broth 1 cup at a time and stirring frequently until absorbed, until the rice is tender but still toothsome (taste a few grains), 20 to 24 minutes from when the first cup of broth is added. You might not need to use all of the broth. Or, if the rice still seems fairly firm when you add the last of the broth, heat and use more chicken broth as needed. Stir in the peas, Parmigiano, vinegar, and half the mint and thyme. Season with salt and pepper to taste and serve immediately, garnished with a sprinkling of the remaining mint and thyme. —*Tony Rosenfeld*

Yields 8 cups; serves four to six as a main course.

- ¾ ounce (scant 1 cup) dried porcini (also called cèpes)
- 1 ounce dried shiitakes (scant 1 cup)
- 5 cups low-salt chicken broth; more as needed
- 2 tablespoons unsalted butter
- 1 medium yellow onion, finely diced
- Kosher salt and freshly ground black pepper
- 2 cups arborio or carnaroli rice
- ⅓ cup dry white wine
- 1½ cups frozen petite peas, thawed
- 1 cup freshly grated Parmigiano-Reggiano cheese
- 1 tablespoon balsamic vinegar
- 3 tablespoons chopped fresh mint
- 1½ teaspoons chopped fresh thyme

Minty Quinoa Tabbouleh

Yields about 8 cups.

1½ cups quinoa

Kosher salt

3 cups water

1½ cups seeded and finely diced
tomato

1 cup finely chopped fresh
flat-leaf parsley

1 cup peeled, seeded, and finely
diced cucumber

½ cup thinly sliced scallion
greens

½ cup extra-virgin olive oil;
more to taste

6 tablespoons fresh lemon
juice; more to taste

¼ teaspoon ground cumin

⅛ teaspoon ground cinnamon

½ cup finely chopped fresh mint

**Tabbouleh, a lemony Middle Eastern parsley and grain salad, is
traditionally made with bulgur wheat. This version, fragrant from a
touch of cumin and cinnamon, uses quinoa instead.**

Rinse the quinoa well in a bowl of cool water and drain. Bring the quinoa,
½ teaspoon kosher salt, and water to a boil in a medium saucepan over high
heat. Cover, reduce the heat to medium low, and simmer until the water is
absorbed and the quinoa translucent and tender, 10 to 15 minutes. (The outer
germ rings of the grain will remain chewy and white. Some germ rings may
separate from the grains and will look like white squiggles.) Immediately fluff
the quinoa with a fork and turn out onto a baking sheet to cool.

When cool, fluff the quinoa again and transfer to a large bowl. Add the
tomato, parsley, cucumber, scallion, oil, lemon juice, cumin, cinnamon, and
1 teaspoon kosher salt. Toss well. Cover and refrigerate to let the flavors
mingle, at least 2 hours or overnight.

Before serving, let sit at room temperature for 20 to 30 minutes. Stir in the
mint. Taste and add more oil and lemon juice (you'll probably need at least
1 tablespoon of each), and more salt as needed. —*Jennifer Armentrout*

Cooking with Quinoa

If you can cook white rice, then you can cook
quinoa. The formula (2:1 liquid to grain) and
method are pretty much the same. Bring the
quinoa and liquid, salted to taste, to a boil,
reduce the heat to a simmer, cover, and cook
until the water is absorbed. It cooks faster than
rice, in about 10 to 15 minutes, making it the
fastest-cooking whole grain out there. Just be
sure to fluff it with a fork before serving.

It's critical to rinse the quinoa well before
cooking it to get rid of its coating of saponin, a
bitter natural substance that protects the plant
from insects and birds. Most of the saponin will
have been removed in processing, but some
grains may need a bit more rinsing: if the water
appears very cloudy, keep rinsing in fresh water
until the cloudiness is almost gone.

White Basmati Rice Pilaf with Whole Spices, Saffron & Mint

Yields about 4 cups;
serves six.

1 cup white basmati rice, preferably Indian or Pakistani

2 tablespoons vegetable oil

1 teaspoon cumin seeds

6 green or white cardamom pods

Two 3-inch-long cinnamon sticks

2 fresh or dried bay leaves

1 medium red onion, halved and thinly sliced lengthwise

1½ cups cold water

2 teaspoons kosher or sea salt

¼ teaspoon saffron threads

1 cup firmly packed fresh mint leaves, finely chopped

"Basmati" means "queen of fragrance" and this aptly named rice does indeed give off a wonderfully nutty aroma during cooking. Basmati rice is great for pilafs because its low starch content helps the long grains stay separate when cooked. Rinsing the rice removes any excess starch left on the surface of the grains after milling.

Put the rice in a bowl and gently rinse with three or four changes of water, until the water runs fairly clear. Fill the bowl halfway with cold water and let the rice soak at room temperature for 30 minutes to soften the kernels. Drain.

Heat a 3-quart saucepan over medium-high heat; pour in the oil and swirl it around. It should appear to shimmer; if not, continue heating until it does. Add the cumin, cardamom, cinnamon, and bay leaves, which will sputter, crackle, and smell aromatic. After 20 to 30 seconds, add the onion and cook, stirring frequently, until it turns golden brown, about 5 minutes.

Add the drained rice and toss gently with the onion mixture. Pour in the water and sprinkle on the salt and saffron and stir once to blend. Leaving the pot uncovered, bring the water to a boil over medium-high heat. After about 3 minutes, when much of the water has evaporated or been absorbed (if you move some of the rice with a fork, the water should look like it comes about halfway up the rice), stir the rice once more to bring the partially cooked layer from the bottom of the pan to the surface. Cover with a tight-fitting lid and turn down the heat to the lowest possible setting. Cook, covered, for another 10 minutes. Without removing the cover, turn off the heat and let the pan stand off the heat, undisturbed, for another 10 minutes.

Remove the lid and add the mint. Fluff the rice with a fork to let the steam escape and to incorporate the mint leaves. Remove the cinnamon sticks and bay leaves and instruct your guests not to eat the cardamom. *—Raghavan Iyer*

Wild Rice Pilaf with Dried Apricots & Pine Nuts

Serves four.

3 tablespoons unsalted butter

1 medium onion, diced

1 teaspoon finely chopped fresh rosemary

1 cup wild rice

2 cups low-salt chicken broth

¾ teaspoon kosher salt; more to taste

⅓ cup diced dried apricots

½ cup pine nuts, toasted

Freshly ground black pepper

Wild rice varies, so check for doneness after 45 minutes—the grains will have popped open and will taste tender—but it may need more than an hour. Try dried cherries or cranberries instead of apricots, or brown rice instead of wild.

In a medium frying pan, melt the butter over medium heat , then sauté the onion and rosemary until the onion is deep golden, about 10 minutes. Add the wild rice and stir to coat with the butter. Add the broth and salt, cover, and bring to a boil. Reduce the heat to medium low and simmer until the grains are slightly open and tender but not mushy, about 50 minutes. Let rest, covered, for 5 minutes. Stir in the apricots, pine nuts, and pepper. Taste and adjust the seasonings and serve. —*Amanda Cushman*

Three Paths to Perfect Rice

The pilaf method

With the pilaf method, the rice is first sautéed in oil along with aromatics and spices. Then a measured amount of liquid is added, the mixture is brought to a simmer, covered, and left to cook until the rice absorbs the liquid. Basmati and wild rice respond beautifully to the pilaf method.

The pasta method

Like pasta, the raw rice goes into a large pot of boiling water and cooks uncovered. When the grains reach the desired tenderness, the water gets poured off. This method keeps brown rice (used in the recipe on p. 140) grains separate and distinct instead of mushy.

The absorption method

The rice cooks in a measured amount of water in a tightly covered pot so that by the time the rice is tender, all the water has been absorbed. As the water level drops, trapped steam finishes the cooking. Instead of a pot, you can use a rice cooker; just follow the manufacturer's directions. Medium-grain rice takes on a creamy, tender texture when cooked by the absorption method.

Brown Rice Salad with Basil & Pistachios

Yields about 6 cups; serves six to eight.

1 cup long-grain brown rice

½ cup golden raisins

¼ cup plus 2 tablespoons mild-tasting olive oil

¼ cup red-wine vinegar

½ cup raw unsalted pistachio nuts

1 small red onion, finely diced

4 medium to large cloves garlic, finely diced

One 15-ounce can chickpeas, drained and rinsed

1 medium red bell pepper, cored, seeded, and finely diced

1 teaspoon kosher or fine sea salt; more to taste

1 teaspoon red pepper flakes

½ cup firmly packed fresh basil leaves, cut into thin strips (chiffonade)

Brown rice adds toothsome texture to this grain salad. It won't get soggy even after being dressed with the vinaigrette, so you can make the whole salad up to a few days in advance. Or make just the rice ahead of time. To create a basil chiffonade, stack the leaves, roll them up from the tip to the stem end, then slice the roll. The slices will unfurl into long, thin strips.

Fill a medium saucepan with water and bring it to a boil over high heat. Add the rice and return to a boil. Cook, uncovered, until the rice grains are cooked and tender but still a little chewy, 20 to 25 minutes. Drain the rice through a sieve and rinse with cold water to stop the cooking. Set aside.

While the rice is cooking, purée the raisins, ¼ cup of the oil, and the vinegar in a blender, scraping down the sides as needed, to make a thick, smooth vinaigrette.

Heat a 10-inch skillet over medium-high heat and toast the pistachios, stirring frequently, until they brown in spots and give off a strong nutty aroma, about 2 minutes. Transfer to a cutting board. When cool enough to touch, chop them coarsely.

Heat the remaining 2 tablespoons oil in the same skillet over medium high heat until very hot. Stir-fry the onion and garlic until honey brown, 2 to 3 minutes. Scrape this into a large bowl along with the pistachios, vinaigrette, chickpeas, bell pepper, salt, and red pepper flakes. Add the rice and fold the ingredients together. The salad can be served at room temperature or chilled.

Just before serving, fold in the basil, taste, and season with more salt, if you like. —*Raghavan Iyer*

Mexican Tomato Rice & Beans

This dish is delicious served with grilled pork tenderloin, or even just rolled up in a flour tortilla as a vegetarian burrito. Vary the spice heat by adding more or less jalapeño; take care when chopping it because the spicy capsaicin can stay on your hands (rubber gloves are the safest bet).

In a 1-quart saucepan, combine the rice and water. Bring to a boil over medium-high heat, cover, reduce the heat to low, and cook for 20 minutes. Remove from the heat and let stand, covered, for another 5 minutes.

While the rice steams, set a fine sieve in a bowl and drain the can of tomatoes. Pour the tomato juices into a 1-cup liquid measure. Add enough water to equal 1 cup.

Heat a 10- to 12-inch skillet over medium-high heat. Pour in the oil and stir-fry the garlic and jalapeño until the garlic browns and the jalapeño smells pungent, about 1 minute. Add the black beans, salt, cumin, and chili powder; stir two to three times to blend and cook the spices, about 30 seconds. Stir in the tomato juice and water mixture and bring to a boil. Adjust the heat to maintain a gentle boil and cook, stirring occasionally, until the beans absorb much of the liquid, 5 to 7 minutes. Add the tomatoes, oregano, cilantro, and cooked rice and cook, stirring occasionally, until the rice is warm, 1 to 2 minutes. Serve immediately. —*Raghavan Iyer*

Yields 6 cups; serves six to eight.

- 1 cup medium-grain white rice
- 2 cups cold water
- One 14.5-ounce can diced tomatoes (preferably "petite-cut")
- 2 tablespoons extra-virgin olive oil
- 6 medium cloves garlic, finely chopped
- 1 medium jalapeño, seeded and finely chopped
- One 15-ounce can black beans, drained and rinsed
- 2 teaspoons kosher or fine sea salt
- 2 teaspoons ground cumin
- 1 teaspoon chili powder
- ¼ cup finely chopped fresh oregano leaves and tender stems
- ¼ cup finely chopped fresh cilantro leaves and tender stems

5
Chicken, Game Hens, Turkey & Duck

p182

p152

Sauteed Chicken Breasts with Tomato-Tarragon Pan Sauce (recipe on page 145)

Mustard & Coriander Chicken Breasts with Lemon-Basil Vinaigrette

Serves four.

2 tablespoons Dijon mustard

2 teaspoons lightly cracked coriander seeds

6 tablespoons extra-virgin olive oil

4 boneless, skinless chicken breast halves (6 to 8 ounces each)

Kosher salt and freshly ground black pepper

4 teaspoons fresh lemon juice

3 tablespoons roughly chopped fresh basil

Rather than cooking the chicken breasts until they are white all the way through, stop when they're just a tad pink in the center. As they rest off the grill, they will continue to cook from the residual heat. By the time you're ready to slice them, they'll be perfect instead of overdone.

Prepare a medium-hot grill fire. In a small bowl, whisk the mustard and coriander seeds. Whisk in 3 tablespoons of the olive oil. If the chicken breasts have the tenders attached, remove them and save for another use. Trim any excess fat from the breasts, then rinse and pat dry. Season the breasts with salt and pepper and rub them all over with the mustard-oil mixture.

When the grill is ready, grill the chicken until one side is nicely browned and grill marks appear, 2 to 3 minutes. (There may be some flare-ups at first; if they don't go out, move the chicken off to the side until they do.) With tongs, rotate the breasts 90 degrees (to get a crosshatch of grill marks) and continue grilling until grill marks form and the sides of the breasts are fully opaque, another 2 to 3 minutes. Flip the breasts and grill in the same way until the second side is browned and the inside has just a trace of pink, another 4 to 6 minutes. Transfer to a clean cutting board, cover loosely with aluminum foil, and let rest for about 5 minutes. Meanwhile, whisk the remaining 3 tablespoons oil with the lemon juice, basil, ¼ teaspoon kosher salt, and a few grinds of pepper. Slice the chicken on an angle and serve drizzled with the vinaigrette. —*Molly Stevens*

Sautéed Chicken Breasts with Tomato-Tarragon Pan Sauce

The sauce here makes about one tablespoon for each breast. If you decide you want more—and you might if you serve this with noodles—you can easily double the sauce ingredients. If you do, whisk in a little more butter at the end.

Remove the tenders from the breasts; save for another use or include them in the sauté. Season the breasts on both sides with ample salt and pepper. Put a handful of flour in a pie pan or other shallow plate and position it near the stove.

Combine the broth, vermouth or wine, tomatoes, and tarragon in a 1-cup Pyrex measuring cup or small bowl.

Heat the oil and 2 tablespoons of the butter in a heavy 12-inch skillet over low heat. Dredge one of the chicken breasts in the flour, coating both sides well but shaking off any excess. Increase the heat of the pan to medium high. When the flecks of milk solids from the butter begin to turn golden brown, add the first floured breast to the pan, then quickly flour the remaining breasts and add them to the pan. Sauté, turning once, until golden on both sides and just cooked through, 6 to 8 minutes. total. Transfer the chicken to heated plates and return the skillet to medium-high heat.

Immediately add the combined ingredients from the measuring cup. Boil rapidly, stirring and scraping up the browned bits in the bottom of the pan, until the liquid reduces to about ¼ cup. Whisk in the remaining 1 tablespoon butter. Remove the pan from the heat and taste the sauce. Adjust the seasoning as necessary. Spoon the sauce over the chicken and serve immediately. *—Pam Anderson*

Serves four.

4 boneless, skinless chicken breast halves (6 to 8 ounces each)

Kosher salt and freshly ground black pepper

All-purpose flour for dredging

¼ cup low-salt chicken broth

¼ cup dry vermouth or dry white wine

4 canned tomatoes, drained, seeded, and coarsely chopped

1 teaspoon minced fresh tarragon, or scant ½ teaspoon dried

1 tablespoon vegetable or olive oil

3 tablespoons unsalted butter

Crisp Curried Chicken Fingers with Honey Mustard Dipping Sauce

Serves two to three as a main course.

½ small shallot, minced

1 tablespoon rice vinegar

1 cup panko

6 tablespoons vegetable oil

Kosher salt and freshly ground
  black pepper

1 pound chicken breast tenders

2 tablespoons mayonnaise

¾ teaspoon mild curry powder

¼ teaspoon Tabasco sauce

2 tablespoons Dijon mustard

2 tablespoons honey

This easy recipe makes excellent use of any chicken tenders you may have collected after trimming chicken breasts. Many grocery stores sell packages of tenders also. Panko are super-dry, light, and flaky Japanese breadcrumbs. Look for them in the Asian section of your grocery store or at an Asian market. In a pinch, you can substitute homemade coarse dry breadcrumbs, but they won't stick to the chicken quite as well and the texture will be more sandy than crisp.

Position a rack 6 inches from the broiler element and heat the broiler on high for at least 10 minutes. Combine the shallot and vinegar in a small bowl and set aside for at least 10 minutes.

Meanwhile, pour the panko into a shallow dish (like a pie pan) and toss with 2 tablespoon of the oil, ¼ teaspoon kosher salt, and a few grinds of pepper. Have ready a heavy baking sheet. Trim off any exposed tendon ends from the wide tips of the tenders, if necessary. In a medium bowl, combine the tenders with the mayonnaise, curry powder, Tabasco, ½ teaspoon kosher salt, and several grinds of pepper. Toss with your hands to coat well. Dredge each tender in the panko and arrange in a single layer on the baking sheet. Broil, flipping once, until the tenders are crisp and golden brown on the outside, cooked through on the inside, 3 to 5 minutes per side.

While the chicken cooks, whisk the mustard and honey into the shallot and vinegar. Slowly whisk in the remaining ¼ cup of oil. Season the sauce to taste with salt and pepper. Serve the chicken fingers with small dishes of the sauce for dipping. —*Jennifer Armentrout*

Chicken Breasts with Red Thai Curry Peanut Sauce

Serves four.

2 tablespoons peeled and chopped fresh ginger

1 tablespoon chopped garlic

½ cup smooth natural peanut butter, preferably at room temperature

¼ cup rice vinegar

2 tablespoons soy sauce

2 tablespoons mirin or granulated sugar

1¾ teaspoons red Thai curry paste

3 tablespoons water

4 boneless, skinless chicken breast halves (about 1½ pounds total)

Kosher salt and freshly ground black pepper

2 tablespoons canola oil; more as needed

½ cup unsweetened coconut milk

3 tablespoons minced fresh cilantro

Natural peanut butter has a richer peanut flavor, but the oil tends to separate naturally and mixing it back in can be a messy and strenuous endeavor. The trick is to turn the jar upside down for a day or two so the oil will filter its way up and essentially mix itself into the peanut butter. When you no longer see oil pooled at the bottom, you know it's ready.

In a food processor, combine the ginger, garlic, peanut butter, rice vinegar, soy sauce, mirin, 1½ teaspoons of the curry paste, and water. Process until smooth, about 30 seconds. Taste to check the heat level and add the remaining ¼ teaspoon curry paste if you like.

If the chicken breasts come with tenders, remove them and reserve for another use. Between two sheets of plastic wrap, lightly pound the breasts to an even thickness with a meat mallet, a heavy pan, or the side of a cleaver. Season the chicken all over with salt and pepper. Set a large, heavy skillet over medium-high heat and add the canola oil. When the oil is very hot, add two of the breasts and cook until nicely browned, 3 to 4 minutes. Flip the chicken and continue to cook until it's cooked through, another 3 to 4 minutes. Transfer to a platter. Repeat with the remaining chicken, adding 1 to 2 tablespoons more oil if the pan is dry.

Reduce the heat to low and add the coconut milk and ½ cup of the peanut sauce to the skillet. (Save the remaining sauce for another use.) Stir to combine and heat through, about 2 minutes. Remove from the heat and stir in the cilantro. Drizzle the sauce over the chicken and serve immediately. —*Kate Hays*

Kung Pao Chicken

Serves four.

¾ cup low-salt chicken broth

2 tablespoons soy sauce

1 tablespoon balsamic vinegar

¼ cup plus 1 tablespoon cornstarch

2 teaspoons Asian sesame oil

1½ teaspoons granulated sugar

1½ pounds boneless, skinless chicken breast halves, cut into 1½-inch pieces

Kosher salt and freshly ground black pepper

¼ cup canola oil

3 small hot red dried chiles, such as Thai chiles or chiles de arbol, split lengthwise (reserve the seeds)

2 tablespoons peeled and minced fresh ginger

6 scallions, thinly sliced, whites and greens kept separate

1 medium red bell pepper, cored, seeded, and cut into 1-inch pieces

2 inner ribs celery, cut crosswise ½ inch thick

¼ cup dry sherry

¼ cup coarsely chopped salted peanuts

Successful stir-frying relies on very high heat and a quick hand. Food can go from perfectly cooked to burnt in a matter of seconds, so make sure all the ingredients are ready to go before you begin.

Whisk the broth, soy sauce, vinegar, 1 tablespoon of the cornstarch, the sesame oil, and sugar in a measuring cup. In a large bowl, toss the chicken with ¾ teaspoon kosher salt and a few generous grinds of pepper. Add the remaining ¼ cup cornstarch and toss with the chicken (you may want to use tongs, as the cornstarch has a chalky texture), shaking off any excess.

Heat 3 tablespoons of the canola oil in a 12-inch heavy skillet over medium-high heat until it's shimmering hot. Sauté the chicken, flipping after 2 minutes, until it's lightly browned on two sides, about 4 minutes total (it's all right if the chicken sticks slightly and if the sides of the chicken are still raw). Add the remaining 1 tablespoon canola oil to the skillet. Add the chiles and their seeds, the ginger, and the scallion whites and cook, stirring, for 1 minute. Add the bell pepper and celery and cook, stirring, until they soften slightly, about 2 minutes. Add the sherry and cook until it almost completely reduces, 30 to 60 seconds, scraping the bottom of the pan to incorporate any browned bits. Give the broth mixture a quick whisk, stir it into the chicken and vegetables, and bring to a boil (the sauce should immediately thicken). Slice into one of the thicker pieces of chicken to see if it's cooked through. If still pink, reduce the heat to a simmer, cover, and cook a few minutes more. Serve immediately, sprinkled with the peanuts and scallion greens. —*Tony Rosenfeld*

Four Steps to a Chinese Classic

1 Lightly dredge chunks of chicken in cornstarch to give them a protective coating and to help them brown evenly.

2 Sear the chicken on both sides to give the dish a deep, rich flavor base.

3 Stir in the aromatics, then the pepper and celery, and cook until they soften slightly.

4 Add a soy-sesame sauce to the pan and, within moments, it will thicken and the dish will be ready to serve.

Chicken Breasts Stuffed with Prosciutto & Fontina

Serves four.

4 large boneless, skinless chicken breast halves (8 ounces each)

4 thin slices prosciutto (2 to 3 ounces total)

1 cup lightly packed grated Fontina cheese

¾ cup unbleached all-purpose flour

2 large eggs

1½ cups fresh breadcrumbs

Kosher salt and freshly ground black pepper

⅔ cup olive oil

For even more flavor, add two tablespoons Dijon mustard to the eggs and four teaspoons dried sage leaves to the breadcrumbs in the breading step.

If the chicken breasts have tenders, remove them and save for another use. Trim, rinse, and pat the breasts dry. Make a pocket on the thicker side of each breast: Using a sharp boning or utility knife, cut into the breast about ½ inch from one end. Cut a pocket, going to within about ¼ inch of the other side. Lay a slice of prosciutto along the length of the pocket, then stuff in ¼ cup of the cheese, distributing it evenly throughout the pocket and to the ends. Press on the top of each breast to close the pocket.

Line up three wide shallow dishes (like soup plates or pie pans). Fill the first with the flour. In the second, whisk the eggs. In the third, toss together the breadcrumbs with ½ teaspoon kosher salt and ½ teaspoon pepper.

Season the breasts generously on both sides with salt and pepper. Dredge one breast well in the flour, shaking off any excess. Dip it into the eggs, turning to coat evenly, then dredge it in the breadcrumbs, pressing to make the crumbs adhere evenly. Gently shake off excess. Set on a plate and repeat with the other breasts. Refrigerate for at least 5 minutes and up to 3 hours to let the breading set. Discard any leftover flour, egg, or crumbs.

Heat the oven to 350°F. Heat the olive oil in a heavy 10-inch nonstick skillet over medium-high heat. When the oil is very hot, carefully place two of the breasts in the pan and cook until golden brown, about 3 minutes per side. If the oil seems to get too hot, reduce the heat to medium. Transfer to a baking sheet. Repeat with the other two breasts. Bake until the chicken and filling reach 165°F on an instant-read thermometer, about 15 minutes. Serve immediately. —*Jennifer C. Martinkus and Derrin Davis*

This chapter includes three recipes for stuffed and coated chicken breasts. The method shown here will also work with your own filling and coating recipes.

1 Make a pocket on the thicker side of each breast: Using a sharp boning or utility knife, cut into the breast about 1/2 inch from one end. Create a pocket, slicing to within about 1/4 inch of the other side.

2 Stuff each breast with some filling, distributing it evenly throughout the pocket and to the ends. Press on the top of each breast to close the pocket.

Line up three wide shallow dishes. Fill the first with the flour. In the second, whisk the eggs. In the third, toss the breadcrumbs with salt and pepper.

3 Season the breasts generously on both sides with salt and pepper. Dredge one breast well in the flour, shaking off any excess. Dip it into the eggs, turning to coat evenly, then dredge it in the breadcrumbs, pressing to make the crumbs adhere evenly. Gently shake off any excess. Set on a plate and repeat with the other breasts. Refrigerate for at least 5 minutes and up to 3 hours to let the breading set. Discard any leftover flour, egg, or crumbs.

Heat the oven to 350°F.

4 Heat the olive oil in a heavy, 10-inch nonstick skillet over medium-high heat. When the oil is very hot, carefully add the breasts to the pan and cook until golden brown, about 3 minutes per side. If the oil seems to get too hot, reduce the heat to medium. Transfer the breasts to a baking sheet. Repeat with the other breasts.

5 Bake until the chicken and filling reach 165°F on an instant-read thermometer, about 15 minutes. Serve immediately.

Chicken Roulades Stuffed with Goat Cheese, Basil & Sun-Dried Tomatoes

Serves four.

4 boneless, skinless chicken breast halves (about 1½ pounds total), rinsed and patted dry

¼ pound fresh goat cheese, crumbled (about 1 cup)

16 large oil-packed sun-dried tomato halves, drained

1 ounce baby spinach leaves

16 large fresh basil leaves, rinsed and patted dry

Kosher salt and freshly ground black pepper

¾ cup unbleached all-purpose flour

2 large eggs, beaten in a small bowl

1¾ cups fresh breadcrumbs seasoned with ½ teaspoon kosher salt and ½ teaspoon ground pepper

⅔ cup olive oil

This is a beautiful dish for a dinner party because the flavor combination is a favorite and the sliced roulades look stunning on the plate. It does require some last-minute cooking, though you can assemble the roulades up to 2 hours ahead of time and then cook them off in between courses.

Set the chicken on a cutting board and, holding a chef's knife parallel to the board, cut each breast in half so you have eight thin cutlets. Lay plastic wrap over the chicken and pound with a heavy skillet to flatten. Remove the plastic, season the chicken with salt and pepper, and top each piece with a quarter of the goat cheese, sun-dried tomatoes, spinach leaves, and basil (try to keep the fillings in the center of the chicken so they don't slide out the sides). Season with salt and pepper and roll up each piece starting with the narrow end. Use a toothpick to secure each roulade.

Line up three wide shallow dishes. Fill the first with flour, the second with the beaten eggs, the third with the breadcrumbs. Dredge one chicken roulade well in the flour, shaking off any excess. Dip it into the eggs, turning to coat evenly, and then dredge it in the breadcrumbs, pressing to make the crumbs adhere evenly. Gently shake off any excess. Set on a plate and repeat with the other breasts. Refrigerate to let the breading set, 10 minutes to 2 hours.

Heat the oven to 350°. Heat ⅓ cup of the olive oil in a heavy 12-inch nonstick skillet over medium-high heat. When the oil is very hot, carefully add half of the breasts to the pan and cook until golden brown on all sides, about 2 minutes per side. If the oil seems too hot, reduce the heat to medium. Transfer the roulades to a baking sheet. Pour out the hot oil, wipe out the pan, and heat the remaining ⅓ cup of oil. Cook remaining roulades and transfer to the baking sheet. Bake until the chicken and filling reach 165°F on an instant-read thermometer, about 15 minutes. Let the roulades rest for a few minutes before removing the toothpicks (with tweezers or pliers, if necessary). Slice the roulades in half on the diagonal and serve four pieces to each person immediately. —*Tony Rosenfeld*

Chicken Piccata with Fried Capers

By quickly pan-frying the capers, you add not only their sharp, bright flavor to the piccata but also a wonderful crisp texture.

Rinse the capers and pat dry with paper towels. Heat the oil in a 10-inch nonstick skillet over medium-high heat. When the oil is hot, add the capers and stir-fry until most of them open like flowers and become crisp and slightly brown, 30 to 60 seconds. Remove from the heat and transfer the capers to a dry paper towel with a soup spoon, tilting each spoonful against the side of the pan to let excess oil drain back into the pan.

Season the chicken cutlets with salt and pepper. Heat the skillet over medium-high heat and sauté the cutlets in batches until golden brown and just cooked through, 1 to 2 minutes per side. Transfer the cooked chicken to a plate and cover to keep warm.

With the pan still over medium-high heat, add the garlic and sauté until lightly golden, about 30 seconds. Add the broth and scrape the pan with a wooden spoon to dissolve any browned bits. Boil the broth until reduced by about half. Stir in the lemon juice and honey. Turn off the heat, add the butter, and swirl the pan until the butter melts and thickens the sauce. Stir in the parsley and about half the capers. Adjust the salt and pepper, if needed. Spoon the sauce over the chicken, scatter the remaining capers over it, and serve. *—Jennifer Armentrout*

Serves two to three.

2 tablespoons drained nonpareil capers

2 tablespoons olive oil

1 pound thin chicken breast cutlets

Kosher salt and freshly ground black pepper

1 clove garlic, finely chopped

½ cup low-salt chicken broth

2 tablespoons fresh lemon juice

½ teaspoon honey

2 tablespoons cold unsalted butter, cut into 3 pieces

1 tablespoon chopped fresh flat-leaf parsley

Chicken with Potatoes, Peas & Coconut-Curry Sauce

Serves two to three.

1 pound boneless, skinless chicken breast halves

Kosher salt and freshly ground black pepper

2 tablespoons vegetable oil; more as needed

½ medium onion, finely diced (to yield about ½ cup)

1 tablespoon minced fresh ginger

2 teaspoons seeded, minced fresh jalapeño

1 tablespoon sweet curry powder (not Madras or hot)

1 cup low-salt chicken broth

1 medium red or yellow potato, peeled and cut into ¼-inch dice (to yield about 1 cup)

One 5.5-ounce can coconut milk, well shaken

½ cup frozen peas

2 tablespoons roughly chopped fresh cilantro

Jalapeños add a fresh-tasting heat to the sweet curry and coconut, but be careful when handling them. Consider wearing gloves to avoid irritating your eyes by rubbing them after you handle the cut chile.

Trim the chicken, removing the tenders. Holding your knife at a 45-degree angle, cut each breast crosswise into ¾-inch-thick slices. Reserve the tenders for another use or sauté them with the sliced chicken (no need to slice them). Season the chicken slices generously with salt and pepper.

In a 10-inch straight-sided sauté pan, heat the oil over medium-high heat until it's hot enough to shimmer. Add half of the chicken and cook, flipping once, until lightly browned and just barely cooked through, 1 to 2 minutes per side. Transfer the chicken to a plate; repeat with the remaining chicken. Cover with foil to keep warm.

Return the pan to medium heat and, if it looks dry, add another 1 tablespoon oil. Add the onion, ginger, and jalapeño and sauté, stirring almost constantly with a wooden spoon, until the vegetables soften, about 2 minutes. Add the curry powder and sauté for 30 seconds. Pour in the chicken broth and scrape the pan with the spoon to loosen any browned bits. Add the potato and ½ teaspoon kosher salt. Bring to a simmer and cook, partially covered, until the potato is barely tender, 7 to 8 minutes. Add the coconut milk and peas; simmer uncovered until the peas are thawed, the potato is fully tender, and the sauce is somewhat thickened, 4 to 5 minutes. Taste the sauce; add salt and pepper as needed. Add the chicken along with any accumulated juices to the sauce and turn to coat with the sauce. Serve immediately, sprinkled with the cilantro. —*Jennifer Armentrout*

For Juicy Chicken, Slice Thin and Sear Quickly

Thin slices mean quick cooking. By slicing the boneless chicken breasts on an angle and searing the slices over medium-high heat, you can cook the chicken in about 6 minutes.

Slice

Holding your knife at a 45-degree angle, cut each breast crosswise into ¾-inch-thick slices.

Sear

White edges signal that it's time to flip the chicken. Slide a metal spatula under each piece to release any areas that are sticking.

Stir-Fried Chicken with Green Beans & Mushrooms

Serves two generously.

6 ounces green beans, ends trimmed, sliced lengthwise into quarters (about 2 cups)

3 tablespoons vegetable oil

1 tablespoon Big Four Paste (recipe follows)

1 boneless, skinless chicken breast half (6 to 8 ounces), sliced thinly against the grain

1 teaspoon minced fresh ginger

1 or 2 fresh bird chiles or 1 fresh serrano chile or 1 small fresh jalapeño, minced

2 tablespoons soy sauce

½ teaspoon granulated sugar

¼ teaspoon sea salt or kosher salt

½ pound fresh brown or shiitake mushrooms, stems trimmed, caps thinly sliced (to yield about 2½ cups)

¼ cup dry white wine

Slicing the green beans lengthwise into quarters and blanching them might seem fussy, but it makes a big difference in their texture, so try not to skip this step.

Bring a medium pot of water to a boil over high heat. Add the quartered green beans and blanch until bright green and still crunchy but no longer raw tasting, about 1 minute. Drain, shock in cold water, drain again, and set aside.

Heat the oil in a large skillet or stir-fry pan over high heat for 1 minute. Add the Big Four Paste; stir-fry for 30 seconds to distribute the paste in the oil. Add the chicken and stir constantly until it turns white. Add the ginger and chiles; stir-fry for 30 seconds. Add the soy sauce, sugar, and sea salt; stir-fry for 30 seconds. Add the green beans and mushrooms. Stir-fry to mix and combine. Add the wine and stir until the chicken is cooked, the beans are slightly soft but crunchy, and the mushrooms are soft, 3 to 5 minutes. Serve hot. *—Su-Mei Yu*

The Big Four Paste

Yields about ¾ cup.

1 tablespoon coriander seeds

2 tablespoons white peppercorns (preferably Thai)

12 to 15 cloves garlic, minced (½ cup)

1 teaspoon coarse sea salt or kosher salt

1 cup minced fresh cilantro stems, roots, or both

This extremely versatile flavoring paste can be made ahead and refrigerated for up to a month. Try adding 1 tablespoon to your other favorite stir-fries or lightly coat meat or fish destined for the grill with a mix of 1 teaspoon of the paste and 1 tablespoon each of olive oil and lemon juice. Meatloaf and meatballs also benefit from the flavoring; use 1 tablespoon of paste for every pound of ground meat. For a less pungent paste, use 2 teaspoons peppercorns and 1 teaspoon coriander.

Heat a small dry skillet over medium heat. Add the coriander seeds and toast them, shaking the skillet, until the seeds are aromatic, about 3 minutes. Pour the seeds into a small bowl to cool. Repeat with the peppercorns. When cool, grind the coriander seeds and peppercorns separately in an electric spice grinder or a mortar and pestle. Finish making the paste in a mortar, which results in a fine texture or in a food processor, or a blender, which will be coarser.

To finish with a mortar and pestle: Put the garlic and salt in a mortar (set a damp towel under the mortar to keep it from sliding) and pound straight up and down with the pestle until a paste forms. Use a spatula to scrape the garlic from the sides into the center of the mortar as often as necessary. Add the cilantro and continue pounding to a fairly smooth paste. Add the ground spices and pound until incorporated. Transfer to a sealed jar and refrigerate.

To finish with a food processor or blender: Pulse the garlic, salt, and cilantro in the processor until finely minced, scraping down the sides of the bowl as needed. Add the ground spices and process to a paste. Transfer to a sealed jar and refrigerate. *–Su-Mei Yu*

Peel Ginger with a Spoon

Of all the little tricks for preparing vegetables, one of the handiest is using a spoon to peel fresh ginger. Most people use a paring knife for this task, but the knife usually ends up trimming off some of the inner good stuff, too. If you just scrape the side of a spoon along the ginger, the skin comes right off, leaving all the aromatic flesh behind. Try it once and you'll never go back to using a paring knife.

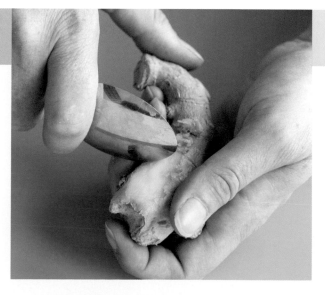

Roasted Poblano & Bell Pepper Chicken Tacos

Serves two amply or four as a light meal.

½ red bell pepper, cored, seeded, and flattened

1 poblano, cored, seeded, and flattened

1 store-roasted chicken

2 tablespoons extra-virgin olive oil

½ teaspoon ground cumin

Pinch cayenne

1 clove garlic, put though a garlic press or minced

Juice of ½ lime

Pinch kosher salt

½ cup sour cream

1 tablespoon finely chopped yellow onion

2 tablespoons finely chopped fresh cilantro; more leaves for garnish

4 small (6- to 7-inch) corn tortillas

¼ cup grated Cheddar cheese

Homemade or purchased tomato salsa for serving

Store-roasted chickens provide a shortcut to tender, shreddable dark meat in this quick and casual dish. Feel free to play around with the topping: Sautéed corn would be a nice addition, while shredded beef or even cooked diced potatoes could take the place of the chicken.

Position an oven rack close to the broiler and heat the broiler. Put the peppers skin side up on a baking sheet and broil until blackened. Transfer them to a small bowl, cover with plastic wrap, and let cool.

Reduce the oven temperature to 400°F.

Remove the skin from the legs, thighs, and wings of the chicken and shred the meat; you should have about 1½ cups. (Save the breasts for another use, such as chicken salad.) In a medium bowl, combine the olive oil, cumin, cayenne, half the garlic, and the lime juice. Season with salt. Add the chicken to the bowl and toss to coat it well with the vinaigrette.

When the peppers are cool enough to handle, remove the blackened skin and chop them finely.

In a small bowl, combine the sour cream, onion, the remaining garlic, the cilantro, and chopped peppers.

Put the tortillas on a baking sheet. Divide the chicken among the tortillas, leaving a little space around the edges. Top with the sour cream mixture, then the cheese. Bake until the cheese is melted, about 5 minutes. Garnish with a little fresh cilantro and serve with some salsa. Eat as is with a knife and fork or roll the tortilla up and eat with your hands. *—Joanne McAllister Smart*

Stacked Green Chile & Grilled Chicken Enchiladas

Serves four.

2 boneless, skinless chicken breast halves

3 tablespoons olive oil; more as needed

Kosher salt and freshly ground black pepper

12 small (5½- to 6-inch) corn tortillas

Green Chile Sauce (recipe follows), heated

6 ounces Monterey Jack cheese, grated

Chopped fresh cilantro for garnish (optional)

Green Chile Sauce

Yields about 4 cups.

You can make this sauce a day ahead. It's also delicious over grilled chicken, swordfish, and pork, or served cold as a condiment.

5 medium tomatillos, papery outer skins removed

1 quart low-salt chicken broth

1¼ to 1½ pounds fresh Anaheim chiles, roasted, peeled, seeded, and coarsely chopped

2 teaspoons minced yellow onion

1 teaspoon dried oregano or 2 teaspoons chopped fresh

1 clove garlic, minced

½ teaspoon kosher salt; more to taste

¼ teaspoon ground white pepper

2 tablespoons cornstarch, dissolved in 2 tablespoons water

Your favorite hot sauce (optional)

Put a medium saucepan of water on to boil. Boil the tomatillos until soft, 5 to 10 minutes. Drain and purée in a blender or food processor. Return the tomatillos to the saucepan along with the broth, chiles, onion, oregano, garlic, salt, and pepper. Bring to a boil over medium-high heat, reduce the heat, and simmer for 10 minutes. Add the cornstarch slurry; stir well. Simmer, stirring occasionally, until thickened slightly and reduced to 4 to 4½ cups, another 5 to 15 minutes. Adjust the seasonings if needed, including hot sauce to suit your taste.

Green chiles and chicken is a favorite combination in West Texas and New Mexico, where these stacked enchiladas are more common than the rolled kind. The chicken can also be cooked under the broiler or on a grill pan.

Heat a gas grill to medium high or build a medium-hot charcoal fire. Coat the chicken with olive oil and season generously with salt and pepper. Grill the chicken breasts until just cooked through, 4 to 5 minutes per side. When cool enough to handle, slice into thin strips. Heat the oven to 450°F.

In a small skillet, heat the 3 tablespoons oil over medium-high heat until very hot (dip the edge of a tortilla in to check; it should sizzle straight away). Using tongs, set a tortilla in the hot oil and cook until soft and lightly brown on each side, 15 to 20 seconds per side. Transfer to paper towels to cool and drain. If the pan gets dry, add another tablespoon of oil.

In a baking dish large enough to accommodate four separate stacks of tortillas (a 10x15-inch Pyrex dish is good), ladle a thin layer of sauce. Lay four tortillas in the dish and ladle about ½ cup of sauce over them. Divide half the chicken among the first layer of tortillas and top with another ½ cup of sauce and a third of the cheese. Stack on another four tortillas and top with the rest of the chicken, more sauce, and another third of the cheese. Finish with a third tortilla layer and top with the remaining sauce and cheese. Bake until the sauce has thickened somewhat, about 20 minutes. The edges of the top tortilla in each stack will turn golden, but if they look like they're drying out too much or burning, occasionally spoon some sauce over them. Let rest for 5 to 10 minutes before serving. To serve, transfer each stack with a metal spatula to a dinner plate. Spoon any sauce left in the baking dish over the stacks and sprinkle with chopped cilantro if you like. *—Robb Walsh*

Chicken-Vegetable Pot Pie with Puff Pastry Crust

Serves four.

4 cups low-salt chicken broth

1½ pounds boneless, skinless chicken thighs

1 tablespoon extra-virgin olive oil

2 slices bacon, cut crosswise into ¼-inch strips

1 medium carrot, cut into medium dice

½ small bulb fennel, cut into medium dice

1½ cups medium cremini or button mushrooms, quartered

One 9-ounce package frozen artichoke hearts, thawed and drained if necessary (about 1 cup)

¾ cup frozen pearl onions, thawed

1 medium clove garlic, finely chopped

3 tablespoons chopped fresh flat-leaf parsley

1 teaspoon finely grated lemon zest

1 teaspoon chopped fresh thyme

6 tablespoons unsalted butter

6 tablespoons all-purpose flour

½ pound frozen puff pastry, thawed in the refrigerator overnight

1 large egg, lightly beaten

As delicious as this pot pie is, it's hard to believe so much of it comes from the freezer section of the supermarket. Frozen puff pastry makes a delicious, light, and crisp crust with no mixing and no mess. (For the best results, let the frozen pastry thaw in the refrigerator overnight before using it.) Frozen pearl onions eliminate fussy peeling, and frozen artichoke hearts mean not having to deal with the prickly choke.

Position a rack in the center of the oven and heat the oven to 400°F.

In a medium saucepan over medium heat, bring the broth to a simmer. Add the chicken thighs, cover, and cook at a gentle simmer over medium-low to low heat until just cooked through, about 15 minutes (check on the broth periodically to make sure it's simmering, not boiling). Transfer the poached chicken to a plate to cool. Boil the broth, uncovered, over medium-high heat until reduced to 2½ cups, about 10 minutes.

Meanwhile, heat the olive oil in a 12-inch skillet over medium-high heat. Add the bacon and cook until just barely crisp, 1 to 2 minutes. Add the carrot and fennel and cook until browned in spots, about 2 minutes. Transfer the mixture to a large bowl with a slotted spoon, leaving behind as much fat as possible. Add the mushrooms to the pan and cook until browned, about 3 minutes. Add the artichokes, onions, and garlic and cook until browned in spots, about 2 minutes, Transfer the mushroom mixture to the bowl with the carrot, fennel, and bacon.

Dice the cooled chicken, discarding any excess fat. Add the diced chicken, parsley, lemon zest, and thyme to the bowl of vegetables.

Melt the butter in the same skillet over medium heat. Add the flour and cook, whisking, until caramel colored, about 4 minutes. Whisk in the reduced broth and simmer, whisking occasionally, for 15 minutes, to thicken the sauce and cook off the raw flour flavor (adjust the heat as necessary to keep the sauce from cooking too rapidly).

While the sauce simmers, remove the puff pastry from the refrigerator and unfold it on a clean work surface. Trim to an 8-inch square, then cut that into four 4-inch squares. Transfer the pastry squares to a parchment-lined or lightly oiled baking sheet. Brush the pastry lightly with the egg (you won't need all of the egg). Bake until puffed and very light golden brown, about 10 minutes.

When the sauce is done simmering, season it to taste with salt and pepper. Stir the sauce into the chicken and vegetable mixture and adjust the seasoning with salt and pepper to taste. Transfer the mixture to an 8-inch-square baking dish and arrange the baked pastry squares on top. Bake the pot pie until the crust is deeply browned and the filling bubbles around the edges, 15 to 20 minutes. *—Allison Ehri*

Spicy Chicken & White Bean Chili

Serves four.

1 ripe avocado, pitted, peeled, and cut into medium dice

1 large white onion, finely diced

Juice of 2 limes

½ cup chopped fresh cilantro

Kosher salt and freshly ground black pepper

Two 15-ounce cans cannellini beans, rinsed and drained

One 14.5-ounce can diced tomatoes and their juice

1½ canned chipotles in adobo, plus 2 tablespoons of the sauce

1½ pounds boneless, skinless chicken thighs, trimmed of excess fat, or 3½ cups shredded store-roasted chicken

2 tablespoons olive oil

1 tablespoon chili powder

1½ teaspoons ground cumin

¾ cup lager beer, such as Corona

Sour cream, for garnish (optional)

Puréeing some of the beans along with the canned tomatoes in this recipe gives the dish a thick texture and a rich, slow-cooked feel. Chipotle chiles are available canned with adobo sauce in many supermarkets and specialty food markets.

Toss the avocado, about one-quarter of the onion, 2½ tablespoons of the lime juice, and 2 tablespoons of the cilantro in a medium bowl. Season with salt and pepper to taste and set aside.

In a food processor, combine 1 cup of the beans, the tomatoes and their juice, and the chipotles and adobo sauce and process until smooth. Set aside.

Season the chicken with 1 teaspoon kosher salt and ½ teaspoon pepper. Heat the oil in a large Dutch oven or casserole over medium-high heat until it's shimmering hot. Add the chicken (the thighs should just fit, evenly spaced) and sear without touching until golden brown, 3 to 4 minutes. Flip and cook the other side until also golden brown, 3 to 4 minutes. Transfer to a large plate and let rest for 10 minutes. Take the pot off the heat and set aside. When the chicken has rested, shred it by hand or chop it coarsely.

Return the pot to medium-high heat. Add the remaining chopped onion to the pot and cook, stirring, until it begins to brown and soften, about 3 minutes. Add the chili powder and cumin and stir for 20 seconds. Add the beer and cook, scraping the bottom of the pan with a wooden spoon to get up any browned bits, until it almost completely reduces, 3 to 4 minutes. Add the remaining white beans and the puréed bean mixture and bring to a boil. Stir in the chicken along with any accumulated juices on the bottom of the plate. Cover, reduce the heat to medium low, and simmer for 15 minutes so the chicken finishes cooking and the flavors mix and meld. Stir in ¼ cup of the cilantro and the remaining lime juice and season with salt and pepper to taste.

Ladle into large bowls and serve immediately with a generous spoonful of the avocado mixture, a dollop of sour cream (if using), and a sprinkling of the remaining cilantro. *—Tony Rosenfeld*

Chicken with Mustard-Fennel Crust

**By adding the crumb crust at the end of cooking, there's no competition
between chicken and crust over which one gets cooked first. You can get
the chicken just right, then raise the heat and cook off the crust so it's
perfectly golden and crunchy.**

Set a rack in the center of the oven and heat the oven to 400°F. Rinse the
chicken parts and pat them dry; season generously with salt and pepper. Heat
1 tablespoon of the oil in a 10-inch sauté pan over medium-high heat until
very hot. Working in two batches, brown the chicken well on both sides, 3 to
4 minutes per side. Transfer the chicken, skin side up, to an 11x14-inch or
similar roasting pan and bake until cooked through, about 15 minutes.

Meanwhile, over medium heat, toast the fennel seeds in a small dry skillet,
stirring frequently, until golden and fragrant, 2 to 3 minutes. Transfer to a
small bowl and add the remaining 2 tablespoons olive oil, the breadcrumbs,
½ teaspoon kosher salt, and ⅛ teaspoon pepper.

Remove the chicken from the oven and raise the oven temperature to
500°F. Turn the chicken pieces over and, with a pastry brush, lightly dab the
mustard on top. With your hands, press the breadcrumb mixture on top of the
mustard. Bake until the crumb crust turns golden, about another 10 minutes.

Transfer the chicken to a serving platter, sprinkle with the parsley, and serve.

—*Arlene Jacobs*

Serves four.

8 bone-in, skin-on chicken thighs
  or drumsticks (or a mix)

Kosher salt and freshly ground
  black pepper

3 tablespoons extra-virgin
  olive oil

1 tablespoon fennel seeds

1 cup coarse fresh breadcrumbs

2 tablespoons Dijon mustard

2 tablespoons chopped fresh
  flat-leaf parsley

Lemony Moroccan-Style Chicken Kebabs

Serves six.

For the marinade:

2 lemons

6 cloves garlic, peeled

Two ⅛-inch-thick slices peeled fresh ginger

1 teaspoon dried marjoram

1 teaspoon ground coriander

1 teaspoon ground cumin

½ teaspoon ground turmeric

⅛ teaspoon ground cinnamon

Pinch saffron threads

1 teaspoon light brown sugar

2½ teaspoons kosher salt

2 teaspoons freshly ground black pepper

3 tablespoons olive oil

For the kebabs:

2½ pounds boneless, skinless chicken thighs, trimmed of excess fat and cut into 2-inch chunks

1 sweet onion (like Vidalia), cut into 1-inch pieces

1 red bell pepper, cored, seeded, and cut into 1-inch squares

1 yellow bell pepper, cored, seeded, and cut into 1-inch squares

2 tablespoons chopped fresh flat-leaf parsley, for garnish

For the yogurt-lemon Sauce:

1 seedless cucumber, cut into ½-inch dice

½ cup chopped fresh cilantro

2 cups plain whole-milk yogurt

Kosher salt

Microwaving the lemons is a quick way to give them the flavor of preserved lemons. The marinade can be prepared in advance and refrigerated until ready to use. Oiling the grate keeps the kebabs from sticking. For an easy way to do it, soak a paper towel in oil and use tongs to rub it over the hot grill.

Make the marinade: Cut four deep, lengthwise gashes, equally spaced, into each lemon. Put them and the garlic cloves in a small microwavable container. Cover and microwave on high until the lemons are soft and juice has exuded from them, about 4 minutes (If not soft, continue to microwave in 30-second intervals). Strain the juice into a small container and let the lemons and garlic cool briefly. When the lemons are cool enough to handle, separate them into sections. Scrape the pulp and most of the white pith away with a spoon; discard. Put the scraped lemon peels, garlic, lemon juice, and remaining marinade ingredients in a blender and purée to make a coarse, soft paste. Set 2 tablespoons aside to use for the yogurt sauce.

Marinate the chicken: Put the chicken into a 1-gallon zip-top bag; scrape in the remaining marinade. Massage the bag to coat all the chicken pieces and marinate for 1 to 2 hours in the refrigerator.

Grill the kebabs: Build a medium-hot charcoal fire or heat a gas grill to medium high. Dump the chicken into a bowl, but don't scrape off any excess marinade. Put the onion and peppers in the marinade bag and massage them to coat with the marinade (it's fine if the onion pieces break apart). Transfer to another bowl. Thread the chicken onto skewers, positioning a piece of onion and pepper between the pieces of chicken. If there's extra pepper or onion, thread them onto separate skewers, if you like.

When ready to grill, oil the grill grate. Grill the kebabs over direct heat (uncovered for charcoal; covered for gas), turning the skewers every 2 to 3 minutes until the chicken is firm and shows no redness when cut into, about 10 to 15 minutes. Check several pieces of chicken to be sure.

Make the sauce: Combine the reserved 2 tablespoons marinade with the cucumber, cilantro, yogurt, and 2 teaspoons kosher salt. Mix well. (Make the sauce no more than an hour before serving or it will get too watery).

To serve: Remove the chicken and vegetables from the skewers and serve them in a mound with the yogurt sauce on the side. *—Bruce Aidells*

tip: For more control on the grill, use flat or double-pronged skewers. They'll keep food from spinning when you turn the kebabs.

Grilled Chicken with Rosemary & Caramelized Lemons

Serves four.

½ cup kosher salt; more as needed

8 cups cold water

One 3½- to 4-pound whole chicken

2 tablespoons extra-virgin olive oil

1 medium lemon, sliced ⅛ inch thick and seeded

2 teaspoons chopped fresh rosemary

Freshly ground black pepper

Butterflying is a simple technique that helps the chicken cook quickly and evenly. It's an especially useful method for grilling, because you're not wasting time heating up the cavity of the bird while other parts of the chicken run the risk of drying out in the sometimes unpredictable heat.

A day ahead: In a large bowl, dissolve the salt in the water. Add the chicken and submerge it in the brine, using a plate to weight it, if needed. Refrigerate for 24 hours.

On the day of grilling: Set up a charcoal or gas grill to cook with direct heat. For gas grills, turn all the burners to low (an oven thermometer set on the grate should read 450° to 500°F; you'll be able to hold your hand 4 or 5 inches above the grate for 5 seconds). For charcoal, light a chimney starter filled with mesquite lump charcoal. When all the coals are lit, pour them in the center of the grill and spread in an even layer. Let them burn down to medium-low heat (you'll be able to hold your hand 1 to 2 inches above the grate for 5 full seconds).

Meanwhile, heat 1 tablespoon of the oil in a 12-inch skillet over medium heat. Add the lemon slices. Cook, turning occasionally, until they're soft and golden brown (it's fine if the pulp starts to dissolve), 5 to 10 minutes. Transfer the slices to a plate and let cool.

Meanwhile, take the chicken out of the brine; pat it dry with paper towels. Cut off the wingtips at the first joint. Remove the backbone by cutting down each side of it; discard it or save it for stock. Lay the chicken flat on a work surface, skin side up, and press on the breastbone to flatten the chicken; you'll feel some of the rib bones breaking. Use your fingers to separate the skin from the breast, thighs, and drumsticks, being careful not to tear the skin. Spread the rosemary under the skin, distributing it evenly over the breasts, thighs, and drumsticks. Working with one slice at a time, slide the lemon slices under the skin of the chicken, keeping them in a single layer. Sprinkle the skin with salt and pepper. Drizzle the remaining 1 tablespoon oil on the chicken and rub the skin so it's completely coated.

Oil the grill grate. Set the chicken on the grill, skin side down. Grill (covered for gas; uncovered for charcoal) until the skin is deeply golden brown, 10 to 15 minutes. Monitor the grill for hot spots and move the chicken as needed. Flip the chicken, cover the grill (keep the vents open for charcoal), and grill until an instant-read thermometer registers 175°F in the thickest part of the thigh (the breast should be at least 165°F) and the juices run clear when the thermometer is removed, another 15 to 35 minutes. Remove from the grill and let rest for 10 minutes before carving and serving. *—Joanne Weir*

Adding Flavor with Lemon Slices

Caramelizing the lemon slices in a skillet sweetens their flavor and gives them a head start on cooking. When the chicken comes off the grill, the lemon slices taste almost preserved. They're sweet and tender enough to eat straight.

1 Cook the lemon slices until soft and golden.

2 Slide the lemons and rosemary under the skin.

3 Grill over direct heat, watching for hot spots.

Grilled Butterflied Chicken Breasts with Cilantro-Lime Butter

Serves two.

2 tablespoons unsalted butter, softened

1½ teaspoons finely chopped fresh cilantro; plus 2 large sprigs for garnish

½ teaspoon finely grated lime zest

¼ teaspoon green Tabasco or other jalapeño hot sauce

Kosher salt

2 large boneless, skinless chicken breast halves (about 1 pound), rinsed and patted dry, tenders removed (reserve the tenders for another use)

2 tablespoons fresh lime juice

1 tablespoons extra-virgin olive oil

You can make this brightly flavored butter a day or two ahead of using it, or even longer if you wrap it well and freeze it. The butter would also taste great paired with grilled skirt steak or shrimp.

In a small bowl, mash the butter, chopped cilantro, lime zest, Tabasco, and ¼ teaspoon kosher salt with a wooden spoon or rubber spatula to form a smooth butter. Scrape onto a piece of plastic wrap and roll and twist the plastic to shape the butter into a short log. Refrigerate until firm enough to slice, 20 to 25 minutes.

Meanwhile, butterfly the chicken breasts by making a horizontal cut through the center of the thickest long side of the breast. Cut almost but not entirely through each breast. Open the breasts like a book. Put the chicken in a shallow, nonreactive pan or on a plate. Season with ¾ teaspoon kosher salt and drizzle with the lime juice and olive oil. Let the chicken sit for 15 minutes.

Heat a gas grill to high. Lay the chicken breasts on the hot grill and cook, covered, until they have grill marks, 1½ minutes. With tongs, rotate the chicken 90 degrees (to get a crosshatch of grill marks) and continue grilling until grill marks form, another 1½ minutes. Flip the breasts and cook the second side in the same way but for a little less time, grilling for 1 minute in one direction and 1 minute in another, until cooked through. Immediately transfer the chicken to two warm serving plates, thinly slice the chilled butter, and arrange the butter slices all over the top of the chicken. Garnish with the cilantro sprigs and serve immediately. —*Susie Middleton*

Grilled Chicken Breasts with Sun-Dried & Fresh Tomato Salsa

Serves two.

½ pound small red and yellow cherry tomatoes, halved or quartered, depending on size

2 tablespoons chopped drained oil-packed sun-dried tomatoes

2 teaspoons capers (roughly chopped if large), drained

½ teaspoon finely chopped garlic

1 tablespoon sherry vinegar

2 teaspoons lightly chopped fresh thyme; plus sprigs for garnish, if you like

3 tablespoons plus 2 teaspoons extra-virgin olive oil

Kosher salt and freshly ground black pepper

2 large boneless, skinless chicken breast halves (6 to 8 ounces each), tenders removed and reserved for another use; breasts butterflied

A double dose of tomatoes lets you enjoy not only the sweet summery flavor of fresh tomatoes but the deeper, richer tones supplied by the sun-dried variety.

In a small bowl, combine the cherry tomatoes, sun-dried tomatoes, capers, garlic, vinegar, 1 teaspoon of the chopped thyme, 3 tablespoons of the olive oil, ¼ teaspoon kosher salt, and a few grinds of pepper. Set aside, stirring occasionally to let the flavors combine.

Heat a gas grill to high. Put the chicken in a shallow nonreactive pan or plate. Rub it all over with kosher salt (about ½ teaspoon for each piece of chicken), a few grinds of pepper, and the remaining 1 teaspoon thyme. Drizzle ½ teaspoon olive oil over each side of each piece of chicken and rub all over.

Lay the butterflied breasts on the hot grill grates and cook, covered, until they have grill marks, 1½ minutes. With tongs, rotate the breasts 90 degrees (to get a crosshatch of marks) and continue grilling until grill marks form, another 1½ minutes. Flip the breasts and cook the second side in the same way but for a little less time, grilling for 1 minute in one direction and 1 minute in another, until cooked through.

Transfer the breasts immediately to two warm serving plates. Stir the tomato mixture and spoon equal amounts (it will be a generous portion) over each piece of chicken. Garnish with a sprig of thyme, if you like.

—Susie Middleton

Little Tomatoes in All Shapes, Colors, and Sizes

In summer, gardens and farmers' markets overflow with all sorts of tomato varieties. In winter, cherry tomato varieties are often the only tomatoes with any hint of flavor. Cherry tomatoes are bright and sweet, with a concentrated flavor that really shines in a quick sauce. To find little tomatoes like these, visit farm markets or pester your gardener friends to share—if you don't grow your own, that is.

Sweet 100

Sun Gold

Brandywine Grape

Red Currant

Matt's Wild Cherry

Wild Cherry

White Currant

Santa Lucia

Black Cherry

Black Huckleberry

Riesentraube

Spicy Beer-Can Chicken on the Grill

Serves four to six.

Spice Rub (recipe follows)

One 4-pound whole chicken

Beer-Can Sauce (recipe follows)

One 12-ounce can beer

Several large leaves romaine lettuce

½ cup thinly sliced scallions (white and green parts)

1 lemon, zested into very thin strips

1 orange, zested into very thin strips

Spice Rub

Yields ¼ cup.

1 tablespoon kosher or sea salt

2 teaspoons ground cumin

1 teaspoon red pepper flakes

1 teaspoon ground coriander

1 teaspoon dry mustard

1 teaspoon garlic powder

1 teaspoon onion powder

1 teaspoon freshly ground black pepper

In a small bowl, combine all the ingredients. Mix until well blended.

Beer-Can Sauce

Yields ¾ cup.

6 tablespoons tomato ketchup

3 tablespoons Dijon mustard

1½ tablespoons molasses

1½ tablespoons red-wine vinegar

1 tablespoon Spice Rub (see above)

½ teaspoon Tabasco sauce

In a small bowl, whisk all the ingredients until they're well blended.

Grilling a chicken set on top of an open can of beer sounds like a joke but it's really an ingenious way to infuse the meat with moisture. The can has the added benefit of helping to keep the bird upright during cooking. Take care when removing the can and pouring out its contents to make the sauce; the can and the liquid are very hot. Flavor-packed condiments and a dash of assertive spices are mixed into a rich sauce, part of which gets added to the can of beer before being set inside the chicken. The flavors mingle with the liquid and get infused into the bird, and the leftovers are used to make a delicious pan gravy. This bold rub is great to have on hand for impromptu grilling. It would taste delicious on beef and pork as well as chicken. Make extra to keep in your spice cabinet.

A day ahead: Make the spice rub; set aside 1 tablespoon for the sauce. Rinse the chicken and pat it dry with paper towels. Sprinkle 1 tablespoon of the rub inside the body and neck cavities. With your fingers, work a little of the rub under the skin. Sprinkle the remaining spice rub all over the skin and rub it in to spread evenly. Tuck the wings behind the neck. Cover the chicken and refrigerate overnight.

On the day of grilling: Make the beer-can sauce.

Set up a charcoal or gas grill to cook with indirect heat. If using charcoal, pour 1 to 2 inches of natural hardwood charcoal over the bottom grate (about a single layer). Light a chimney starter full of coals and, when they're covered with ash, pour them over the unlit coals in the grill. When the fire has burned down and the coals are glowing embers covered with ash, use long tongs or a grill rake to divide them into two equal piles on opposite sides of the grill.

If using gas, set the outside burners to medium high and leave the center burner off. (For a two-burner grill, light only one burner.)

While the grill is heating, open the can of beer and poke several holes on top of the can using a churchkey-style can opener. Pour out (or drink) half of the beer. Using a funnel, fill the can with the beer-can sauce. Gently swirl the can to mix. Put the can in the center of a 10- to 12-inch ovenproof skillet. Holding the chicken upright with the opening of the body cavity facing down, lower the chicken onto the beer can, pushing the can up into its cavity. Stabilize the chicken with its legs so that it stands up.

Grill the chicken: Set the skillet in the center of the grill, or in the area where there's no direct heat. Put an oven thermometer on the grate next to it. Cover the grill. Adjust the vents or burners to keep the temperature between 350° and 375°F and grill until an instant-read thermometer registers 175°F at the thickest part of the thigh, 45 minutes to 1¼ hours. If the grill temperature is correct, the chicken should start to lightly brown

after 15 minutes. (If using charcoal, check every 15 minutes and if the temperature drops below 300°F or if the coals have burned down very far, add a handful of fresh charcoal to each pile of coals.)

Carefully transfer the chicken and beer can to a cutting board. Let it rest for 5 minutes. Meanwhile, line a platter with the lettuce leaves. Using wads of paper towels to protect your hands, carefully remove the chicken from the beer can (ask for help if the can is stuck). Discard all but 1 tablespoon of fat in the skillet, then pour the contents of the can into the skillet. (If the skillet drippings have burned, pour the contents of the can into a clean saucepan.) Bring to a boil over medium-high heat and cook, whisking, until it has reduced slightly and thickened to a nice gravy consistency, 2 to 3 minutes.

Carve the chicken into eight pieces, arrange on the platter, and garnish with the scallions and citrus zest. Put the sauce in a sauceboat or bowl and serve alongside.

—Waldy Malouf

Putting a Spicy Spin on Beer-Can Chicken

This recipe adds sweet and spicy ingredients to the beer and an aromatic spice rub to the chicken. After grilling, the beer mixture gets simmered into a rich, complex sauce.

1 Pour out half the beer; pour in a spicy-sweet sauce.

2 Set the chicken over the can so it grills vertically.

3 Reduce the spicy beer mixture to create an intense sauce.

Creamy Tomato & Fennel Chicken

Serves four.

2 tablespoons unsalted butter

3 tablespoons vegetable oil

2 large cloves garlic, smashed and peeled

Kosher salt

1 medium-large bulb fennel (1½ pounds), trimmed and cut into wedges ½ to ¾ inch thick (leave the core intact so the wedges hold together)

2½ to 3 pounds skin-on, bone-in chicken legs and thighs

Freshly ground black pepper

½ cup low-salt chicken broth

One 14.5-ounce can diced tomatoes and their juices

⅓ cup fresh basil leaves, torn into ½-inch pieces, plus 2 tablespoons chopped basil

⅓ cup heavy cream

For the deepest flavor, be sure to brown the fennel really well.

In a 12-inch frying pan, heat the butter and 2 tablespoons of the oil over medium-low heat. Add the garlic, season with salt, and cook gently until softened, about 10 minutes. Transfer the garlic with a slotted spoon to a plate and reserve.

Increase the heat to medium high and arrange the fennel in the pan in a single layer (a little overlap is fine). Season with salt and cook until nicely browned on the bottom, 4 to 5 minutes. Flip the fennel and brown the other side, 3 to 4 minutes. Transfer to a plate or bowl.

Season the chicken with salt and pepper. Add the remaining 1 tablespoon oil to the pan. When it's hot, put the chicken in the pan, skin side down, and brown on both sides, 12 to 15 minutes total. Transfer to a plate.

Discard all the fat from the pan and set it over high heat. Pour in the broth and scrape the pan with a wooden spoon to release the browned bits clinging to the bottom. Simmer until the broth reduces to about ¼ cup, 1 to 2 minutes. Add the tomatoes with their juices and return all the chicken and the garlic to the pan. Bring to a boil, then reduce the heat to medium low and cover the pan. Cook for 15 minutes, turning the chicken once.

Tuck in the fennel around the chicken and sprinkle on the torn basil. Cover and cook for another 15 minutes, turning the chicken once, or until the chicken is cooked through.

Transfer the chicken to a plate. Increase the heat to high and stir the cream into the sauce. Let the sauce boil until slightly thickened, 3 to 4 minutes. Season to taste with salt and pepper. Pour the sauce into a deep serving platter and nestle the chicken into the sauce. Garnish with the chopped basil.

—Nancy Verde Barr

Perfect Roast Chicken with Pan Sauce

Serves four.

One 3½- to 4-pound chicken
2 tablespoons kosher salt
1½ tablespoons olive oil
2 teaspoons granulated sugar
Freshly ground black pepper
Ingredients for pan sauce recipe

Salting the chicken beforehand is similar to brining. It adds flavor, keeps the meat moist and makes it tender. Cooking at high heat results in deliciously crisp skin and a quick cooking time. Just make sure to use a smaller bird for this method. At this heat, a large bird will end up dried out by the time it's fully cooked. Serve with either one of the delicious pan sauces.

Sprinkle the chicken inside and out with the salt; set it on a wire rack and set the rack over a plate. Refrigerate uncovered for at least 2 hours (4 hours is better) or up to two days.

Apricot & Prune Sauce with Moroccan Spices

Yields about 1½ cups.

To make cutting the sticky dried fruits easier, try using kitchen shears doused with a light spray of vegetable oil. If you don't have vermouth, you can substitute dry white wine.

1 cup low-salt chicken broth
¼ cup orange juice concentrate
¼ cup dry vermouth
2 tablespoons olive oil
4 cloves garlic, minced
1 teaspoon ground cumin
1 teaspoon ground ginger
½ teaspoon ground cinnamon
⅛ teaspoon ground cloves
½ cup dried apricots, halved
½ cup prunes, halved
Degreased juices from the roasting pan
3 tablespoons chopped fresh cilantro
Kosher salt and freshly ground black pepper

While the chicken roasts, combine the broth, orange juice concentrate, and vermouth; set aside. When you're ready to make the sauce, heat the olive oil in a 10-inch skillet or sauté pan over medium-high heat. Add the garlic and spices; sauté until fragrant and golden, less than 1 minute. Add the apricots and prunes and sauté for about 1 minute. Add the broth mixture and degreased pan juices; simmer until reduced to 1½ to 1⅔ cups, 5 to 8 minutes. Stir in the cilantro and season to taste with salt and pepper. Pour into a serving vessel and serve alongside the carved chicken.

Position a rack in the lower middle of the oven and heat the oven to 450°F. Cross the chicken legs and tie them together; tuck the wings under the chicken. Brush the breast side of the chicken all over with some of the olive oil; sprinkle with 1 teaspoon of the sugar and a few grinds of pepper. Set the chicken, breast side down, on a V-rack set in a small metal roasting pan (don't use ceramic or Pyrex). Brush the back side of the chicken with the remaining oil and sprinkle with ½ teaspoon sugar and a few more grinds of pepper. Have ready 1 cup water and turn on the exhaust fan.

Roast the chicken, breast side down, until the back is deep golden brown, about 30 minutes. Check frequently and if the chicken drippings appear to be burning, add ¼ to ½ cup of the water to the pan.

Remove the chicken from the oven. With a wad of paper towels in each hand, turn the chicken so it's breast side up. Sprinkle with the remaining ½ teaspoon sugar and add all or what remains of the water to the pan. Return the chicken to the oven and roast, breast side up, until it's golden brown and an instant-read thermometer inserted in the thigh registers 175°F, another 15 to 20 minutes.

Transfer the chicken to a cutting board to rest for at least 15 minutes and up to 30 minutes for chicken served warm (or up to 2 hours if serving the chicken at room temperature).

Meanwhile, make the sauce. Remove the V-rack from the roasting pan and tilt the pan so the juices collect in one corner. Spoon off and discard as much of the clear fat as possible. Set the pan and its drippings aside. Choose one of the pan sauce recipes that follow.

When ready to serve, carve the chicken. Serve with the warm pan sauce.

–Pam Anderson

Lemon Artichoke Sauce with Garlic & Parsley

Yields 2 cups.

For a cleaner flavor, look for artichoke hearts in water or brine rather than those marinated in oils and spices.

1 cup low-salt chicken broth
¼ cup fresh lemon juice
¼ cup dry vermouth
2 teaspoons olive oil
4 cloves garlic, minced
1 teaspoon dried oregano
One 14- to 15-ounce can whole artichoke hearts, rinsed, drained, and cut into sixths
Degreased juices from the roasting pan
2 tablespoons chopped fresh flat-leaf parsley
Kosher salt and freshly ground black pepper

While the chicken roasts, combine the broth, lemon juice, and vermouth; set aside. When you're ready to make the sauce, heat the olive oil in a 10-inch skillet over medium-high heat. Add the garlic and oregano; sauté until fragrant and golden, less than 1 minute. Add the artichokes and sauté until any moisture has evaporated, about 1 minute. Add the broth mixture and degreased pan juices; simmer until reduced to about 2 cups, 3 to 5 minutes. Stir in the parsley and season to taste with salt and pepper. Pour into a serving vessel and serve alongside the carved chicken.

Two Tricks Get Crisp Skin and Juicy Breast Meat

Salt the bird and let it sit overnight in the fridge, uncovered. This will help dry the skin, which encourages a crisp finished result.

Start by roasting breast side down and flip over halfway through. This keeps the breast meat from drying out before the rest of the chicken has cooked. Use wads of paper towels to protect your hands while flipping the chicken.

How to Carve Roast Chicken

There's more than one way to carve a roast chicken, but this technique is a good choice because it gives you boneless breast meat that you can slice across the grain, if you like.

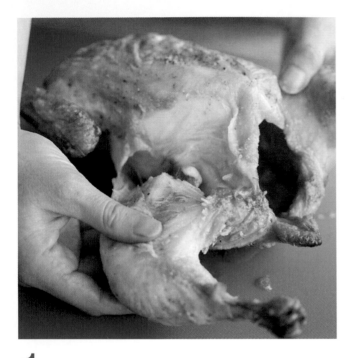

1 Forcefully bend a leg away from the body until the joint pops apart. Use a sharp boning knife to sever the leg from the body, cutting through the separated joint.

2 As you separate the leg, be sure to get the "oyster," a tasty nugget of meat toward the back of the chicken just above the thigh. Use the tip of the knife to scrape it free from its indentation in the body.

5 Finish separating the breast by simultaneously pulling back on the meat and using little flicks of the knife tip to cut the meat away from the body. Finally, cut through the last of the skin holding the breast onto the body. If you want smaller pieces, set the breast on the cutting board and, holding the knife at a 45-degree angle, slice it crosswise, either in half or into thin slices.

3 Separate the drumstick from the thigh by cutting through the joint with a chef's knife. It should be fairly easy to cut through the joint. If the knife meets resistance, reposition the blade slightly and try again.

4 Begin separating one side of the breast from the body by cutting along the breastbone with the tip of your boning knife. Work from the tail end of the bird toward the wing end. When you hit the wishbone, angle the knife and cut down along the wishbone toward the wing. Then make a cut between the breast and the wing.

6 Trim off the wingtips with a chef's knife, then cut the wing pieces from the body.

Herbes de Provence Roast Chicken with Mushroom & Water Chestnut Dressing

Serves four.

One 4-pound chicken, with giblets

1 tablespoon dried herbes de Provence, crumbled

2 teaspoons kosher salt; more as needed

Freshly ground black pepper

½ pound good-quality baguette, cut into ¼-inch cubes (about 4 cups)

3 tablespoons olive oil

2 cups low-salt chicken broth

¼ cup unsalted butter

1 large rib celery, cut into small dice

1 small yellow onion, cut into small dice

6 ounces medium cremini or button mushrooms, trimmed and cut into eighths

1 large clove garlic, finely chopped

¾ cup small diced water chestnuts (from an 8-ounce can of sliced water chestnuts; you won't need the whole can)

2 tablespoons chopped fresh flat-leaf parsley

2 teaspoons chopped fresh sage

1 teaspoon poultry seasoning, preferably Bell's brand

½ teaspoon celery seeds

Let the flavor of the herbs penetrate the bird's skin overnight while the bread for the dressing dries out.

Remove the giblets and neck from the chicken and reserve. Combine the herbes de Provence, salt, and several grinds of pepper in a small bowl. Rub the spices all over the chicken, then set it on a rack in a small roasting pan and refrigerate, uncovered, overnight. Spread the bread cubes out on a rimmed baking pan and leave out on the counter to dry overnight.

Heat 1 tablespoon of the oil in a medium saucepan over medium heat. Pat the giblets and neck dry and cook without flipping until golden brown on one side, about 2 minutes. Turn and sear the other side and continue cooking until the liver is just cooked through, another 2 minutes. Remove the liver and reserve it. Pour off the excess fat, add the broth, and simmer until the liquid tastes rich and flavorful, about 30 minutes. Strain the broth into a liquid measuring cup, reserving the giblets and neck; you should have about ¾ cup liquid. If you have less, compensate with water. If you have more, return it to the pan and simmer until you have ¾ cup.

Position a rack in the center of the oven and heat the oven to 400°F. Rub the chicken all over with the remaining 2 tablespoons oil, tuck the wings back behind the neck, and tie the legs together. Let sit while the oven heats.

Meanwhile, melt 2 tablespoons of the butter in a 10-inch sauté pan over medium heat. Add the celery and onion and cook until slightly softened, about 3 minutes. Transfer to a large bowl. Increase the heat to medium high, melt the remaining 2 tablespoons butter, and add the mushrooms. Sauté until golden brown, about 5 minutes. Add the garlic and water chestnuts and sauté 1 minute. Transfer the mushrooms, garlic, and water chestnuts to the bowl of vegetables. Pull as much meat as you can off of the reserved neck. Mince the neck meat, liver, and other giblets, and add them to the bowl, along with the bread cubes, parsley, sage, poultry seasoning, celery seeds, 1 teaspoon kosher salt, and several grinds of pepper. Toss to combine. Pour the strained broth over the dressing and toss again. Add salt and pepper to taste.

Wrap the dressing in a double layer of aluminum foil. Put the chicken in the oven and place the package of dressing on the same rack near the roasting pan. Roast until an instant-read thermometer inserted in a chicken thigh reads 170°F and the juices run clear, 50 to 60 minutes. Let the chicken and dressing rest at room temperature for 10 minutes. Carve the chicken and serve with the dressing. —*Allison Ehri*

Dry-Brined Roasted Turkey

Serves ten.

One 10- to 12-pound turkey

¼ cup kosher salt

2 medium to large yellow onions, left unpeeled and cut into eighths

2 medium carrots, left unpeeled and cut into 1-inch chunks

2 medium ribs celery, cut into 1-inch chunks

Silky Pan Gravy (recipe folows)

To dry-brine the turkey, sprinkle it with salt and refrigerate it overnight. This gives the flavor and tenderness of wet-brining, but it's less cumbersome.

The night before, remove the giblets from the turkey, cut off the tail, if attached, and reserve the giblets and tail for making the turkey broth. Rinse the turkey thoroughly. Sprinkle the salt all over it, starting on the back side, then the cavity, and finally the breast. Put the turkey, breast side up, on a wire rack set over a rimmed pan or platter and refrigerate, uncovered, overnight.

Remove the turkey from the refrigerator an hour before you intend to roast it and let stand at room temperature. Fifteen to 20 minutes before roasting, position a rack in the lowest part of the oven and heat the oven to 400°F. Put half of the onions, carrots, and celery in the turkey cavity. Tie the legs together with kitchen twine. Tuck the wings behind the neck and under the turkey. Scatter the remaining onions, carrots, and celery in a large flameproof heavy roasting pan fitted with a large V-rack. Set the turkey, breast side down, on the V-rack.

Roast for 30 minutes. Pour 1 cup of water into the roasting pan and roast for another 30 minutes. Remove the turkey from the oven and close the oven door. With two wads of paper towels, carefully turn the turkey over so that it's breast side up. Add another ½ cup water to the roasting pan. Return the turkey to the oven and continue to roast until an instant-read thermometer inserted in the thigh registers 170°F, about another 45 minutes for a turkey in the 10-pound range, or about another 1 hour for a 12-pounder. (Keep a close eye on the vegetables and pan drippings throughout the cooking process. They should be kept dry enough to brown and produce rich brown drippings to make gravy, but moist enough to keep from burning, so add water as needed throughout.) Transfer the turkey to a carving board or platter, tent with aluminum foil, and let rest for at least 45 minutes and up to 1 hour before carving and serving. Meanwhile, make the gravy from the drippings. —*Pam Anderson*

Silky Pan Gravy with Cream, Cognac & Thyme

Yields about 3 cups.

Drippings and vegetables from Dry-Brined Roasted Turkey

2 tablespoons Cognac

½ cup dry vermouth

2½ cups low-salt turkey or chicken broth

2 teaspoons lightly chopped fresh thyme

½ cup heavy cream

¼ cup unbleached all-purpose flour

This gravy gets its silky texture from being strained and then thickened with a cream/flour mixture. Saturating the flour with cream before whisking it into the gravy keeps it from forming those dreaded lumps.

Set the roasting pan with the turkey drippings and vegetables over two burners set on medium high. Add the Cognac, vermouth, and ½ cup of the broth; cook, stirring with a wooden spoon or wooden spatula to loosen the browned bits in the pan, until the liquid comes to a simmer. Strain the contents of the roasting pan through a large sieve and into a large saucepan. Add the remaining 2 cups broth and the thyme to the saucepan and bring to a boil over medium-high heat; reduce the heat and let simmer to blend the flavors, about 5 minutes.

Meanwhile, put the heavy cream in a small bowl and whisk the flour into the cream to make a smooth paste. Gradually whisk the cream mixture into the broth mixture. Bring to a boil over medium-high heat, reduce the heat to low, and gently simmer to thicken the gravy and cook off the raw flour flavor, about 10 minutes. Keep hot until ready to serve.

Heavy Cream is the Secret to This Rich, Silky Gravy

Deglaze

Pour in the Cognac, vermouth, and some of the turkey broth; stir with a wooden spatula to scrape the browned bits from the bottom of the pan.

Strain

Pour the contents of the roasting pan through a sieve set in a large saucepan. Press gently to extract all the juices.

Enrich

To add extra body, whisk in heavy cream combined with a little flour, and let the gravy simmer to thicken.

Roasted Apricot-Ginger Glazed Game Hens

Serves four.

2 Cornish game hens, (about 1½ pounds each)

4 teaspoons Asian sesame oil

Kosher salt and freshly ground black pepper

1 tablespoon peeled and minced fresh ginger

1 clove garlic, minced

½ cup apricot preserves

2 teaspoons honey

2 teaspoons soy sauce

2 teaspoons fresh lemon juice

1 teaspoon cornstarch, dissolved in 1 teaspoon water

Soy sauce, sesame oil, and ginger give this dish a decidedly Asian flavor. If you don't have a ginger grater, use a sharp, fine zester, such as one from Microplane, to cut through the root's tough fibers. The sweetness of the hens would go well with a basmati rice and scallion pilaf and baby spinach salad.

Set a rack in the center of the oven and heat the oven to 450°F. With a sharp knife or poultry shears, remove the backbones from the hens and slice through the breastbone, cutting the hens in half. Brush the skin of the hens with 2 teaspoons of the sesame oil and set them, skin side up, on a wire rack set in a rimmed baking sheet. Sprinkle the skin with ½ teaspoon kosher salt and several grinds of pepper. Roast until the hens are almost cooked through (an instant-read thermometer inserted in the thickest part of the thigh should register 165°F), about 25 minutes.

Meanwhile, heat the remaining 2 teaspoons sesame oil in a small saucepan over medium heat. Add the ginger and garlic and cook, stirring often, until soft and fragrant, 2 to 3 minutes. Stir in the preserves, honey, soy sauce, and lemon juice; bring to a boil and cook, stirring occasionally, until thickened slightly, 4 to 5 minutes. Add the cornstarch slurry to the saucepan and cook until the mixture thickens, another 1 minute.

Brush the hens with the apricot-ginger glaze and continue to roast until the glaze has browned in spots and the thermometer registers 170°F in the thigh, another 5 to 7 minutes. Season to taste with salt and pepper and serve immediately. *—David Bonom*

Is It Done? Poultry Roasting Times & Temperatures

Type of chicken	Oven temperature and estimated time	Meat temperature
Whole chicken (about 3½ pounds)	400°F for about 1 hour	170°F in the thickest part of the thigh
Butterflied chicken (about 3½ pounds)	475°F for about 40 minutes or 425°F for about 50 minutes	170°F in the thickest part of the thigh
Bone-in chicken parts	425°F for 50 to 60 minutes	Well-browned and 165°F for white meat, 170°F for dark
Cornish hens (about 1½ pounds each)	425°F for 40 to 45 minutes unstuffed; 45 to 50 minutes stuffed	170°F in the thickest part of the thigh (the center of the stuffing should be 165°F)

Port-Glazed Roasted Game Hens with Couscous Stuffing

If you can't find dried apples for the stuffing, dried plums or cherries are good substitutes.

Make the stuffing: In a small skillet over medium heat, melt the butter. Add the onion and cook until soft, 5 to 7 minutes; set aside. In a medium saucepan, bring the broth to a boil; remove from the heat. Stir in the couscous, cover, and let sit off the heat for 10 minutes. Fluff the couscous with a fork. Stir in the cooked onion, pistachios, cranberries, apricots, apples, cinnamon, ginger, parsley, salt, and pepper. Set aside to cool completely.

Stuff the hens: Heat the oven to 425°F. Season the cavity of each hen with salt and pepper. Make sure the stuffing is thoroughly cool and pack each hen loosely with about ½ cup of stuffing. With kitchen twine, tie each hen's legs together. Tuck the wings underneath. Arrange the hens breast side up on a wire rack set in a shallow roasting pan (or two) filled with ¼ inch water (to prevent the glaze drippings from smoking).

Glaze and roast the hens: Brush the 2 tablespoons melted butter over the hens; season with salt and pepper. Roast the hens for 20 minutes. Meanwhile, in a small saucepan, combine the glaze ingredients and bring to a boil. Reduce the heat to a simmer and cook until reduced to ¾ cup, about 3 minutes. Strain. Brush the hens generously with the glaze and continue to roast, basting with more glaze every 10 minutes, until the juices run clear when you prick the thickest part of the thigh and an instant-read thermometer inserted in the thigh registers 170°F, another 30 to 35 minutes. Transfer the hens to a platter, tent with aluminum foil, and let stand for 10 minutes before serving. —*Joanne Weir*

Serves six.

2 tablespoons unsalted butter

½ cup finely minced yellow onion

1 cup low-salt chicken broth

¾ cup couscous

½ cup unsalted pistachios, lightly toasted and coarsely chopped

¼ cup dried cranberries

¼ cup chopped dried apricots

¼ cup chopped dried apples

½ teaspoon ground cinnamon

½ teaspoon ground ginger

2 tablespoons chopped fresh flat-leaf parsley

1 teaspoon kosher salt; more as needed

Freshly ground black pepper

6 Cornish game hens (about 1½ pounds each)

For the glaze:

2 tablespoons unsalted butter, melted

1 cup port

¼ cup granulated sugar

6 cinnamon sticks

12 whole cloves

12 slices fresh ginger

Duck Breast & Orange Salad

Serves four.

2 navel oranges

2 tablespoons sugar

3 tablespoons white-wine vinegar

1 tablespoon fresh lemon juice

1 teaspoon finely grated lemon zest

3 tablespoons minced shallot

6 tablespoons canola oil

Kosher salt and freshly ground black pepper

4 boneless, skin-on duck breasts halves (about 2 pounds total)

1 medium head frisée, washed, dried, and torn into bite-size pieces

1 large or 2 small heads bibb lettuce, washed, dried, and torn into bite-size pieces

2 tablespoons sliced fresh chives (¼-inch pieces)

One of the great things about duck is that the skin is loaded with very flavorful fat. To help render it, the skin gets scored before cooking. This has the added benefit of keeping the skin from buckling, so the duck breast maintains a nice shape and is easy to slice.

Finely grate one of the oranges to get 1 teaspoon zest; set aside. Slice off the ends of both oranges, stand each orange on one of its cut ends, and slice off the skin in strips, getting all the bitter white pith. Working over a bowl, cut the segments free from the membrane, letting each segment fall into the bowl.

Put the sugar and vinegar in a small saucepan over medium-high heat and boil until the sugar is completely melted, the bubbles become large and thick, and the mixture turns golden brown, 3 to 5 minutes. Take the pan off the heat and stir in the orange zest, lemon juice, and lemon zest. Let cool slightly. Add the shallot and gradually whisk in the oil; season with salt and pepper.

Rinse the duck and pat dry. Trim any silverskin from the meat side. With a sharp knife, score the skin in a ½-in. crosshatch pattern. Cut only through the skin and not the meat. Trim any excess skin, leaving a ¼-inch overhang. Season well with salt and pepper on the flesh side and very lightly on the skin side.

Heat a 12-inch skillet over medium-high heat for 1 minute. Put the duck in the pan, skin side down, and let it sear. As fat collects in the pan, spoon it off. When the skin turns medium brown (6 to 8 minutes), reduce the heat to medium and continue to cook until much of the fat has rendered and the skin is golden brown, 2 to 4 minutes. Flip the breasts and cook briefly on the flesh side, 2 to 3 minutes for medium rare (or 3 to 4 minutes for medium). Transfer to a cutting board and cover loosely with aluminum foil.

Meanwhile, toss the frisée and bibb lettuce with enough of the vinaigrette to lightly coat. Slice the duck crosswise on a slight diagonal into ¼-inch-thick slices. Mound the greens on each plate and arrange the duck slices and orange segments all around. Drizzle each salad with a little more of the vinaigrette and garnish with the chives. *—Arlene Jacobs*

Pan-Roasted Duck Breasts with Sherry, Honey & Thyme Sauce

You can dress up this dish by adding a few dried figs, if you like. Trim off the figs' stems and, depending on their size, halve or quarter them. Soak the figs in the sherry for 10 minutes, then drain them, reserving the sherry. Add the sherry as directed and add the figs to the sauce along with the broth.

Heat the oven to 425°F. Rinse the duck and pat dry. Trim any silverskin from the meat side of the breasts. Scrape the tendon out of the tender, if it's still attached, and pat the tender back in place. Trim the edges of the skin so there's about ¼-inch overhang. With a sharp knife, score the skin in a ½-inch crosshatch pattern. Cut only through the skin and not into the meat. Season the breasts on both sides with salt and pepper.

Heat a large ovenproof sauté pan or skillet (don't use nonstick) over medium-high heat for 1 minute. Put the duck in the pan, skin side down, and let it sear. As fat collects in the pan, spoon it off once or twice. When the skin turns medium brown, after about 6 minutes, reduce the heat to medium. Continue to cook until much of the fat is rendered from the duck and the skin looks crisp and deep golden brown, another 2 to 4 minutes.

Flip the breasts skin side up, spoon off any remaining fat, and put the pan in the oven. Roast until the duck is cooked to your liking: 3 to 4 minutes for medium rare and 5 to 6 minutes for medium well. To check for doneness, cut into a breast or use an instant-read thermometer: 135°F for medium rare, 155°F for medium well.

Transfer the duck to a plate or platter and tent with aluminum foil to keep warm. Set the pan on medium-high heat and pour in the sherry and sherry vinegar. Immediately scrape the pan with a wooden spoon to loosen any cooked-on bits. Boil until the liquid has reduced to about 2 tablespoons, about 3 minutes. Add the broth, honey, thyme, and ¼ teaspoon kosher salt. Boil until the liquid is reduced by about half, about 3 minutes. Reduce the heat to low and blend the butter into the sauce by constantly stirring or swirling the pan. Slice the duck thinly on an angle, arrange it on heated plates, and spoon the sauce over or around it. Serve immediately.

—Jennifer Armentrout

Serves four.

4 boneless, skin-on duck breast halves (about 2 pounds total)

Kosher salt and freshly ground black pepper

¼ cup dry sherry

¼ cup sherry vinegar

½ cup low-salt chicken broth

2 teaspoons honey

1 teaspoon lightly chopped fresh thyme

1 tablespoon unsalted butter

6
Beef, Lamb & Pork

p204

p228

Dry-Aged Beef Rib Roast with a Mustard, Garlic & Thyme Crust (recipe on page 217)

Seared Flank Steak
with Shallot-Mustard Sauce

Serves four.

1 flank steak, about 1½ pounds

Kosher salt and freshly ground black pepper

1 tablespoon corn oil

6 tablespoons cold unsalted butter (4 tablespoons cut into ½-inch cubes)

3 tablespoons finely minced shallot

3 medium cloves garlic, minced

½ cup dry red wine

¾ cup low-salt beef broth

1 teaspoon chopped fresh thyme

1 teaspoon Dijon mustard

1 tablespoon chopped fresh tarragon

Searing the steak before finishing it in the oven creates a beautiful crust and concentrates the beefy flavor. Serve with oven-roasted potatoes and an arugula salad.

Set a rack in the center of the oven and heat the oven to 400°F. Season the steak generously with salt and pepper. Heat an ovenproof 12-inch sauté pan over high heat until very hot. Add the oil to coat the pan and sear the steak on one side until well browned, about 1½ minutes. Flip with tongs and cook until the second side is well browned, about another 2 minutes. Put the pan in the oven and roast until the steak is cooked to your liking, 5 to 7 minutes for medium rare. Transfer the steak to a cutting board and let rest, lightly covered with aluminum foil, while you make the sauce.

Set the same skillet over medium heat and add 2 tablespoons of the butter. When it melts, add the shallot and garlic and cook until soft and translucent but not browned, about 2 minutes. Add the wine, increase the heat to medium high, and boil until syrupy, 2 to 4 minutes. Add the broth and thyme and boil until about ⅓ cup of liquid remains, 6 to 8 minutes. Reduce the heat to low and whisk in the mustard. (Don't let the sauce boil after the mustard is added.) Stir in the butter cubes, a few at a time. Stir in half the tarragon and season the sauce to taste with salt and pepper.

With a sharp knife, slice the steak thinly across the grain on the diagonal, drizzle with the sauce, and sprinkle with the remaining tarragon.

—Arlene Jacobs

Pan-Seared Rib-Eye Steak with Balsamic Onion & Tomato Salsa

Serves four.

1 tablespoon extra-virgin olive oil

1 medium onion, cut into medium dice

2 teaspoons granulated sugar

1 tablespoon balsamic vinegar

1 pint grape tomatoes, halved

¼ cup thinly sliced fresh basil leaves

Kosher salt and freshly ground black pepper

2 tablespoons unsalted butter

4 boneless rib-eye steaks, ¾ to 1 inch thick (6 to 8 ounces each)

Tender, well-marbled rib-eye steaks are the perfect platform for this flavorful salsa, which you can make in advance. A mixed salad of bibb lettuce, spinach, and torn basil makes a great partner for this dish.

Heat the oil in a 12-inch skillet over medium-high heat until hot; add the onion and sugar. Cook, stirring occasionally, until the onion begins to soften but not brown, 4 to 5 minutes. Add the vinegar and cook until the onion is soft, 2 to 3 minutes. Add the tomatoes and cook, stirring, until they just begin to soften, 1 to 2 minutes. Remove from the heat, stir in the basil, and season the salsa to taste with salt and pepper. Transfer to a bowl and keep warm.

Season the steaks generously on both sides with salt and pepper. Wipe out the skillet and melt the butter over medium-high heat. Cook two of the steaks until nicely browned on both sides and cooked to your liking, about 3 minutes per side for medium rare. Transfer the steaks to plates or a platter and keep warm while you cook the remaining two steaks. Serve the steaks topped with the onion and tomato salsa. *—David Bonom*

Seared Beef Tenderloin with Sun-Dried Tomato Butter, Mushrooms & Arugula

If you can't get medallions, buy 1-inch-thick filet mignon (tenderloin steaks) and cut them in half to a ½-inch thickness.

Mix the minced sun-dried tomatoes with 2 tablespoons of the butter and the vinegar. Season with a pinch or two of salt, wrap in plastic, and shape it into a 2-inch-long cylinder. Put in the freezer to firm.

Season the beef well on both sides with salt and pepper. In a large skillet, heat the olive oil over medium-high heat until quite hot. Sear the medallions until well browned on both sides and cooked to rare, about 2 minutes per side (or longer if you like your steak cooked more). Transfer to a plate and tent with aluminum foil to keep warm. Add the remaining 2 tablespoons butter to the pan. When it's foaming, add the shallots, cook for 30 seconds, and then add the mushrooms and a good pinch of salt. Cook, stirring, until the mushrooms are well browned, 2 to 3 minutes. Add the arugula to the pan and toss with the mushrooms, cooking just until the leaves have wilted.

Arrange the sautéed vegetables on dinner plates, top with the beef, and serve with a slice or two of the chilled butter on the meat. *—Ali Edwards*

Serves two.

- 3 oil-packed sun-dried tomatoes, minced
- ¼ cup unsalted butter, well softened
- ¼ teaspoon sherry vinegar
- Kosher salt and freshly ground black pepper
- 4 beef tenderloin medallions, ½ inch thick (¾ pound total)
- 1 tablespoon olive oil
- 2 shallots, minced
- ¼ pound cremini mushrooms, stems trimmed; caps wiped clean and sliced about ¼ inch thick
- ½ pound arugula, trimmed, washed, and dried, or 10 ounces packaged baby arugula

Herb-Marinated Skirt Steaks

Serves six to eight.

4 pounds skirt steaks
(about 3 or 4 steaks)

12 cloves garlic

Four 5-inch sprigs fresh
rosemary

16 sprigs fresh thyme

1 tablespoon freshly cracked
black pepper

Extra-virgin olive oil

Sea salt

Pesto-Style Salsa Verde (recipe
follows)

For the best flavor and tenderness, cook these steaks to medium rare or just barely medium. Thinner skirt steaks will cook more quickly. If you can't grill these steaks, sear-roast them; there are instructions for both methods.

Trim the steaks of excess fat and cut into pieces of relatively even thickness and manageable size. Smash the garlic cloves with the flat part of a heavy knife, then peel the cloves. Crush and tear the rosemary sprigs with your hands to release their perfume. In a medium-large bowl, combine the steaks with the herbs, garlic, pepper, and 6 tablespoons olive oil. Toss to coat well. Cover and refrigerate for one to two days.

Take the steaks out of the refrigerator 30 minutes before grilling and brush off the herb sprigs and garlic.

To grill the steaks: Prepare a medium-hot gas or charcoal grill fire. Season the steaks with salt. Oil the grill and then grill the steaks for 2 to 3 minutes on each side for medium rare (thicker steaks will be medium rare after 3 to 5 minutes per side). Let rest for 10 minutes on a clean cutting board before slicing thinly across the grain. Serve with the salsa verde.

To sear-roast the steaks: Heat the oven to 400°F. Put a rack in a rimmed baking sheet or roasting pan. Heat a 12-inch sauté pan over high heat until very hot. Add a small amount of olive oil and as many pieces of steak as will fit without crowding (and use a splatter screen if you have one). Sear until the first side is well browned, 2 to 3 minutes. Flip and sear the other side until well browned, 2 to 3 minutes. (Reduce the heat to medium high if the pan is too hot and smoky.) Transfer the steaks to the rack on the baking sheet and continue searing the remaining steaks in batches. When all the steaks are seared, roast them in the oven until done to your liking, 5 to 10 minutes.

Let the steaks rest for 10 minutes before slicing thinly across the grain.

Serve with the salsa verde.

—Maria Helm Sinskey

Pesto-Style Salsa Verde

Yields 1 cup.

This smooth herb sauce is delicious with anything grilled: fish, shellfish, chicken, pork, beef, even vegetables.

¼ cup blanched almonds

Kosher salt and freshly ground black pepper

1 cup packed fresh flat-leaf parsley leaves

½ cup packed fresh basil leaves

½ cup packed fresh cilantro leaves

2 medium cloves garlic, coarsely chopped

¼ teaspoon red pepper flakes

¾ cup extra-virgin olive oil

1 tablespoon white-wine vinegar

Heat the oven to 400°F. Spread the almonds in a pie pan and toast them in the oven until lightly golden, about 8 minutes. Transfer to a plate and let cool.

Bring a large pot of water to a boil and salt the water heavily (it should taste like sea water). Add the parsley and basil and blanch for 1 minute. Drain and immediately transfer the leaves to a colander under cold running water or to an ice bath. When they have cooled, squeeze them dry with your hands.

Put the toasted almonds, the blanched parsley and basil, the cilantro, garlic, red pepper flakes, ½ teaspoon kosher salt, and a few grinds of pepper in a blender or food processor. With the machine on, gradually pour the olive oil into the feed tube and process until the mixture becomes a thick purée. The salsa verde may be made to this point a day ahead and refrigerated.

Return the salsa verde to room temperature, if chilled, and stir in the vinegar just before serving to prevent discoloration.

Getting the Most from Fresh Herbs

Storage

Treat fresh herbs like a bouquet of flowers: stems down in a few inches of water. Keep the bouquet loosely tented with a plastic produce bag and store in the refrigerator. This treatment keeps herbs hydrated but not too wet. Many herbs, like parsley, mint, and cilantro, may last up to two weeks this way. Exception: Cut basil is happiest around 55°F, which is colder than room temperature but warmer than the fridge. If basil is purchased already refrigerated, it should stay that way. If cut fresh or bought unrefrigerated, keep the basil at room temperature unless it's very hot out. Regardless, cut basil rarely keeps longer than a week.

Cleaning

When ready to use the herbs, hold them by their stems and vigorously swish them around in a bowl of cool water until they seem free of dirt. Shake the herbs over the sink and then spin dry or blot dry with paper towels. (Curly parsley can be squeezed partially dry before blotting with paper towels.) The drier the herbs, the better they'll withstand chopping.

Chopping

Use a sharp chef's knife in a rock-chopping motion (the front part of the knife should be moving in a slight slicing motion as you chop). The idea is to cut through the herbs cleanly, rather than bashing and bruising them, which happens if you use a dull knife. Bruised herbs bleed a lot of their flavor out onto the cutting board, and their color dulls or blackens quickly.

Bourbon & Brown Sugar Marinated Steak

Serves four.

½ cup soy sauce

⅓ cup bourbon or other whiskey

⅓ cup firmly packed dark brown sugar

1 tablespoon Dijon mustard

1 teaspoon hot sauce, such as Tabasco

1½ to 2 pounds beef steak, preferably flank, or 1½-inch-thick New York strip steaks

You can marinate the steaks in the refrigerator for up to 2 hours before grilling. Just bring the steaks back to room temperature before grilling. Serve with grilled vegetable skewers.

Prepare a medium-hot grill fire. Meanwhile, combine the soy sauce, bourbon, sugar, mustard, and hot sauce in a large zip-top bag. Seal and shake to combine the ingredients and dissolve the sugar. Add the steak to the bag, seal, massage to cover the steaks with marinade, and set aside for 15 to 20 minutes at room temperature.

When the grill is ready, remove the steak from the marinade and shake off any excess, but don't pat it dry. Reserve the marinade. Grill the steak until good sear marks appear, 3 to 4 minutes. With tongs, rotate the steak 90 degrees (to get a crosshatch of grill marks) and continue grilling until grill marks form and the edges are a little crisp, another 3 to 4 minutes. Flip the steak and grill the other side in the same way until the exterior is nicely seared and the steak is cooked to your liking, 10 to 12 minutes total cooking time for medium rare. Let the steaks rest for about 5 minutes.

Meanwhile, pour the marinade into a small saucepan and boil over medium high heat until syrupy, about 3 minutes (watch carefully to prevent burning). For flank steak, slice the meat thinly across the grain. For strip steaks, slice thickly or serve in chunks. Serve with a drizzle of the sauce. *—Molly Stevens*

Stir-Fried Beef with Snow Peas & Shiitakes

Ponzu is a piquant Japanese sauce made with vinegar, rice wine, seaweed and dried bonito flakes. Its savory flavor forms the backbone of this stir-fry.

In a small bowl, stir the cornstarch into 1 tablespoon of the broth until smooth. Stir in the remaining 5 tablespoons broth, along with the ponzu and sesame oil.

Season the sliced beef with ½ teaspoon kosher salt and several grinds of pepper. Heat 2 tablespoons of the oil in a large skillet or stir-fry pan over medium-high heat. When the oil is very hot (it should shimmer), add the beef and stir-fry just until it loses its raw color, 2 to 3 minutes. Transfer the beef to a bowl. Return the pan to medium-high heat, add the remaining 1 tablespoon oil, and then add the mushrooms and peas. Stir-fry until the mushrooms are tender and the peas are crisp-tender, 4 to 5 minutes. Add the scallions, ginger, and garlic and stir-fry for 30 seconds. Return the beef to the pan. Give the broth mixture a quick stir to recombine and pour it into the pan. Cook, stirring, until the sauce thickens, about 1 minute. Serve immediately. *—Jennifer Armentrout*

Serves four.

- 2 teaspoons cornstarch
- 6 tablespoons low-salt chicken broth
- ¼ cup ponzu sauce
- 1 tablespoon Asian sesame oil
- 1¼ pounds boneless beef rib-eye steaks, trimmed and thinly sliced across the grain (⅛ to ¼ inch thick)
- Kosher salt and freshly ground black pepper
- 3 tablespoons neutral oil, like canola or vegetable
- 7 to 8 ounces fresh shiitake mushrooms, stems discarded and caps thinly sliced
- ½ pound snow peas, trimmed
- 3 small or 2 medium scallions (white and green parts), thinly sliced
- One 1½-inch piece fresh ginger, peeled and minced
- 2 medium cloves garlic, minced

Argentine-Style Burger

Yields four burgers.

2 tablespoons extra-virgin olive oil

½ cup finely chopped yellow onion

2 tablespoons finely chopped garlic

1 tablespoon finely chopped jalapeño

Kosher salt and freshly ground black pepper

1½ pounds ground round (85% lean)

1½ teaspoons ground cumin

1½ teaspoons dried oregano

¼ cup finely chopped fresh cilantro

Four 5- to 6-inch pita pockets

Thin red onion slices (optional)

Lettuce leaves (optional)

Chimichurri Sauce (recipe follows)

Chimichurri Sauce

Yields about 1 cup.

This sauce—a version of the classic Argentine condiment—can be made up to two days in advance and refrigerated in a sealed container.

1 cup packed fresh flat-leaf parsley leaves (from 1 large bunch)

1 cup packed fresh mint leaves (from 1 large bunch)

⅓ cup extra-virgin olive oil

¼ cup fresh lime juice

2 tablespoons coarsely chopped garlic

1 teaspoon coarsely chopped jalapeño

1 teaspoon ground cumin

1 teaspoon kosher salt; more to taste

Put the parsley, mint, olive oil, lime juice, garlic, jalapeño, cumin, and salt in a food processor. Process, stopping to scrape the bowl as often as needed, until puréed into a thick sauce. Add more salt to taste if needed and refrigerate until ready to use.

Chimichurri sauce is a zesty Argentinian staple that accompanies all manner of grilled meats. Here it perks up a burger flavored with garlic, cumin and jalapeno. Creating a dent in the center of the patties helps the middle cook in the same amount of time as the edges.

In a medium skillet, heat 1 tablespoon of the oil over medium heat. Add the onion, garlic, jalapeño, and ¼ teaspoon kosher salt. Cook, stirring occasionally, until softened, about 3 minutes. Transfer to a medium bowl, let cool for 10 minutes, and then add the beef, cumin, oregano, cilantro, 1 teaspoon kosher salt, and several grinds of pepper. Mix gently with your hands until just combined. Shape the meat into four burgers, ¾ inch thick and 4 inches across, working the meat as little as possible. Make a ¼-inch dent in the center of each burger with the tips of your middle three fingers. Sprinkle both sides with salt.

On the Stovetop

Put a large skillet or griddle, preferably cast iron, over high heat and let it get very hot, about 2 minutes. (The pan is hot enough when a drop of water evaporates instantly.) Add the remaining 1 tablespoon oil and tilt the pan to spread it evenly. Arrange the burgers so there's as much space as possible between them, reduce the heat to medium high, and cook, uncovered, for 5 minutes. Turn and cook until the burger feels springy but not mushy when poked, about 3 minutes for medium rare (or longer if you're concerned about undercooked meat).

On the Grill

Charcoal: Prepare a medium-hot fire. Cook the burgers, uncovered, on one side for 5 minutes. Turn and cook until the burgers feel springy but not mushy when poked, another 4 to 5 minutes for medium rare.

Gas: Heat the grill to high. When the interior temperature is about 500°F, cook the burgers for 3 minutes with the lid closed. Turn, close the lid, and cook until the burgers feel springy but not mushy when poked, another 3 to 4 minutes for medium rare. Cut the top inch or so off the pitas to open up the pockets wide enough to fit the burgers. Serve each burger in a pita with red onion and lettuce, if using, and some of the chimichurri sauce. *—Bob Sloan*

Hamburgers with Watercress & Roquefort Butter

Serves four.

- 1½ pounds ground beef (preferably chuck)
- Kosher salt and freshly ground black pepper
- 3 ounces Roquefort cheese, crumbled (a generous ⅓ cup)
- 2 tablespoons unsalted butter, at room temperature
- 4 hamburger buns or kaiser rolls, split
- 4 very thin slices red onion
- 1 cup loosely packed watercress sprigs, tough stems removed, well rinsed, and dried

Using watercress to top this rich blue-cheese burger adds a welcome peppery bite. Be sure to wash and dry the watercress well.

Heat the oven to 400°F. Season the beef with salt and pepper and shape it into four patties about 1 inch thick. Season both sides of each patty with salt and pepper.

In a small bowl, mix the Roquefort and butter with a rubber spatula.

Heat a large, heavy sauté pan over medium-high heat for 1 minute. Set the hamburgers in the pan, reduce the heat to medium, and cook until well browned on the first side, 4 to 5 minutes. Flip the burgers and cook to your liking: another 4 minutes for medium rare, or another 6 minutes for medium.

Meanwhile, toast the buns or rolls, split sides up, on a baking sheet in the oven until crusty and very light gold, 6 to 8 minutes. Spread each cut side of each bun with about 1 tablespoon of the Roquefort butter. Serve the hamburgers on the toasted buns, topped with the onion and watercress.

—Tasha DeSerio

Southwestern Beef Stew with Squash, Peppers & Beans

Sort of a cross between beef chili and beef stew, this dish would be at home served with either warm cornbread or mashed or roasted potatoes.

Position a rack in the lower middle (but not the bottom) of the oven and heat the oven to 450°F.

Pat the beef dry with paper towels, trim away any thick pieces of fat, and cut into 1-inch cubes. Season generously with salt and pepper. Heat 2 tablespoons of the oil over medium-high heat in a heavy Dutch oven 9 to 10 inches in diameter. As soon as the oil is very hot, add a quarter of the beef cubes, taking care not to crowd the pan. Sear the beef until two sides form an impressive dark-brown crust, 8 to 10 minutes. Transfer the beef to a bowl and continue to sear the remaining beef in batches, adding more oil to the pan if needed. It's fine for the pan bottom to darken, but if it smells like it's burning, lower the heat just a little. Set all the seared beef aside in a bowl.

Reduce the heat to medium and add the onions and garlic to the empty pot, adding another 1 tablespoon oil if the pan is dry. Cook, stirring frequently, until soft, about 5 minutes. Add the chili powder, cumin, and oregano, and continue to cook, stirring, until fragrant, 30 seconds to a minute. Season with salt and pepper. Stir in the flour, then the tomatoes with their juices, the wine, and water. Return the beef and any accumulated juices to the pot.

Lay a large sheet of heavy-duty aluminum foil over the pot and, using a potholder or a thick towel, press it down in the center so it almost touches the stew. Crimp the foil around the pot's rim for a tight seal. Cover snugly with the lid. Turn the burner to medium high until you hear the juices bubble. Put the pot in the oven and cook for 1 hour and 15 minutes. Check the stew: If the meat is fork-tender, it's done; if not, cook for another 15 minutes, adding a little more water to the pan if it looks dry.

Meanwhile, heat a large sauté pan over medium-high heat. Add enough oil to cover the bottom of the pan and sauté the squash and bell peppers until just tender and lightly browned. Remove from the heat and set aside.

Remove the pot from the oven, carefully remove the foil, and stir in the cooked vegetables and the beans. Remembering that the pot and lid are hot, cover again with the foil and the lid. Let stand so that the meat rests and the vegetables marry, about 15 minutes. When ready to serve, the stew juices might need thinning to achieve a thin gravy texture. If so, stir in water—¼ cup at a time—as needed. Season with salt and pepper to taste. Gently reheat, if necessary, and serve garnished with the cilantro. *—Pam Anderson*

Serves six to eight.

- 3 pounds boneless beef chuck
- Kosher salt and freshly ground black pepper
- 3 tablespoons olive or vegetable oil; more as needed
- 2 large or 3 medium onions, diced
- 3 large cloves garlic, minced
- ¼ cup chili powder
- 2 teaspoons ground cumin
- 1 teaspoon dried oregano
- 3 tablespoons all-purpose flour
- One 14.5-ounce can diced tomatoes
- 1 cup dry white wine
- 1 cup water
- 4 cups mixed yellow squash (peeled and cut into bite-size pieces), and red and green bell pepper (cored, seeded, and cut into bite-size pieces)
- 1 cup canned pinto beans, drained and rinsed
- 2 to 3 tablespoons coarsely chopped fresh cilantro, for garnish

Beef & Bean Chili with Individual Nachos

Serves three to four.

For the chili:

1 to 1½ tablespoons chili powder

1 tablespoon ground cumin

2 teaspoons paprika

1 teaspoon dried oregano

Pinch to ⅛ teaspoon cayenne

3 tablespoons olive oil

1 pound ground beef

1 teaspoon kosher salt; more to taste

1½ to 2 tablespoons seeded and chopped fresh jalapeño

1½ cups chopped onion

4 large cloves garlic, chopped

One 14-ounce can diced tomatoes, with their juices

¼ cup water

One 15-ounce can kidney or black beans, drained and rinsed

1 tablespoon molasses

1 teaspoon balsamic vinegar

Sour cream, for serving

Fresh cilantro leaves, for serving

For the nachos:

8 large "restaurant-style" tortilla chips or more smaller chips (choose ones that will lie fairly flat on a baking sheet)

1 fresh jalapeño, sliced paper thin into rings

About ¾ cup grated Cheddar or Monterey Jack cheese, or a mix

Mixing the spices together before adding them to the chili helps to disburse them evenly. If you like your chili picante, use the larger amounts of the hot ingredients. The small amounts of molasses and balsamic vinegar add some complexity to this otherwise straightforward chili.

Make the chili: In a small bowl, combine the chili powder, cumin, paprika, oregano, and cayenne.

In a deep sauté pan or Dutch oven, heat about 1 tablespoon of the oil. Add the ground beef, breaking up the chunks of meat, season it with the 1 teaspoon of kosher salt, and cook, stirring occasionally until the meat is no longer pink. Drain the meat in a colander placed over a bowl to catch the grease.

Add another 1 tablespoon oil to the pan, then the onion and chopped jalapeño, and season with a pinch of salt. Cook, stirring occasionally, over medium-high heat until just tender, about 4 minutes. Add the garlic and cook, stirring, for about 1 minute. Add another 1 tablespoon oil and the spices and cook, stirring, for about 1 minute. Return the meat to the pan. Add the diced tomatoes and their juices and the water. Stir well and bring to a boil. Reduce the heat to a simmer, cover, and cook for at least 20 minutes, although longer is fine.

Stir in the beans and cook, uncovered, for another 15 to 20 minutes. Stir in the molasses and vinegar.

Make the nachos: Heat the broiler. Lay the tortilla chips on a small baking sheet. Top each with a few slices of jalapeño. Cover each chip with a small handful of cheese (about 2 tablespoons for large chips); it's fine if the cheese doesn't cover the chip completely. Slide the baking sheet under the broiler to melt the cheese and brown the edges of the chips slightly. Remove from the oven and let cool briefly while you plate the chili.

To serve: Portion the chili into four deep bowls. Stand a nacho or two in the chili. Top the chili with a dollop of sour cream and a sprinkling of cilantro leaves. —*Joanne McAllister Smart*

Texas Beef Chili with Poblanos & Beer

Serves eight.

3 tablespoons olive oil; more as needed

2 large sweet onions, diced

2 large fresh poblano chiles or green bell peppers, stemmed, seeded, and diced

5 cloves garlic, minced

Kosher salt

4½ pounds boneless beef chuck, cut into 1-inch cubes

2 bay leaves

2 cinnamon sticks, 3 to 4 inches long

3 tablespoons New Mexico chile powder or 2 tablespoons ancho chile powder

1 tablespoon chipotle chile powder

1 tablespoon ground cumin

⅛ teaspoon ground cloves

One 12-ounce bottle amber ale, such as Shiner Bock®, Dos Equis® Amber, or Anchor Steam Liberty Ale®

1½ quarts low-salt beef broth

For the garnishes:

Two 14-ounce cans kidney beans, rinsed and drained

1 medium red onion, chopped

3 medium, ripe tomatoes, cored, seeded, and chopped

⅓ cup coarsely chopped fresh cilantro

12 ounces sour cream or whole-milk plain yogurt

This chili has a pleasant kick. It thickens as it sits overnight and the flavors round out and deepen. It's best made with chipotle and New Mexico chile powders, but ancho, another pure chile powder, is a good substitute for New Mexico. Both ancho and chipotle powders are available in grocery stores.

In a 12-inch skillet, heat 2 tablespoons of the oil over medium-high heat. Add the onions and sauté until softened, translucent, and starting to brown, 8 to 10 minutes. Add the poblanos, reduce the heat to medium, and cook, stirring occasionally, until the they soften, another 8 to 10 minutes. If the pan seems dry, add a little more olive oil. Add the garlic and 1 teaspoon kosher salt and sauté for another 5 minutes. Set aside.

Meanwhile, heat the remaining 1 tablespoon olive oil in an 8-quart or larger Dutch oven (preferably enameled cast iron) over medium-high heat. Sear the beef cubes until browned and crusty on two sides, working in batches to avoid crowding the pan. With tongs or a slotted spoon, transfer the browned beef to a bowl. During searing, it's fine if the pan bottom gets quite dark, but if it smells like it's burning, reduce the heat a bit. If the pan ever gets dry, add a little more oil.

Once all the beef is seared and set aside, add the onions and peppers to the pan, along with the bay leaves, cinnamon sticks, chile powders, cumin, and cloves and cook, stirring, until the spices coat the vegetables and are fragrant, 15 to 30 seconds. Slowly add the beer while scraping the pan bottom with a wooden spoon to dissolve the coating of spices. Simmer until the beer is reduced by about half and the mixture has thickened slightly, 5 to 7 minutes. Add the beef, along with any accumulated juices, and the beef broth. Bring to a simmer, then reduce the heat to medium low. Simmer, partially covered, for 3 hours, stirring occasionally. Test a cube of meat—you should be able to cut it with a spoon. Discard the cinnamon sticks and bay leaves.

If not serving immediately, chill overnight. The next day, skim any fat from the top, if necessary, before reheating.

To serve, heat the chili gently. Using a slotted spoon, transfer about 2 cups of the beef cubes to a plate. Shred the meat with a fork and return it to pot. (The shredded meat will help create a thicker texture.) Taste and add more salt if needed. Heat the beans in a medium bowl covered with plastic in the microwave (or heat them gently in a saucepan). Arrange the beans, chopped onion, tomatoes, cilantro, and sour cream in small bowls to serve as garnishes with the chili. —*Paula Disbrowe and David Norman*

Chile Powder Profiles

Pasilla

Heat level: moderate
Flavor: sweet, berry-like
Use in: *mole* sauce, chili, braised pork, beef stews

Ancho

Heat level: moderate
Flavor: fruity, sweet
Use in: black beans, *mole* sauce, spice rubs for grilled pork or shrimp

New Mexico

Heat level: moderate
Flavor: earthy, fruity
Use in: enchiladas, sauces, ground beef taco filling

Chipotle

Heat level: hot
Flavor: smoky, sweet
Use in: barbecue sauce, grilling spice rubs, mayonnaise

Cayenne

Heat level: very hot
Flavor: intense, sharp
Use in: dips, soups, crab cakes, roasted potato wedges

Sirloin Tacos

Serves eight.

1 tablespoon kosher salt

1 teaspoon Hungarian paprika

1 teaspoon dried granulated garlic

1 teaspoon coarsely ground black pepper

1 teaspoon dried thyme

2 pounds sirloin steak, about 1 inch thick

12 to 16 small (5½- or 6-inch) flour or corn tortillas, warmed

Roasted Tomato Salsa (recipe follows)

Serve these tacos with the Roasted Tomato Salsa, as well as chopped lettuce, cilantro sprigs, sour cream, and your other favorite taco condiments.

In a small bowl, combine the salt, paprika, granulated garlic, pepper, and thyme; blend well. Sprinkle both sides of the steak with the dry rub, then rub it in. Let the meat sit for half an hour at room temperature.

To cook on a charcoal grill, light the charcoal (preferably hardwood) in a chimney starter. Pour the hot coals into the grill so they are banked to one side. Put the grill grate on the grill. When the coals are coated in gray ash and you can hold your hand 1 to 2 inches above the grate for 2 seconds, set the meat directly above the coals to sear it until dark grill marks form, about 3 minutes per side. Or, heat one area of a gas grill on high and another on low. Set the meat on the grates on the high side and sear it until dark grill marks form, about 3 minutes per side.

When the steak is nicely marked by the hot grill on both sides, move the meat away from the coals (or to the cooler side of a gas grill) and cover the grill so it can cook indirectly. Remove the steak from the grill when it's slightly firm to the touch and registers 130° to 135°F on an instant-read thermometer for medium rare (about another 5 to 8 minutes), or 140° to 145°F for medium. Let the steak rest on a cutting board for at least 5 minutes before carving. To serve, trim the fat from the steak and slice the meat on the diagonal into thin strips. Serve with warm tortillas and the roasted tomato salsa and let your guests assemble their own tacos. *—Robb Walsh*

Roasted Tomato Salsa

Yields about 2 cups.

Serranos are generally hotter than jalapeños, but they're also smaller, so you can use either, in the same quantity.

½ medium yellow onion, finely diced

1½ tablespoons fresh lime juice; more to taste

6 medium Roma tomatoes

3 fresh jalapeño or serrano chiles, halved lengthwise, stemmed, and seeded

1 clove garlic, peeled

1 cup coarsely chopped fresh cilantro

1½ teaspoons kosher salt; more to taste

In a small bowl, soak the onion in the lime juice for 15 minutes. In a dry, heavy skillet (preferably cast iron) over high heat, "roast" the tomatoes, chile halves, and garlic clove until charred on all sides, 2 to 5 minutes for the garlic, 8 to 10 minutes for the chiles, and 12 to 15 minutes for the tomatoes. Pulse in a blender; the mixture should remain slightly chunky. Transfer to a serving bowl and add the onion, lime juice, cilantro, and salt. Taste and add more salt or lime juice if needed. Use immediately or cover and refrigerate for up to a week.

Six-Spice Braised Short Ribs

Serves six to eight.

½ cup peeled and sliced fresh ginger (¼ inch thick)

8 large cloves garlic, peeled

½ cup dry red wine

¼ cup red-wine vinegar

1½ tablespoons coriander seeds, finely ground

1 tablespoon sweet Hungarian paprika

1½ teaspoons cayenne

1½ teaspoons ground ginger

1½ teaspoons allspice berries, finely ground

¾ teaspoon black peppercorns, finely ground

¼ cup canola oil

½ cup tomato ketchup

¼ cup pure maple syrup

2½ tablespoons fresh thyme leaves

Leaves from 1 sprig fresh rosemary

2 tablespoons kosher salt; more as needed

6 pounds bone-in beef short ribs (3 to 4 inches long)

2 quarts low-salt beef or chicken broth

¼ cup coarsely chopped fresh cilantro

Serve the ribs and sauce over a pile of creamy mashed potatoes. A side of sautéed spinach or chard also pairs well.

In a blender, grind the fresh ginger, garlic, wine, and vinegar to create a smooth paste. Add the coriander, paprika, cayenne, ground ginger, allspice, and black pepper; blend just to combine.

To bloom the spices, heat the oil in a medium, heavy saucepan over medium heat. When the oil is hot, carefully add the spice paste and cook, stirring constantly and carefully (the mixture will bubble and splatter), until thick and very aromatic and the oil separates out of the paste, 5 to 8 minutes. Remove from the heat, let the spice paste cool, then stir in the ketchup, maple syrup, thyme, rosemary, and salt. Rub this paste over the ribs.

Put the ribs in a nonreactive container, cover well, and refrigerate for at least one and up to two days.

When ready to cook, put the ribs, marinade, and broth in a heavy 8-quart (or larger) pot over medium heat. Bring the liquid to a boil, reduce the heat to medium low or low, cover, and simmer until the meat is very tender when pierced with a fork, about 2½ hours. Uncover and simmer for another 15 minutes.

Remove the ribs from the liquid and transfer to a 9x13-inch Pyrex dish or other similar container. Cover with aluminum foil. Use a ladle to skim the fat (there will be a lot) from the braising liquid. Bring the liquid to a boil, reduce the heat to a gentle simmer and cook, uncovered, until it reduces to about 4 cups and becomes a slightly thick, velvety sauce, about 45 minutes. If serving right away, return the ribs to the sauce to reheat briefly.

If making ahead, pour as much of the sauce over the ribs as will fit in the dish and pour the remaining sauce into another container. Let cool, uncovered, at room temperature for 1 hour, then cover and refrigerate until ready to serve, for up to two days.

When ready to serve, reheat the ribs and sauce in a large pot over medium heat until the sauce is bubbling and the meat is warm all the way through. Taste the sauce and add salt if needed. Sprinkle with the cilantro and serve.

—Floyd Cardoz

Roast Beef with a Classic Breadcrumb, Garlic & Herb Crust

Serves eight to ten.

One 5-pound boneless strip loin roast or 5- to 6-pound boneless top sirloin roast with the cap removed, trimmed if necessary and patted dry

Kosher salt and freshly ground black pepper

2 tablespoons vegetable oil

1 cup coarse fresh breadcrumbs, preferably from a baguette

4 cloves garlic, minced

2 medium shallots, minced

1 tablespoon roughly chopped fresh thyme

1 tablespoon roughly chopped fresh marjoram

3 tablespoons unsalted butter, melted

⅓ cup Dijon mustard

Creamy Horseradish-Mustard Sauce, for serving (recipe follows)

Creamy Horseradish-Mustard Sauce

Yields 1⅓ cups.

The sauce can be stored, covered, in the refrigerator for up to four days. Be sure to stir it before using.

1 cup crème fraîche

3 tablespoons drained prepared horseradish

3 tablespoons Dijon mustard

½ teaspoon kosher salt

Pinch cayenne

In a small bowl, whisk all the ingredients. Let the sauce sit for 20 minutes for the flavors to meld before serving.

Searing the meat before encasing it in a flavorful crust caramelizes the surface and seals in the juices. The crust has the added benefit of providing an extra layer of protection to keep the meat moist. You can make the horseradish-mustard sauce in advance.

Let the roast sit at room temperature for 30 minutes. Meanwhile, position a rack in the center of the oven and heat the oven to 400°F. Put a roasting rack in a roasting pan or a heavy rimmed baking sheet. (Line the pan with aluminum foil for easier clean-up, if you like.)

Season the roast liberally with salt and pepper on all sides. Turn on the exhaust fan. Heat the oil in a large sauté pan over medium-high heat. When the oil is hot, brown the meat well on all sides, including the ends, about 4 minutes per side. Transfer the meat to the pan. Set aside while you prepare the crust.

In a medium bowl, combine the breadcrumbs, garlic, shallots, thyme, marjoram, ½ teaspoon kosher salt, and ¼ teaspoon pepper. Pour the melted butter into the mixture; toss to combine. Using a rubber spatula, smear the top and sides of the beef with the mustard. With your hands, lightly press the breadcrumb mixture into the mustard.

Roast the beef until an instant-read thermometer inserted into the thickest part of the meat reads 125°F for medium rare, about 60 minutes for a strip loin roast or 60 to 80 minutes for a top sirloin roast, depending on its thickness. (To keep the crust from overbrowning, start checking on the roast after 30 minutes of cooking and, when the crust is golden brown, tent it with foil.)

Meanwhile, make the horseradish-mustard sauce.

Remove the roast from the oven and let the meat rest for 10 to 20 minutes (the meat will continue to cook as it rests) before carving, across the grain, into ½-inch-thick slices. *—Gordon Hamersley*

Tips for a Successful Crust

1 First sear, then crust

Searing the roast before you apply the crust creates flavorful browning on the surface of the meat.

2 Coat the meat with something sticky

A crust needs something to stick to: mustard, yogurt, mayonnaise, and roasted garlic purée all make great "glues." Or the crust itself can be a sticky paste.

3 Not too thick, not to thin

Apply the crust about ¼ to ½ inch thick, patting it on lightly with a little extra pressure as needed.

4 Just the top and sides

You don't need to apply crust to the bottom of the roast, only the top and sides.

5 Don't be crust-fallen

No matter how careful you are, it's inevitable that some of the crust will fall off when you carve the roast. This goes with the territory, so don't sweat it. Just make sure everyone gets some of the crust on the plate with their portion of meat and everyone will be happy.

Individual Beef Croustades with Boursin & Mushrooms

Serves six.

For the mushroom filling:

1 pound fresh white button or cremini mushrooms, cleaned

2 medium shallots

1 clove garlic, cut in half

2 tablespoons unsalted butter

1 tablespoon olive oil

¼ cup chopped fresh flat-leaf parsley

Kosher salt and freshly ground black pepper

For the croustades:

6 filets mignons, 6 ounces each and about 1¾ inches thick

Kosher salt

1 tablespoon unsalted butter

1 tablespoon vegetable oil

2 cakes (5.2 ounces each) peppercorn Boursin cheese, slightly softened at room temperature

1-pound package phyllo dough (with at least 24 sheets, preferably more), thawed in the refrigerator overnight

¼ pound (½ cup) unsalted butter, melted; more if needed

¼ cup thinly sliced fresh chives

Mushroom Filling

Ask for filets from near the tail end of the tenderloin so they're tall and narrow, rather than short and wide.

Make the mushroom filling: Trim the mushroom stems close to the caps. Put the mushrooms, shallots, and garlic in a food processor and pulse until finely chopped but not puréed; scrape the bowl as needed. Transfer the chopped mushrooms to the center of a clean dishtowel. Gather up the sides of the towel and twist, keeping the mushrooms well contained in the cloth, bonbon style. With one hand, hold the ball of mushrooms over the sink; with the other hand, twist the gathered cloth, squeezing out as much liquid as possible.

Heat the butter and oil in a 10-inch skillet or sauté pan over medium heat. Add the mushrooms, cover, and cook, stirring occasionally, until the mushrooms are very soft and fragrant, 3 to 5 minutes. Don't let them brown. Uncover and cook until the pan is mostly dry, 2 to 3 minutes. Add the parsley; season with ½ teaspoon kosher salt and pepper to taste. The filling can be refrigerated for up to a week or frozen for up to two weeks. If frozen, thaw overnight in the refrigerator and, if necessary, cook gently in an uncovered skillet to evaporate any juices that may have developed in the freezer.

Make the croustades: Season the filets mignons generously on all sides with salt. Heat the butter and oil in a 10-inch skillet or sauté pan over medium-high heat until very hot and sizzling.

Put three of the filets in the pan and sear on one side until well browned, 1 to 2 minutes. Turn and brown the other side. Then quickly sear along the sides, using tongs to turn, about another 1 minute per side. Transfer to a plate lined with paper towels. Repeat with the remaining filets. Cover and refrigerate for at least 1 hour.

Mash the Boursin with a fork in a small bowl until spreadable. Remove at least 24 sheets of phyllo from the package and cut them into 10-inch squares. Cover them with plastic wrap and a damp dishtowel while you work to keep them from drying out. Lay a single phyllo sheet on a clean, dry surface. With a pastry brush, lightly paint an even coat of the melted butter over the entire surface of the square. Sprinkle with about ½ teaspoon of the chives. Set a second sheet at a 90-degree angle over the first. Brush butter over it as well and sprinkle with another ½ teaspoon chives.

Make four layers, omitting the chives from the last layer, with the corners of the phyllo pointing in different directions, starlike. Blot one filet dry with a paper towel, set it in the center of the star, and sprinkle it with salt. Spread

about 2 tablespoons of the Boursin on the filet and top that with 2 generous tablespoons of the mushroom filling.

Pick a starting point and work your way around the filet, gathering the edges of the phyllo star together, beggar's purse style. Lightly pinch together the gathered phyllo close to the surface of the meat to hold it in place. Pull the corners open slightly as if making a paper flower. Brush the whole exposed surface lightly with more butter, being sure that the bottom is buttered as well. Transfer to a heavy baking sheet. Repeat this "packaging'" for the remaining filets. If you're working ahead, chill the croustades uncovered on the baking sheet until ready to bake, up to 8 hours.

To bake: Take the croustades out of the refrigerator about 20 minutes before you're ready to bake them. Position an oven rack in the lower third of the oven and heat the oven to 400°F. Bake the croustades, rotating the baking sheet after 10 minutes to ensure evening browning, until an instant-read thermometer inserted through the side of each packet and into the center of the filet reads 130°F for medium rare, 17 to 22 minutes. Serve immediately.

–Randall Price

Roasted Beef Tenderloin with Caramelized Shallots & Red Wine

Serves six.

One 2½- to 3-pound beef tenderloin roast (preferably the head piece), trimmed of silverskin, at room temperature

1 tablespoon extra-virgin olive oil

Kosher salt and freshly ground black pepper

¼ cup cold unsalted butter

3 large shallots, halved and thinly sliced lengthwise

¾ cup dry red wine, preferably a fruity California Cabernet Sauvignon

1 sprig fresh rosemary, plus ½ teaspoon chopped

¾ cup low-salt beef broth

It's important to let the beef rest before slicing it; this allows the juices to redistribute from the outside of the roast throughout the whole roast, making this lean cut very juicy.

Position a rack in the center of the oven and heat the oven to 450°F. Brush or rub the beef with the oil and place in a 9x13-inch roasting pan lined with aluminum foil. Season generously with salt and pepper.

Roast the beef until an instant-read thermometer registers 120° to 125°F for rare, about 25 minutes; 125° to 130°F for medium rare, about 30 minutes. (The temperature of the beef will rise 5°F as it rests.) Wrap the beef in the foil that lines the pan and let rest on a carving board for 10 to 15 minutes.

While the beef roasts, make the sauce. Melt 2 tablespoons of the butter in a 12-inch skillet over medium heat. Add the shallots and cook, stirring often, until softened and turning golden brown, 8 to 10 minutes. Add the wine and rosemary sprig and bring to a boil over medium-high heat. Boil until the volume of wine and shallots reduces to ½ cup, about 3 minutes. Add the broth and continue to boil until reduced to 1 cup, about 5 minutes. Reduce the heat to low. Remove the rosemary sprig and stir in the chopped rosemary. Cut the remaining 2 tablespoons cold butter into small cubes and add a few of them at a time to the sauce, stirring to melt each addition.

Unwrap the tenderloin and stir any accumulated juices into the sauce. Season the sauce to taste with salt and pepper. Slice the meat and serve with the sauce. *–Jennifer McLagan*

Dry-Aged Beef Rib Roast with a Mustard, Garlic & Thyme Crust

If you lack the time or inclination to dry-age the beef, you can skip that step, though the roast won't be quite as delicious. (Start with a 4- to 4½-pound roast if not dry-aging.)

Three to seven days ahead: Dry-age the beef as described in How to Dry-Age Beef at Home, steps one through four.

Roast the beef: Mince the garlic with a chef's knife and sprinkle with the salt. Using the side of the knife, scrape and mash the garlic and salt together until they turn into a paste. In a small bowl, combine the garlic paste with the mustard, thyme, olive oil, and pepper. Trim the aged beef as described in step four of the aging method and rub the garlic mixture over all sides of the beef. Put the roast, fat side up, on a rack set in a heavy-duty rimmed baking sheet or small roasting pan. Let sit at room temperature for 1 hour. Meanwhile, position a rack in the center of the oven; heat the oven to 450°F.

Roast the beef for 15 minutes. Without opening the door, reduce the oven temperature to 375°F. Continue to roast until a thermometer inserted in the center of the roast registers 130°F for medium rare, 1 to 1½ hours.

Let the beef rest for 20 minutes. Carve and serve with the crème fraîche sauce. *—Jennifer Armentrout*

How to Dry-Age Beef at Home

Dry-aged beef has a remarkable depth of flavor, unfortunately it can be hard to come by. But the good news is that if you have a refrigerator, you can dry-age beef at home.

1 Buy a prime or choice boneless beef rib or loin roast from the best meat source in your area.

2 Unwrap the beef, rinse it well, and pat it dry with paper towels. Do not trim. Wrap the roast loosely in a triple layer of cheesecloth and set it on a rack over a rimmed baking sheet or other tray.

3 Refrigerate for three to seven days; the longer the beef ages, the tastier it gets. After the first day, carefully unwrap and then rewrap with the same cheesecloth to keep the cloth fibers from sticking to the meat.

4 When ready to roast, unwrap the meat and, with a sharp knife, shave off and discard the hard, dried outer layer of the meat. Shave away any dried areas of fat, too, but leave behind as much of the good fat as possible. Roast whole or cut into steaks.

Horseradish-Chive Crème Fraîche

Yields about 1 cup.

This sauce is best made one day ahead and keeps well for a week. If you can't find crème fraîche, substitute ⅔ cup sour cream and ⅓ cup mayonnaise.

¼ cup prepared horseradish

1½ tablespoons thinly sliced chives

½ pound crème fraîche (or ⅔ cup sour cream plus ⅓ cup mayonnaise)

Kosher salt

Stir the horseradish and chives into the crème fraîche. Season to taste with salt, cover, and refrigerate for at least 6 hours or until needed.

Sautéed Lamb Chops with Herbes de Provence

Serves four.

5 tablespoons extra-virgin olive oil

2 tablespoons dried herbes de Provence

2 cloves garlic, mashed to a paste

12 lamb rib chops (¾ inch thick)

Kosher salt and freshly ground black pepper

A mortar and pestle or mini food processor makes quick work of the garlic-herb paste. Serve with mashed potatoes and haricots verts.

In a small bowl, combine 4 tablespoons of the oil with the herbes de Provence and mashed garlic to make a wet paste. Rub this all over the lamb chops and set aside at room temperature for 20 minutes.

Generously season both sides of the chops with salt and pepper. Heat the remaining 1 tablespoon oil in a 10-inch sauté pan over high heat until very hot. Sear the chops in batches until browned on one side, 2 to 3 minutes. Flip and cook until the second side has browned, 2 to 3 minutes for medium rare. Transfer the chops to a platter, cover loosely with aluminum foil, and let rest for 5 minutes before serving. —*Arlene Jacobs*

Lamb Chops with Pomegranate Red-Wine Sauce

Pomegranate juice, often used in Middle Eastern cooking, adds a rich, sweet flavor to this garnet-colored sauce.

Liberally season the lamb chops with salt and pepper on both sides. Heat the olive oil in a 12-inch sauté pan over medium-high heat until very hot. Sear the chops in two batches until well browned on both sides, about 2 minutes per side for medium rare, 3 minutes per side for medium. Keep the chops warm on a platter covered with aluminum foil. Pour off and discard all but about 1 or 2 tablespoons fat from the pan.

Add the shallot to the pan and cook, stirring constantly, until browned, 1 to 2 minutes. Add the pomegranate juice, wine, broth, vinegar, thyme, and honey and cook, stirring, until the liquid is reduced by half, 3 to 5 minutes. Reduce the heat to medium low and swirl in the butter until it melts. Taste and adjust the seasoning with salt and pepper. Transfer the chops to dinner plates and serve with the sauce. *–Kate Hays*

Serves four.

12 lamb rib chops

Kosher salt and freshly ground black pepper

2 tablespoons extra-virgin olive oil

¼ cup minced shallot

½ cup pomegranate juice (such as Pom brand)

¼ cup full-bodied dry red wine

¼ cup low-salt chicken broth

1½ tablespoons balsamic vinegar

1 tablespoon fresh thyme leaves, finely chopped

½ tablespoon honey

2 tablespoons cold unsalted butter, cut into small cubes

Tender Lamb Meatballs in Fragrant Tomato Sauce

Serves four.

¾ cup fresh soft breadcrumbs

2 tablespoons dry white wine or water

1 pound ground lamb

⅓ cup freshly grated Parmigiano-Reggiano cheese, lightly packed

2 tablespoons finely chopped oil-packed sun-dried tomatoes

2 medium cloves garlic, minced

1 teaspoon kosher salt

⅛ teaspoon freshly ground black pepper

¼ cup olive oil

½ cup finely chopped onion

3 cloves garlic, crushed

½ cup dry white wine

1 cup low-salt chicken broth

One 14-ounce can peeled whole tomatoes

One 5-inch sprig fresh rosemary

1 teaspoon balsamic vinegar

6 drops hot sauce

¼ cup plain yogurt

¼ cup chopped fresh flat-leaf parsley or mint, or a mix

These meatballs are light in texture but very deep in flavor, and the tangy tomato sauce is savory and rich. Ladle them over plain couscous or rice.

Put the breadcrumbs in a small bowl and sprinkle with the wine. Toss to moisten them evenly. In a large bowl, gently mix the lamb, breadcrumbs, Parmigiano, sun-dried tomatoes, minced garlic, salt, and pepper together with your hands. Don't squeeze or overwork the mixture, but do try to distribute all the ingredients evenly. Roll the mixture into about 16 balls.

In a large skillet, heat 2 tablespoons of the olive oil over medium heat and add a layer of meatballs, leaving enough room between them so you can turn them without breaking. (Because of the cheese, the meatballs may stick a little, so use a metal spatula to gently dislodge them as you turn them. Take care not to burn the browned bits that stick to the pan; they'll add flavor to the sauce.) Brown the meatballs gently on all sides; if the pan is crowded, do this in batches. It should take about 6 minutes per batch.

Transfer the meatballs to a plate, pour off any fat from the pan, and add the remaining 2 tablespoons olive oil and the onion. Cook over medium-high heat, stirring almost constantly until the onion is very soft and starting to brown lightly, about 5 minutes. Add the garlic cloves, turn the heat to high, pour in the wine, and boil until it's reduced to a glaze, about 1 minute. Add the broth, all the tomatoes, ⅓ cup of the juice from the tomatoes (discard or freeze the rest of the juice for later), and the rosemary. Crush the tomatoes with a wooden spoon or a spatula until they're in small pieces.

Nestle the meatballs in the sauce, cover the pan, and adjust the heat to a lively simmer. Cook the meatballs until they're no longer pink inside, shaking the pan so they get evenly moistened, about 5 minutes. Transfer the meatballs to a clean plate, increase the heat to high, and boil the sauce until it's fairly thick and very tasty, about 5 minutes. Add the vinegar and hot sauce, then taste and add salt if necessary.

Return the meatballs to the sauce and gently reheat them. Serve immediately over rice or couscous, with a spoonful of yogurt drizzled over each serving and a sprinkling of the fresh herbs. *—Martha Holmberg*

Grilled Butterflied Leg of Lamb with Garlic & Curry Spices

Serves eight to ten.

7 cloves garlic

2 teaspoons kosher salt

1 tablespoon coriander seeds, cracked or coarsely ground

1½ tablespoons sweet curry powder

2 tablespoons peeled and finely chopped fresh ginger

1 cup dry sherry

¼ cup extra-virgin olive oil

3 tablespoons honey

1 tablespoon freshly cracked black peppercorns

1 boneless butterflied leg of lamb, 3 to 5 pounds, trimmed of excess fat, rinsed, and patted dry

6 sprigs fresh cilantro, roughly chopped

You can prepare the spice rub and meat up to a day in advance. **Sweet curry powder is a mild mix of spices, including coriander, cumin, ginger, nutmeg, and cinnamon.**

Prepare the lamb: Finely chop the garlic, sprinkle the salt over it, and mash with the flat side of the knife to make a paste.

Put the cracked coriander and curry powder in a cold, dry sauté pan and set it over medium-low heat. Shake the pan a few times while the spices toast until they have a strong nutty smell, 1 to 3 minutes. Don't let them burn.

In a small bowl, mix the garlic paste, toasted spices, ginger, sherry, olive oil, honey, and pepper together until the mixture resembles a somewhat thin, grainy soup.

If you like, separate the lamb along its natural seams into smaller, easier-to-handle pieces. Put it in a shallow nonreactive baking dish and pour the marinade over the meat. Cover with plastic wrap, set aside, and let the flavors penetrate the meat for 2 hours at room temperature (or up to 24 hours in the refrigerator). Turn the meat twice during the marinating time.

Grill the lamb: Prepare a medium-hot charcoal fire or gas grill. Grill the lamb (covered if using a gas grill, uncovered if using charcoal) on one side until nicely charred, about 10 minutes. Turn the meat over and continue grilling (again, covered if using a gas grill, uncovered if using charcoal) until an instant-read thermometer inserted into a thick section of the meat registers 130° to 135°F for medium rare, 7 to 12 minutes, depending on what type of grill you use. (If you like your lamb cooked to medium, continue grilling until the meat's temperature reaches 140° to 145°F; for medium well, 150° to 155°F.) Transfer the lamb to a tray or carving board and let it rest for 8 to 10 minutes. Carve the lamb across the grain into ¼-inch-thick slices. Arrange the slices on a platter, drizzle with the juices that accumulated during resting, and sprinkle with the cilantro before serving. *–Gordon Hamersley*

A Butterflied Leg is Perfect for a Party

A grilled butterflied leg of lamb is perfect for entertaining because some sections of the meat cook to medium rare, others to medium, and still others to medium well, so everyone's taste is sure to be satisfied. A butterflied leg has been completely boned and cut open into one sheet. It's relatively thin, so it cooks much faster than a traditional leg, and the large, flat cut of meat practically begs to be rubbed with flavorings or doused in marinade. Choose a fairly lean piece with medium- to deep-red meat and little connective tissue. To make the cut easier to handle, separate it into smaller pieces at the seams, if you like.

Boneless Leg of Lamb with Mint, Pine Nut & Currant Stuffing

Serves six to eight.

½ cup dried currants

½ cup tawny Port, or as needed

1 cup coarse breadcrumbs, toasted

½ cup lightly packed coarsely chopped fresh mint

½ cup lightly packed coarsely chopped fresh flat-leaf parsley

3 tablespoons extra-virgin olive oil

½ cup pine nuts, toasted to a light golden brown

Sea salt and freshly ground black pepper

2 large eggs, lightly beaten (the eggs won't be cooked hotter than 130°F, so if salmonella is a concern, use pasteurized eggs, or omit the eggs)

One 3- to 4-pound boneless rolled and tied leg of lamb

Red Onion Jam (recipe follows)

Packed with sweet currants and fresh mint, this flavorful stuffing is a natural partner to roast lamb. You can make the stuffing and the Red Onion Jam in advance.

In a small bowl, soak the currants in enough Port to cover for at least 2 hours and up to overnight.

When ready to roast the lamb, drain the currants; discard the Port. Position a rack in the lower middle of the oven and heat the oven to 400°F.

In a large bowl, combine the breadcrumbs, mint, parsley, olive oil, pine nuts, and currants. Season to taste with salt and pepper. Add the beaten eggs and mix well.

Untie the lamb and unroll it. Lay the meat flat and pat dry with paper towels. Trim any excess fat and, if necessary, butterfly portions of the lamb to make it roughly rectangular and evenly thick. Sprinkle the inside of the lamb with salt and pepper and pat the stuffing evenly over the meat. Roll up the lamb tightly, from one short end to the other, and tie the roast snugly at 1-inch intervals with kitchen twine. Sprinkle the outside of the lamb with more salt and pepper, then set it, seam side up, on a rack in a small roasting pan. Gather up any stuffing that escaped and poke it back in at the ends of the lamb roll. Roast until an instant-read thermometer inserted into a thick part of the roast reads 125° to 130°F (for medium rare), 60 to 70 minutes.

Let rest for 15 minutes, then carve into medium-thin slices. Serve topped with the jam. *–Luke Mangan*

Red Onion Jam

Yields about 1½ cups.

Make this jam while the lamb roasts. Or make it a day ahead and refrigerate; warm it gently before serving.

7 tablespoons unsalted butter

2 medium-large red onions, halved and thinly sliced crosswise into half moons (about 6 cups)

½ cup dry white wine

6 tablespoons honey

3 tablespoons balsamic vinegar

Sea salt and freshly ground black pepper

Melt the butter in a heavy 3- or 4-quart saucepan over medium heat. Add the onions and cook, stirring occasionally, until very soft and stringy looking but not brown, 12 to 15 minutes. (Reduce the heat to medium low if they start to brown.) Add the wine and honey, reduce the heat to medium low if you haven't already, and simmer, stirring occasionally, until the mixture is thick and jammy, another 20 to 30 minutes. Remove from heat, stir in the vinegar, and season with salt and pepper to taste.

Pork Tenderloin with Apples

Serves four.

2 medium Granny Smith apples

½ medium lemon

7 tablespoons unsalted butter

1 tablespoon granulated sugar

2 pork tenderloins (about
    1 pound each), trimmed and
    halved crosswise

Kosher salt and freshly ground
    black pepper

1 tablespoon extra-virgin
    olive oil

2 large shallots, finely minced

¼ cup Calvados or Cognac

¼ cup apple cider

½ teaspoon fresh thyme leaves

⅓ cup heavy cream

Apples and pork are a classic duo. Here the apple flavor comes in three guises—apple brandy and apple cider in the pan sauce, and caramelized apples served alongside.

Set a rack in the center of the oven and heat the oven to 400°F.

Peel, core, and cut each apple into 8 wedges, rubbing the cut edges with the cut side of the lemon half as you go, then juice the lemon half into a small bowl and set aside. In a 10-inch skillet, melt 2 tablespoons of the butter with the sugar over medium-high heat. Add the apples and cook, turning halfway through, until soft and a rich amber color, about 8 minutes (reduce the heat to medium if they start to burn). Set aside and keep warm.

Pat the tenderloins dry with paper towels and season generously with salt and pepper. Heat the oil in a 12-inch ovenproof skillet (don't use nonstick) over medium-high heat until very hot. Sear the pork on all sides until nicely browned, about 5 minutes total. Put the skillet in the oven and roast until an instant-read thermometer inserted in the center of the pork registers 140° to 145°F, 10 to 15 minutes. Transfer to a warm plate (don't clean the skillet), tent with aluminum foil, and let rest for 10 minutes.

Set the skillet over medium heat and add 2 tablespoons of the butter. When it melts, add the shallots and cook until soft and translucent but not browned, about 3 minutes. Remove from the heat and add the Calvados. Return the pan to the stove, raise the heat to medium high, and boil until the Calvados is almost gone, 1 to 2 minutes. Add the cider and thyme; simmer until the liquid is reduced by about half, 2 to 3 minutes. Add the cream and cook over very low heat until the sauce is golden and coats the back of a spoon, about 5 minutes. Cut the remaining 3 tablespoons butter into ½-inch cubes and swirl them into the sauce. Season to taste with salt, pepper, and ½ teaspoon of the reserved lemon juice or to taste. Slice the pork and serve with the warm apples and sauce.

—Arlene Jacobs

Pork Tenderloin with Tequila-Hot Pepper Glaze & Grilled Peaches

Building a two-level fire in the grill allows you to use the sear-roast method on the barbecue. Sweet, smoky peaches are the perfect foil to the spicy pork. Serve with rice pilaf or a couscous salad.

Prepare a medium-hot grill fire. In a small bowl, whisk the jelly, tequila, orange juice, and orange zest. Generously season the pork with salt and pepper. Coat the pork and peaches with a thin film of the olive oil.

If using charcoal, bank the coals so one side of the grill is cooler. Grill the pork over the hotter side of the grill, turning it until all sides develop grill marks, about 2½ minutes per side. Move the pork to the cooler side of the grill (on a gas grill, lower the heat to medium or medium low) and brush the glaze all over the pork. Cover the grill or set a disposable aluminum pan over the pork. Grill for 5 minutes, then turn once and brush again with the glaze. Cover and continue grilling until the pork's internal temperature reaches 145°F, about another 5 minutes. Brush the pork with the glaze again, transfer it to a clean cutting board, and cover it loosely with aluminum foil to rest for about 5 minutes.

Meanwhile, grill the peaches, cut side down, over the hotter part of the grill (on a gas grill, raise the heat to medium high) until grill marks appear, 3 to 4 minutes. Turn the peaches over and brush with the glaze. Continue grilling until warmed through, another 3 to 4 minutes.

Carve the pork into 1- to 2-inch-thick slices and arrange on a platter with the peaches. Sprinkle lightly with salt, drizzle with any leftover glaze and juices from the pork, and serve. *—Molly Stevens*

Serves four to six.

3 tablespoons hot pepper jelly

2 tablespoons silver or gold tequila

2 tablespoons orange or pineapple juice

1 teaspoon finely grated orange zest

2 pork tenderloins (1 to 1¼ pounds each), trimmed of excess fat and silverskin and patted dry

Kosher salt and freshly ground black pepper

2 to 3 medium-size, firm-ripe peaches or nectarines, halved and pitted

2 tablespoons extra-virgin olive oil

Pan-Seared Pork Chops with Pear-Ginger Chutney

Serves four.

3 ripe but firm Bosc pears, peeled, cored, and cut into ½-inch dice

1 medium yellow onion, thinly sliced

⅓ cup raisins

3 tablespoons peeled and minced fresh ginger

1 cup packed light brown sugar

1 cup cider vinegar

¼ cup unsalted butter

⅛ teaspoon cayenne

Kosher salt and freshly ground black pepper

4 boneless center-cut pork loin chops, about 1 inch thick

1 tablespoon olive oil

3 tablespoons chopped fresh cilantro

This versatile chutney is easy to make and will keep for a couple weeks in the refrigerator, or freeze it for longer storage. It goes well with poultry as well as pork.

In a large saucepan, combine the pears, onion, raisins, ginger, brown sugar, vinegar, 3 tablespoons of the butter, the cayenne, and ½ teaspoon kosher salt. Bring to a boil, reduce the heat to maintain a lively simmer, and cook until the solids are very tender and the liquid reduces to a juicy, syrupy glaze, 20 to 25 minutes.

When the chutney has been simmering for about 15 minutes, season the chops with salt and pepper. In a 12-inch skillet, heat the remaining 1 tablespoon butter with the oil over medium-high heat until the butter foams and begins to turn a nutty brown. Add the chops and cook until the first side is deeply browned, 3 to 5 minutes. Flip the chops and continue cooking until the second side is well browned and the chops are cooked through, 3 to 5 minutes.

Stir the cilantro into the chutney and season to taste with salt. Serve the chops topped with the chutney. *—Jennifer Armentrout*

Quick-Braised Pork Chops with Escarole, Sun-Dried Tomatoes & Pine Nuts

Finishing the chops in a very low oven makes them very tender. Just be sure not to cook them too far while browning; a quick sear is all you want.

Heat the oven to 250°F. Season the chops well with salt and pepper. Heat the oil and 1 tablespoon of the butter in a large (12-inch) skillet over medium-high heat. Sear the chops, turning once, until browned, about 3 minutes on one side, 2 minutes on the other. Transfer to a plate and set aside.

Reduce the heat to medium low, put the garlic in the pan, and cook, stirring until fragrant, about 15 seconds. (Watch that those nicely browned butter solids, which add flavor to the final dish, don't burn.) Stir in the red pepper flakes. Add about half the escarole and toss with tongs to mix it with the garlic and pepper flakes. Increase the heat to high, add the broth, and cook for a minute so the greens wilt and create more room in the pan. Add the rest of the escarole, toss, and cook for a couple of minutes. Take off the heat.

Return the chops to the skillet, burying them in the escarole. Cover the pan, put it in the oven, and cook for 25 minutes. Remove the pan from the oven and put it on the stove (being mindful of the pan's hot handle).

Transfer the pork chops and most of the escarole (a slotted spoon makes this easy) to a platter. If necessary, boil the liquid in the pan over high heat until there's about ½ cup to concentrate the flavor of the sauce, 4 to 7 minutes, depending on how much liquid the escarole has given off. Add the remaining 1 tablespoon butter to the pan and swirl to blend it. Add the sun-dried tomatoes, then return the escarole to the pan and toss to coat it with the sauce. Arrange the chops on a platter or on individual plates. Spoon the escarole and tomatoes over and around the chops. Sprinkle on the nuts, drizzle a little vinegar over each chop, and serve.

–Joanne McAllister Smart

Serves four.

4 bone-in pork chops, about 8 ounces each, ¾ to 1 inch thick

Kosher salt and freshly ground black pepper

1 tablespoon olive oil

2 tablespoons unsalted butter

1 tablespoon finely chopped garlic

¼ teaspoon red pepper flakes

1 small bunch escarole (about ½ pound), cut crosswise into 1-inch-wide strips, well washed and dried

½ cup low-salt chicken broth

½ cup chopped oil-packed sun-dried tomatoes

¼ cup pine nuts, toasted in a dry skillet until lightly browned

1 tablespoon balsamic vinegar

Roast Rack of Pork with a Cranberry-Walnut Crust & Sauce

Serves eight.

One 8-bone pork rack (about 5 pounds), chine bone removed

Kosher salt and freshly ground black pepper

2 tablespoons vegetable oil

2 tablespoons unsalted butter

1 medium onion, roughly chopped

1 cup ruby Port

½ cup plus 2 tablespoons balsamic vinegar

¾ cup dried cranberries

¾ teaspoon red pepper flakes

Pinch ground allspice

1½ cups walnuts, toasted and chopped medium-coarse

2 tablespoons roughly chopped fresh flat-leaf parsley

3 cups low-salt chicken or beef broth

When you go to buy a rack of pork, be sure to ask the butcher to remove the chine bone so you can easily carve the rack into chops after cooking.

Let the rack of pork sit at room temperature for 30 minutes. Position a rack in the center of the oven and heat the oven to 400°F. Put a roasting rack in a roasting pan or a heavy rimmed baking sheet. (Line the pan with aluminum foil for easier cleanup, if you like.)

Season the pork liberally with salt and pepper on all sides. Turn on the exhaust fan. Heat the oil in a 12-inch skillet over medium-high heat. When the pan is hot, sear the rack of pork until browned on all sides, including the ends, 2 to 3 minutes per side. Transfer the meat to the roasting pan, meaty side up. Set aside to cool while you prepare the crust.

Pour off all the fat in the sauté pan, return the pan to medium-high heat, and add the butter. When it stops bubbling, add the onion and reduce the heat to medium low. Cook the onion, stirring occasionally, until soft and medium brown, 10 to 15 minutes. Add the Port, ½ cup of the vinegar, the cranberries, red pepper flakes, and allspice. Raise the heat to medium high and boil until the liquid has almost completely evaporated, about another 10 minutes. Transfer the cranberry mixture to a food processor and pulse 12 to 15 times to create a slightly chunky paste. Scrape it into a small bowl and fold in the walnuts and parsley. Season with salt and pepper to taste. Reserve 3 tablespoons of the cranberry mixture in a dish to make a sauce later. Pat the remaining cranberry mixture onto the top and sides of the pork rack.

Roast the pork for 30 minutes, then tent a sheet of foil over it for the remaining cooking time to keep the crust from overbrowning. Continue to roast until an instant-read thermometer inserted into the thickest part of the meat reads 140°F, about another 30 minutes.

Meanwhile, in a medium saucepan over medium-high heat, bring the broth to a boil. Add the remaining 2 tablespoons vinegar and boil until the mixture is reduced by half, about 10 minutes. Lower the heat to medium and whisk in the reserved cranberry paste. Season with salt and pepper to taste.

Let the meat rest for 10 minutes (it will continue to cook as it rests) before carving into chops and serving with the sauce. *–Gordon Hamersley*

Mustard, Sage & Maple-Glazed Pork Roast with Garlic-Roasted Potatoes

Serves six.

For the glaze:

1 tablespoon olive oil

1 medium-small yellow onion (6 ounces), cut into medium dice (to yield 1 cup)

4 cloves garlic, coarsely chopped

⅓ cup coarsely chopped fresh sage (about 1½ bunches)

½ cup Dijon mustard

½ cup pure maple syrup

1 tablespoon soy sauce

¼ teaspoon kosher salt

Pinch freshly ground black pepper

For the pork:

One 6-bone center-cut pork roast (about 5½ pounds), chine bone removed

Kosher salt and freshly ground black pepper

For the potatoes:

2 pounds medium red or yellow potatoes, rinsed (you can use a combination, but they may cook at slightly different rates)

1 head garlic, cloves peeled

3 tablespoons olive oil

Kosher salt and freshly ground black pepper

¼ cup unsalted butter, cut into small pieces

1 tablespoon chopped fresh flat-leaf parsley

When ordering the pork, be sure to have the chine bone removed, so you'll be able to slice the roast between the rib bones. But since most people love to chew the crusted meat and crackling pork fat off the rib bones, don't have them scraped clean (butchers call this frenching).

Make the glaze: Heat the oil in a medium sauté pan over medium heat. Add the onion and garlic and cook, stirring frequently, until softened, about 5 minutes. Cool to room temperature, then purée the onion and garlic with all of the remaining ingredients in a blender or food processor until somewhat smooth. Keep covered in the refrigerator until ready to use on the pork roast.

Prepare the pork and potatoes: Position racks in the center and bottom of the oven and heat the oven to 425°F.

Let the roast sit at room temperature while the oven heats. Season the meat generously with salt and pepper. Put the pork in a small roasting pan, bone side down, and roast on the center oven rack to an internal temperature of 115°F, 50 to 60 minutes. Remove the roast from the oven and let it rest for 20 minutes. (This rest will give the juiciest results.)

Meanwhile, shortly before the pork hits 115°F, cut the potatoes lengthwise into wedges 1½ to 1¾ inches wide at their thickest part. In a medium bowl, toss them with the garlic cloves, olive oil, 1 teaspoon kosher salt, and several grinds of pepper. Arrange in a roasting pan or rimmed baking sheet, one cut side down, evenly spaced. Sprinkle with the pieces of butter. When you take the roast out of the oven, put the potatoes on the bottom rack and reduce the oven temperature to 350°F.

After 20 minutes of resting, cover the roast evenly with the mustard glaze and return it to the center oven rack. At this time, turn the potatoes with a metal spatula onto their other cut side. Roast the pork until the internal temperature is 140°F. Roast the potatoes until golden and crisp on the outside and fork-tender inside. Both should take about 30 minutes (check the potatoes at 20 minutes and, if necessary for even browning, flip them back to their other cut side.) Transfer the roast to a carving board, tent with aluminum foil, and let rest for at least 20 minutes before carving. Set the potatoes aside in a warm place, uncovered (so they stay crisp and don't steam), until ready to serve.

To serve: Slice the roast between the bones into individual chops. Toss the potatoes with the chopped parsley. Arrange the meat and potatoes on a platter. *—Ris Lacoste*

Pork Stew with Green Chiles, Orange & Cilantro

This stew freezes well, so make a double batch (in two pots) and put some away for next month. Serve the stew over steamed, crushed new potatoes, rice, or polenta. Or serve with a big chunk of cornbread or a stack of warmed tortillas for dunking.

Toss the chunks of pork with the salt. Heat 1 tablespoon of the oil in a large Dutch oven or heavy stew pot; when it's very hot, add about half the pork or however much will fit in one layer. Lower the heat to medium and cook until well browned on all sides, 8 to 10 minutes. Take care not to burn the layer of cooked-on juices that will form in the bottom of the pan. Transfer the pork to a bowl, add more oil if needed, and brown the remaining pork in the same way. Transfer to the bowl.

While the pork is browning, cut about a 4x1-inch strip of zest from one of the oranges. Juice all the oranges, to get about 1 cup.

Pour off any oil in the pot, then add the water and dissolve the cooked-on juices. Pour out the liquid and reserve it to use in the stew (unless the juices seemed burned; if so, just discard it).

Wipe out the pan, heat it to medium high, and add 2 tablespoons oil. Add the onion and cook, stirring frequently, until soft and light golden, about 8 minutes. Add the garlic, cumin, coriander, and chile powder and stir for a few seconds. Add the flour, stir constantly for about 1 minute to cook off the raw floury taste, then add the orange juice, broth, and reserved dissolved pan juices. Stir to blend, bring to a boil, add the pork chunks, and immediately turn down the heat to a low simmer. Add the orange zest, cilantro stems, and bay leaf. Cover the pot and gently simmer for about 1 hour.

Add the tomatillos, tomatoes, and green chiles and continue to simmer until the pork is completely tender (tasting a piece is the best test), another 30 to 60 minutes.

Remove the meat and vegetables with a slotted spoon to a bowl; discard the bay leaf and zest. Spoon off any visible fat from the sauce. Increase the heat so the sauce boils gently and reduces in volume by about a third, 8 to 10 minutes. It should be very flavorful and have a nice coating consistency. Return everything to the pot, add the chopped cilantro, taste for seasoning, and serve sprinkled with more cilantro, if you like. *—Martha Holmberg*

Serves six.

- 3 pounds boneless pork shoulder, preferably pork butt, or boneless pork butt country ribs, trimmed of any big pieces of fat and cut into 1-inch cubes
- 2 teaspoon kosher salt
- ¼ cup olive oil
- 2 to 3 medium navel or juice oranges
- ½ cup water
- 1 large onion, thinly sliced
- 1 tablespoon chopped garlic
- 1 tablespoon ground cumin
- 1 teaspoon ground coriander
- ¼ teaspoon chipotle chile powder or other hot chile powder; more to taste
- 2 tablespoons all-purpose flour
- 2 cups low-salt chicken broth
- 8 cilantro stems
- 1 bay leaf
- 1 cup roughly chopped fresh or canned tomatillos
- 1 cup roughly chopped fresh or canned tomatoes
- One 4-ounce can whole green chiles, roughly chopped
- ½ cup chopped fresh cilantro leaves; more for serving

Spicy-Smoky Mexican Pork Kebabs

Serves six.

For the marinade:

1 dried hot red chile, stemmed and seeded

1 tablespoon grated lime zest

2 tablespoons fresh lime juice

½ cup diced yellow onion

½ cup fresh orange juice

¼ cup chopped fresh cilantro

1 teaspoon dried oregano

1 teaspoon ground cumin

1 teaspoon light brown sugar

1 tablespoon chopped canned chipotle in adobo

1 teaspoon minced garlic

2 teaspoons kosher salt

¼ cup vegetable oil

For the kebabs:

2 pork tenderloins (1 to 1¼ pounds each), trimmed of fat and silverskin, halved lengthwise, and sliced into 1½-inch-thick half-rounds

1 red onion, cut into 1-inch pieces

2 fresh poblano chiles, cored, seeded, and cut into 1-inch squares

16 medium radishes, trimmed

16 scallions, root ends trimmed

¼ cup vegetable oil

Kosher salt and freshly ground black pepper

These kebabs are great with grilled butternut squash, though the spicy pork and poblano combination also makes a natural filling for warm tortillas.

Make the marinade: Soak the red chile in very hot water to cover until softened, about 15 minutes. Drain and put the chile in a blender, along with all the remaining marinade ingredients. Blend until smooth. Set aside ½ cup of the marinade for basting. Put the remaining marinade and the pork in a large zip-top bag, seal, and massage the contents to coat. Marinate for 1 to 2 hours in the refrigerator. Remove the pork; discard the marinade.

Make the kebabs: Thread the meat onto skewers, alternating with the onion, the poblano pieces, and the whole radishes.

Build a medium-hot charcoal fire or heat a gas grill to medium high and oil the grill grate. Grill the kebabs (uncovered for charcoal; covered for gas), turning every 2 to 3 minutes. Once the pork loses its raw look, baste with the reserved marinade each time you turn the skewers. Grill until the pork is firm to the touch and the edges have begun to brown and the vegetables have begun to color and soften, about 15 minutes. Mound the skewers on a warm platter; tent with aluminum foil to keep warm. Brush the scallions with oil and sprinkle with salt and pepper. Grill until they begin to brown and soften, turning frequently, 3 to 5 minutes.

To serve: Remove the meat and vegetables from their skewers, mound them on the platter and arrange the scallions around the edges.

—Bruce Aidells

Grill Butternut Squash to Serve on the Side

Bring a large pot of water to a boil. Peel a medium butternut squash and scoop out the seeds; cut into 1-inch pieces. Boil the squash until tender but still firm, about 10 minutes. Drain and cool under cold water. Toss with olive oil and season with salt and pepper. Thread the squash onto skewers and set aside. After you've grilled the pork, grill the squash skewers, basting with the reserved marinade, until browned and tender, 5 to 7 minutes.

7 Fish & Shellfish

p248

p245

Sear-Roasted Salmon with Lemon-Rosemary Butter Sauce (recipe on page 252)

Baked Shrimp with Fennel & Feta

Serves four.

¼ cup extra-virgin olive oil

1½ cups ½-inch diced fennel bulb

2 cloves garlic, minced

¼ cup dry white wine

One 14.5-ounce can diced tomatoes, with their juices

Kosher salt and freshly ground black pepper

½ cup fresh breadcrumbs

3 tablespoons chopped fresh flat-leaf parsley

¼ pound feta cheese, crumbled

1¼ to 1½ pounds large shrimp (21–25 count), peeled and deveined

To give this zesty dish a more complex flavor, use the best Greek, French, or Bulgarian feta cheese you can find. Serve on top of rice or orzo.

Position a rack in the center of the oven and heat the oven to 425°F. In a 12-inch ovenproof skillet, heat 2 tablespoons of the olive oil over medium heat. Add the fennel and cook, stirring occasionally, until slightly softened and lightly browned, 7 to 8 minutes. Add the garlic and sauté until fragrant, 1 minute. Add the wine and bring to a boil. Add the tomatoes and their juices, season with salt and pepper, and stir to heat through. Using a wooden spoon or spatula, spread the tomato mixture into an even layer in the skillet.

In a small bowl, stir the breadcrumbs, parsley, feta, the remaining 2 tablespoons olive oil, and salt (about ½ teaspoon, depending on the saltiness of the feta) and pepper to taste. Arrange the shrimp in a single layer on the tomato mixture and sprinkle with the breadcrumb mixture. Bake until the shrimp are cooked through and the cheese is melted, 12 to 15 minutes.

—Molly Stevens

Shrimp & Asparagus with Cheddar Grits

Old-fashioned grits, made from ground hominy or corn, have a coarser texture than the quick-cooking variety. If you can't find them, you can substitute coarse-ground cornmeal, such as polenta.

Melt ½ tablespoon of the butter in a medium saucepan over medium heat. Add the garlic and cook until fragrant, 30 to 60 seconds. Add the broth and bring to a boil. While stirring constantly, pour in the grits and ¼ teaspoon kosher salt. Reduce the heat to low, cover, and cook, stirring occasionally, until the grits are thickened, 15 to 20 minutes. Stir in the Cheddar and ¼ teaspoon of the hot sauce. Season to taste with salt, pepper, and more hot sauce. Cover and set aside in a warm spot.

Melt 1 tablespoon of the butter in a 12-inch skillet over medium high heat. Add the asparagus, sprinkle with a little salt, and cook, stirring frequently, until crisp-tender and a little browned, 3 to 4 minutes. Add the shrimp and cook until it's opaque and the asparagus is tender, 2 to 3 minutes. Reduce the heat to low and add the Worcestershire and the remaining ¼ teaspoon hot sauce. Melt the remaining 2½ tablespoons butter into the shrimp and asparagus. Season to taste with salt, pepper, and more hot sauce. Serve the shrimp and asparagus over the grits, sprinkled with the scallions. –*Jennifer Armentrout*

Serves two to three.

¼ cup unsalted butter

1 clove garlic, minced

2⅓ cups low-salt chicken broth

½ cup old-fashioned (not quick-cooking) grits

Kosher salt and freshly ground black pepper

½ cup grated extra-sharp Cheddar cheese

½ teaspoon Tabasco or other hot sauce; more to taste

½ pound medium-thick asparagus, bottoms trimmed, spears sliced on the diagonal into 1-inch pieces

1 pound large shrimp (21–25 count), peeled and deveined

2 tablespoons Worcestershire sauce

1 to 2 scallions (green parts only), thinly sliced

Spicy Thai Shrimp Kebabs with Chile-Lemongrass Dipping Sauce

Serves four.

For the grilling sauce:

1 tablespoon chopped garlic

1 tablespoon peeled and chopped fresh ginger

1 teaspoon finely chopped jalapeño

1 tablespoon chopped scallion greens

1 teaspoon kosher salt

¼ cup peanut oil

For the dipping sauce:

3 stalks lemongrass, ends trimmed, tough outer leaves removed, and tender white core finely chopped

3 tablespoons fresh lime juice

2 tablespoons finely sliced scallion whites

1 tablespoon Asian fish sauce

1 tablespoon chopped fresh cilantro

1 tablespoon chopped fresh basil

1½ teaspoons soy sauce

1 teaspoon minced garlic

1 teaspoon light brown sugar

2 teaspoons Sriracha chile sauce; more to taste

3 tablespoons water

For the kebabs:

1½ pounds large shrimp (21-25 count), peeled and deveined

4 Japanese or Chinese eggplant, peeled and cut into ¾-inch-thick rounds

Because shrimp cooks so quickly, it's the lone element on the skewer. Tender Japanese or Chinese eggplant, also grilled on its own skewers, is the perfect accompaniment.

Combine all the grilling sauce ingredients in a food processor and process until well combined; the mixture will still be chunky.

In a small serving bowl, combine all the dipping sauce ingredients; stir well. (Both sauces can be made up to 6 hours ahead and refrigerated.)

Thread the shrimp onto flat or parallel skewers so the skewers are perpendicular to the length of the shrimp. (The double skewers should help to keep the shrimp from spinning when you turn the kebabs on the grill.)

Thread the eggplant pieces onto skewers so that the skewer is parallel to the cut surface of the eggplant. (Use two parallel skewers to prevent the eggplant slices from twirling when you turn them).

Build a medium-hot charcoal fire or heat a gas grill to medium high. Oil the grill grate. Brush the grilling sauce all over the shrimp and eggplant skewers. Grill the shrimp skewers (uncovered on a charcoal grill; covered on a gas grill) until just cooked through, about 2 minutes per side. Grill the eggplant skewers until soft and nicely browned, 2 to 4 minutes per side. If they begin to burn before softening, transfer to a cooler part of the grill (if using gas, lower the heat a bit).

Remove the shrimp and eggplant from the skewers and arrange on a platter. Drizzle with 2 tablespoons of the dipping sauce and serve with the remaining dipping sauce on the side. (For the sauce, use one communal bowl or individual condiment bowls). *—Bruce Aidells*

Indian-Spiced Shrimp

Serves four.

2 tablespoons coriander seeds

2 teaspoons cumin seeds

¼ to ½ teaspoon red pepper flakes

½ cup unsweetened coconut milk

3 tablespoons minced garlic

3 tablespoons peeled and minced fresh ginger

1½ pounds large shrimp (21-25 count), peeled and deveined

2 tablespoons canola or vegetable oil

¼ cup chopped fresh cilantro

2 tablespoons fresh lime juice; plus 4 lime wedges for serving

Kosher salt and freshly ground black pepper

You can prepare the marinade up to a day in advance. When you're ready to cook, toss in the shrimp and allow them to marinate while you prepare a side dish, such as a basmati rice pilaf.

Heat a small, heavy sauté pan over medium high heat until hot. Add the coriander seeds, cumin seeds, and red pepper flakes and cook, shaking the pan constantly, until the spices are very fragrant, 30 to 60 seconds. Transfer to a plate, then grind to a fine powder in a spice grinder.

In a medium bowl, combine the coconut milk, garlic, ginger, shrimp, and spice powder and marinate in the refrigerator for at least 10 and up to 30 minutes.

In a 12-inch nonstick skillet, heat the oil over medium high heat. Add the shrimp and marinade and cook, stirring and shaking the pan, until the shrimp are pink and cooked through, 3 to 5 minutes, adding 1 tablespoon water at a time if necessary to keep the marinade from scorching. Remove from the heat and stir in the cilantro and lime juice. Season with salt and pepper and serve garnished with the lime wedges. *–Kate Hays*

Buy Frozen Shrimp for the Freshest Flavor

Because most shrimp are frozen soon after being caught, you're better off buying shrimp that are still frozen instead of shrimp that have been thawed at the market for your convenience. Shrimp are highly perishable, and you don't really know how long the thawed stuff has been thawed. If you buy frozen shrimp, you can thaw it yourself just before you need it. Let it thaw overnight in the fridge or, for faster thawing, take the shrimp out of its package, put it in a bowl of cold water, and let a trickle of cold water run into the bowl while excess water goes down the drain. The shrimp should be ready to cook in about 15 minutes.

Lemon Barley "Risotto" with Shrimp, Bacon & Spinach

Quick-cooking barley is simply pearl barley that has been presteamed to shorten its cooking time. It cooks up less creamy and a bit chewier than traditional risotto rices, such as arborio and carnaroli.

Cook the bacon in a 12-inch skillet over medium high heat until browned and crisp. Drain on paper towels and crumble into small pieces.

Increase the heat under the skillet to medium high. Sprinkle the shrimp with ¼ teaspoon salt and a few grinds pepper. Working in two batches to avoid crowding, cook the shrimp in the bacon fat until lightly browned and opaque, 1½ to 2 minutes per side. Transfer to a plate.

Add the shallot to the skillet and cook until softened, about 1 minute. Add the barley and stir until coated with the fat, about 30 seconds. Add the lemon juice and cook, stirring, for 15 seconds. Pour in the broth and bring to a boil, scraping up any browned bits in the pan. Reduce the heat to medium low, cover, and simmer until the barley is tender, 12 minutes. Uncover the pan, raise the heat to medium high, and cook, stirring occasionally, until most of the liquid has evaporated, 1 to 2 minutes. Stir in the spinach and cook until wilted, 1 minute. Stir in the bacon, shrimp, Pecorino, and lemon zest and heat through, 1 to 2 minutes. Season to taste with salt and pepper and serve immediately. *–David Bonom*

Serves four.

6 slices bacon

1 pound large shrimp (21-25 count), peeled and deveined

Kosher salt and freshly ground black pepper

½ cup chopped shallot or onion

1⅓ cups quick-cooking barley

1 tablespoon fresh lemon juice

2½ cups low-salt chicken broth

¼ pound baby spinach, washed and spun dry

⅓ cup freshly grated Pecorino Romano cheese

1 tablespoon finely grated lemon zest

Spicy Clams & Sausage in Marinara

Serves four to six.

4 dozen hard-shell clams, about 2 inches wide (littlenecks are good)

2 tablespoons olive oil; more for the bread

8 large cloves garlic, minced; plus 1 clove, halved, for the bread

¼ teaspoon red pepper flakes

2 teaspoons fennel seeds

¼ pound hot Italian sausage (casings removed), broken into pieces

¾ cup dry white wine

2 cups homemade or good-quality jarred marinara sauce

Eight ½-inch-thick slices French or Italian bread

3 tablespoons minced fresh flat-leaf parsley

Briny clams and spicy sausage make a great match. Because they flavor the marinara so exquisitely, this recipe doesn't give you the option of serving bread to mop up the sauce; instead it calls for toasted garlic bread as an integral part of the dish.

Cover the clams with cold water and use a stiff brush to scrub the shells; discard any clams that are open and won't close when thumped against another clam. Lift the them out of the water, discard the water, and repeat washing two or three times, until no sand remains in the water.

Heat the oil in a 5-quart pot over medium low heat. Add the minced garlic, red pepper flakes, and fennel seeds, and cook, stirring often, until the garlic is translucent, about 5 minutes. Increase the heat to medium; add the sausage and cook until the outside is no longer pink, about 2 minutes. Increase the heat to medium high, pour in the wine, and boil until reduced to about 3 tablespoons, about 7 minutes. Stir in the marinara and bring to a quick boil. Put the clams in the pan, cover, and cook until they've opened, about 5 minutes; check often to avoid overcooking.

Meanwhile, toast the bread. Rub each toasted slice with the cut side of the garlic clove and brush with olive oil.

Serve the clams in wide bowls with the parsley sprinkled on top and the toast tucked into the sides.—*Nancy Verde Barr*

Steamed Mussels with Lime & Cilantro

A bowl of steamed mussels looks impressive, but it's ridiculously easy to prepare. A little cream and some hot chiles and lime juice transform the broth into a delicious sauce for crusty bread or jasmine rice.

Rinse the mussels in a colander under cold water, scrub the shells thoroughly, remove the tough, wiry beards, and discard any mussels with broken or gaping shells. While they drain, heat the oil in a large, wide pot over medium high heat. Add the carrot and jalapeño and cook, stirring occasionally, until softened and light brown, about 2 minutes. Add the garlic and ½ teaspoon of the lime zest, and sauté until fragrant, 30 seconds. Pour in the wine and raise the heat to high. As soon as the wine boils, add the mussels and cover the pot. Steam the mussels, shaking the pot once or twice, until the shells open, 5 to 6 minutes.

Remove the pot from the heat. With a slotted spoon, transfer the mussels to a large bowl and keep warm. Return the pot to the heat, add the cream, and boil until the sauce reduces just a bit, 2 to 3 minutes. Add 1½ tablespoons of the lime juice, the cilantro, and chile sauce, if using. Taste and add more lime juice and salt if needed. Ladle the mussels into wide, shallow bowls, pour some of the sauce over each portion, and serve immediately. *–Molly Stevens*

Serves four as a main course; eight as an appetizer.

- 4 pounds mussels
- 2 tablespoons extra-virgin olive oil
- 1 medium carrot, peeled and cut into small dice
- 1 large jalapeño, seeded and minced
- 2 cloves garlic, minced
- Finely grated zest and juice of 1 lime
- ½ cup dry white wine or white vermouth
- ½ cup heavy cream
- ⅓ cup loosely packed fresh cilantro leaves and tender stems, coarsely chopped
- ½ to 1 teaspoon Asian chile sauce, such as sriracha, or other hot sauce (optional)
- Kosher salt

Steamed Mussels with Wine, Garlic & Parsley

Serves six to eight.

3½ to 4 pounds mussels

2 tablespoons extra-virgin olive oil

1 tablespoon unsalted butter

6 medium cloves garlic, finely chopped

4 shallots, thinly sliced

¼ teaspoon red pepper flakes

1½ cups dry white wine, such as Sauvignon Blanc or any other crisp, herbal white wine

¾ cup chopped fresh flat-leaf parsley

Good-quality crusty bread, sliced or torn into pieces, for serving

Wine, garlic, and red pepper flakes create an aromatic broth for steaming mussels. During cooking, the shellfish become infused with the flavors of the liquid, while imparting their own briny character to it at the same time.

Rinse the mussels well under cold water. Pick them over, pulling off any beards and discarding any mussels that are broken or gaping open.

In a large pot with a lid, heat the oil and butter over medium heat. Add the garlic, shallots, and red pepper flakes and cook until fragrant and soft but not colored, 3 to 5 minutes. Add the mussels, wine, and half the parsley. Increase the heat to high and cover the pan. After 2 minutes, remove the lid and toss the mussels well with a large spoon. Cover the pot again and cook until the mussels have opened wide, 3 to 4 minutes longer. Add the remaining parsley, give the mussels a final toss, and portion them and the broth into bowls. Serve the bread alongside. —*Joanne McAllister Smart*

Handling Hard-shell Clams & Mussels

Spotting the good ones

At the fish counter, use your eyes and your nose to guide you. Fresh hard-shell clams and mussels should look tightly closed or just slightly gaping open. If they're yawning wide, they're dead or close to it. Once you have them in hand, take a sniff. They should smell like the sea. If they're really fishy smelling, don't buy them.

Keeping them fresh

Shellfish will suffocate in plastic, so take them out of the bag as soon as you get home, put them in a bowl, cover with a wet towel, and refrigerate. It's best to cook them as soon as possible, but if they were fresh to begin with, they should keep stored this way for up to two days.

Cleaning them up

Just before cooking, look for any shellfish that have opened and tap them on the counter. If they don't close, discard them. Check closed mussels by pressing on the two shells in opposing directions. Dead ones will fall apart. Once you've weeded out the bad ones, scrub the remaining shellfish under cold running water with a stiff brush to get rid of any grit. If the mussels have "beards"—black hairy fibers sticking out of their shells—pinch them and yank them off.

Seared Scallops

Serves two to three.

1 pound dry large sea scallops

Ingredients for 1 sauce recipe (recipes follow)

2 tablespoons extra-virgin olive oil, peanut oil, or a mix of oil and unsalted butter (see the sauce recipes for recommendations)

Kosher salt and freshly ground black pepper

Classic Herb Butter Sauce

Yields enough for 1 pound seared scallops.

3 tablespoons unsalted butter, cut into 6 pieces

2 tablespoons finely diced shallot

¼ cup dry white vermouth or dry white wine

¼ cup finely chopped mixed fresh herbs, such as flat-leaf parsley and chives

¼ teaspoon finely grated lemon zest

Kosher salt and freshly ground black pepper

2 to 3 lemon wedges for serving

When searing the scallops, use 1 tablespoon each extra-virgin olive oil and unsalted butter. When the scallops have been transferred to a plate and the pan has cooled somewhat, return the pan to medium heat. Add a piece of the butter (½ tablespoon) and the shallot and sauté until it begins to soften, about 1 minute. Add the vermouth and simmer until reduced by about half, another 1 to 2 minutes. Add the herbs and lemon zest. Reduce the heat to low, add the remaining butter, and whisk constantly until the butter melts into the sauce. Return the scallops and any accumulated juices to the pan and gently roll them in the sauce to warm them through. Taste for salt and pepper and serve immediately with lemon wedges on the side to squeeze over the scallops

It's important that the scallops are absolutely dry before searing. If not, they will steam instead of sear, and you won't get the sweet, caramelized crust that makes seared scallops so enticing.

Wash the scallops and dry them well. Remove any patches of tough muscle from the sides. Prepare the ingredients for the sauce. Heat a 10- or 12-inch nonstick skillet over medium high heat for 1 to 2 minutes. Add the oil and butter, if using, and heat until quite hot. Pat the scallops dry once more and put them in the pan in a single, uncrowded layer. Season with salt and pepper and let sear undisturbed until one side is browned and crisp, 2 to 4 minutes. Using tongs, turn the scallops and sear until the second side is well browned and the scallops are almost firm to the touch, 2 to 4 minutes. Take the pan off the heat, transfer the scallops to a plate, and set them in a warm spot. Let the pan cool for a minute before you make the sauce. *–Molly Stevens*

Spicy Red Pepper & Cilantro Sauce

Yields enough for 1 pound seared scallops.

This is not so much a sauce as a flavorful coating; you'll have just enough liquid to moisten the scallops as you roll them around in the pan.

2 tablespoons extra-virgin olive oil

1 tablespoon minced garlic

1 serrano chile or small jalapeño, cored, seeded, and minced

½ small red bell pepper, cored, seeded, and finely diced

1 tablespoon fresh lime juice

2 heaping tablespoons coarsely chopped fresh cilantro

Kosher salt and freshly ground black pepper

When searing the scallops, use 2 tablespoons extra-virgin olive oil. Once the scallops have been transferred to a plate and the pan has cooled somewhat, return the pan to medium heat. Add the oil, garlic, and chile and sauté until fragrant, about 30 seconds. Add the bell pepper and cook, stirring often, until the pepper is barely soft, about 1 minute. Add the lime juice and simmer to reduce slightly, 30 to 60 seconds. Stir in the cilantro. Reduce the heat to low and return the scallops and any accumulated juices to the pan. Gently roll them around to coat in the sauce and to warm through. Taste for salt and pepper and serve immediately.

Dry Scallops Well to Ensure a Golden Crust

If you feel any grit on the scallops, rinse them under cold running water. Remove patches of tough muscle from the sides. Pat the scallops dry with paper towels; surface moisture impedes browning.

For a deeply golden sear, use medium high heat and don't crowd the pan. To avoid tearing the scallops while turning them, use a nonstick skillet and handle them gently.

Grilled Salmon with Wasabi-Ginger Mayonnaise

Serves four.

1½ limes

½ cup mayonnaise

1½ tablespoons wasabi paste; more to taste

2 teaspoons finely grated fresh ginger

Kosher salt and freshly ground black pepper

Four 6-ounce skinless salmon fillets

Vegetable oil for the grill

If you can't find wasabi paste, you can use the same amount of wasabi powder. Just add an equal amount of water to the powder to form a paste. Then let it sit for a few minutes to allow the flavor to develop. You can find wasabi paste and powder at Asian groceries, or try the Asian section of your supermarket.

Prepare a medium-hot grill fire. Be sure the grill grate has been scrubbed clean with a wire brush.

Cut the half lime into four wedges and set aside. Finely grate the zest from the whole lime. Cut the zested lime in half and squeeze the juice from one half into a small bowl (save the other half for another use). In a medium bowl, combine 1 teaspoon of the lime juice with the lime zest, mayonnaise, wasabi paste, ginger, and ¼ teaspoon kosher salt. Stir to combine. Taste and add more wasabi paste if you'd like a zippier flavor.

Run your finger along each salmon fillet to feel for tiny bones; use tweezers or needlenose pliers to pull out any you find. Season the fillets lightly with salt and pepper. Spoon about 2 tablespoons of the mayonnaise mixture onto the salmon fillets and refrigerate the rest. With your hands, spread it in a thin layer over all sides of the fillets.

When the grill is ready, oil the grill grate using tongs and a paper towel dipped in oil. Grill the salmon until crisp and slightly charred on one side, about 4 minutes. Turn and continue to grill until it is just cooked through, another 3 to 6 minutes. Serve the salmon topped with a dollop of the mayonnaise and a lime wedge on the side. Pass the remaining mayonnaise at the table.
—*Molly Stevens*

Asian-Style Glazed Salmon with Roasted Mushroom Salad

Tamari is similar to soy sauce except thicker and mellower in flavor. Mirin is a sweet rice wine. Both can be found at Asian markets or on the international foods aisle at some grocery stores. You can serve this dish alongside jasmine rice.

Position a rack in the center of the oven and heat the oven to 400°F. In a large bowl, toss the mushrooms with 1 tablespoon of the sesame oil. Arrange the mushrooms in a single layer on a rimmed baking sheet and roast until softened, 10 to 15 minutes. When cool enough to handle, slice them ¼ inch thick and return them to the bowl.

Meanwhile, in a small bowl, whisk the remaining ½ tablespoon sesame oil with the tamari, mirin, rice vinegar, and ginger. Set aside ⅓ cup of this mixture and transfer the rest to a small saucepan. Bring to a boil. Add the cornstarch slurry and cook, stirring, until thickened, about 30 seconds. Remove from the heat.

Line a 9x13-inch baking dish with aluminum foil. Arrange the salmon in the dish, skin side down and evenly spaced. Using a pastry brush, thickly dab the tops and sides of the salmon with the warm glaze. Use all the glaze and don't worry if some of it slides off of the fish. Bake until the salmon is cooked to your liking, about 10 minutes for medium rare, 12 minutes to medium, 14 minutes for medium well. (Cut into the thickest part of a fillet to check.)

While the salmon cooks, add the red pepper, scallions, and reserved soy mixture to the mushrooms. Toss to combine and season to taste with pepper.

Drizzle the fish with any glaze that has pooled in the baking dish and serve topped with the mushroom salad. *—Kate Hays*

Serves four.

1 pound fresh shiitake or a mix of shiitakes and oyster mushrooms, stemmed

1½ tablespoons Asian sesame oil

⅓ cup tamari or good-quality soy sauce

⅓ cup mirin

¼ cup rice vinegar

1 tablespoon peeled and finely grated fresh ginger (use a rasp-style or ginger grater)

1½ teaspoons cornstarch combined with 1½ teaspoons water

1½ pounds salmon fillet, preferably center cut, pin bones removed; cut into 4 portions

½ cup finely diced red bell pepper

½ cup thinly sliced scallions (white and green parts)

Freshly ground black pepper

Sear-Roasted Salmon with Lemon-Rosemary Butter Sauce

Serves four.

4 skinless salmon fillets (about 1½ pounds total)

Kosher salt and freshly ground black pepper

2 tablespoons olive, canola, or peanut oil

Lemon-Rosemary Butter Sauce (recipe follows)

Lemon-Rosemary Butter Sauce

Yields about ½ cup.

The big flavor brought on by searing the salmon, coupled with the richness of the butter sauce, means this dish can handle a dry rosé or light red, like a Pinot Noir.

¾ cup dry white wine

3 tablespoons finely diced shallot

1 teaspoon chopped fresh rosemary

6 tablespoons unsalted butter, cut into small cubes

1 teaspoon fresh lemon juice

Kosher salt and freshly ground black pepper

After sear-roasting the salmon, pour off any excess fat from the skillet. Using a large wad of paper towels, blot any remaining oil from the pan but leave any browned bits. Return the pan to high heat and add the wine, shallot, and rosemary. Cook, stirring, until the wine is almost completely evaporated, 3 to 4 minutes. Remove from the heat and whisk in the cubes of butter, adding a few at a time until they're all thoroughly incorporated and the sauce is thick and creamy looking. (If the butter is slow to melt, set the pan over low heat.) Stir in the lemon juice, season with salt and pepper to taste, and serve immediately, spooned over the sear-roasted salmon.

Be sure that the oven has reached 425°F before starting to sear—most ovens take 20 to 30 minutes to heat up thoroughly.

Heat the oven to 425°F. Turn the exhaust fan on to high. Pat the fish dry thoroughly with paper towels. Season both sides generously with salt and pepper (about 1 teaspoon of each total). Heat a 12-inch heavy ovenproof skillet over medium high heat until a droplet of water vaporizes in 1 or 2 seconds. (If the water skitters around and doesn't evaporate, the pan is too hot; take it off the heat for about 30 seconds to cool.)

Add the oil, swirl it around the pan, then evenly space the salmon fillets in the pan. Cook without touching for 2 minutes. Using a metal spatula, lift a corner of the fish, check that it's well browned and easily releases from the pan, and flip it over. (If it sticks or isn't well browned, cook for 1 to 2 more minutes before flipping.) Cook the second side for 1 minute, then transfer the skillet to the oven.

Roast until the salmon is slightly firm to the touch (for medium) and registers 135°F on an instant-read thermometer; this should take 4 to 7 minutes. Using potholders, carefully remove the pan from the oven, transfer the salmon to a large plate (don't wash the skillet), tent with aluminum foil, and let it rest while you prepare the sauce. —*Tony Rosenfeld*

Grilled Salmon with Fresh Tomatoes, Herbs & Olives

Serves four.

3 tablespoons extra-virgin olive oil

3 large cloves garlic, lightly smashed and peeled

3 tablespoons chopped mixed fresh herbs (a nice mix is equal parts oregano, rosemary, and thyme)

1 cup coarsely chopped pitted Gaeta or Kalamata olives

1½ pounds cherry tomatoes, halved

Kosher salt and freshly ground black pepper

Four 5- to 8-ounce salmon steaks or fillets

Olive oil

This bright, garlicky sauce is also excellent with fresh tuna. Or, instead of fresh, use drained, oil-packed canned tuna and toss with fusilli, gemelli, or any other short, sturdy pasta.

In a 10- or 11-inch sauté pan, heat the extra-virgin olive oil and garlic together over medium low to medium heat, stirring occasionally, until the garlic infuses the oil but doesn't brown, 3 to 5 minutes. Using a fork, fish out and discard the garlic. Sprinkle in the herbs and olives and raise the heat to medium. Stir to combine and sauté for about a minute. Add the tomatoes, ½ teaspoon kosher salt, and pepper to taste. Simmer, stirring occasionally and adjusting the heat to maintain a lively but not too vigorous simmer, until the tomatoes have been reduced to a thick, pulpy sauce, 15 to 20 minutes.

Prepare a medium-hot grill fire. Rub the salmon with olive oil to coat, then season generously with salt and pepper. Grill until nicely browned on both sides and the flesh is just lightly translucent in the center, 3 to 4 minutes on each side. (Tip: To prevent the salmon from sticking to the grill grate, don't move it for the first 2 minutes.)

Arrange the salmon on plates; if you like, remove the center bones by wiggling and prying them out with a paring knife. Spoon the tomato sauce on top. *—Domenica Marchetti*

Lemony Sole with Capers & Croutons in Brown Butter Sauce

Serves two.

4½ tablespoons unsalted butter

1 slice white bread, cut into ¼-inch cubes

Kosher salt and freshly ground black pepper

1½ medium lemons

4 sole fillets (2 to 3 ounces each)

Unbleached all-purpose flour for dredging

2 tablespoons corn, canola, or vegetable oil

2 tablespoons capers, rinsed and drained

1 tablespoon chopped fresh flat-leaf parsley

Browned butter, lemons, and capers make a quick and flavorful pan sauce for this mild fish. Partner it with an herbed rice pilaf.

Heat the oven to 200°F. Melt 1½ tablespoons of the butter in a 10- to 12-inch nonstick skillet over medium heat. Add the bread cubes, stirring and tossing almost constantly with a wooden spoon, until golden brown and crisp, 3 to 5 minutes. Drain on paper towels and sprinkle with salt. Wipe out the skillet.

Segment the whole lemon. Cut each segment into four pieces. Transfer to a small bowl and add 1 tablespoon juice squeezed from the lemon half.

Season the sole fillets lightly on each side with salt and pepper and dredge the fillets in the flour, shaking off any excess. Heat the oil in the nonstick skillet over medium high heat. Working in batches to avoid crowding the pan, cook the fillets until the first side is light golden, about 2 minutes. Using two spatulas to support the delicate fish, flip them and cook until the second side is light golden and the fillets are opaque, another 2 minutes. Transfer to two dinner plates and keep warm in the oven.

Wipe out the skillet with a paper towel and add the remaining 3 tablespoons butter. Over medium high heat, melt the butter and cook, swirling the pan until the butter turns a medium brown, about 2 minutes. Immediately remove from the heat and add the lemon segments and lemon juice, the capers, and parsley; season to taste with salt and pepper. Drizzle the sauce over the fish and sprinkle on the croutons. *—Arlene Jacobs*

Adding Zing with Capers

Capers are especially good with fish and other foods that tend to be oily or rich. In addition to this fish recipe, try adding them to a vinaigrette, or toss a small handful into a pasta dish or potato salad. For an unusual garnish or salad addition, pat capers dry, then lightly fry them in a little olive oil. They'll get crisp and open up like the little flowers they are.

Rinse brined capers before using. Salt-packed capers are too salty to be eaten straight from the jar; soak them in cool water for about 15 minutes and rinse in several changes of water. If the capers are large, you can chop them roughly unless you want a big burst of caper flavor.

Swordfish with Red Pepper, Cucumber & Mint

Serves four.

1 medium cucumber, peeled, seeded, and diced

Kosher salt

2 tablespoons olive oil

1 small onion, diced

2 cloves garlic, minced

1 large red bell pepper, roasted, peeled, seeded, and diced

1 tablespoon white-wine vinegar

1 teaspoon granulated sugar

Pinch cayenne

Pinch ground cinnamon

Leaves from 5 sprigs fresh mint, chopped; whole sprigs for garnish

2 tablespoons unsalted butter

4 swordfish steaks (about 4 ounces each)

The chopped vegetables that dress up this fish have a lively sweet-sour flavor. Great with swordfish, they can also be served with other fish, as well as grilled chicken or pork.

Toss the cucumber slices with about ½ teaspoon kosher salt and let drain in a colander for at least 20 minutes. In a large frying pan, heat the olive oil over medium high heat. Toss in the onion and cook until it just starts to brown, about 10 minutes. Add the garlic and cook about another 1 minute. Stir in the cucumber and cook for 3 minutes. Stir in the roasted red pepper, vinegar, sugar, cayenne, cinnamon, and salt to taste. Cook until the liquid evaporates, 3 to 5 minutes. Add the chopped mint. Transfer to a bowl.

In the same frying pan, melt the butter over medium high heat. Sprinkle the swordfish with salt and place in the pan. Cook until browned on one side, about 5 minutes. Flip and continue cooking until done, about 3 minutes longer. If there's excess oil in the pan, drain some of it off.

Transfer the swordfish to warm plates or a platter. Return the vegetable sauce to the pan to heat through and absorb the swordfish cooking juices. Spoon over the swordfish and garnish with mint sprigs, if you like. Serve immediately. —*Erica De Mane*

Roasted Cod with Basil Pesto & Garlic Breadcrumbs

Serves four.

For the pesto:

4 cups lightly packed fresh basil leaves (from about 1 large bunch)

⅓ cup pine nuts, toasted

¼ cup lightly packed fresh flat-leaf parsley leaves

1 small clove garlic, peeled

Kosher salt and freshly ground black pepper

¼ cup extra-virgin olive oil

For the cod:

1 large ripe tomato, cored and very thinly sliced (about ⅛ inch)

Kosher salt and freshly ground black pepper

2 tablespoons extra-virgin olive oil

1½ cups coarse fresh white breadcrumbs (from about 4 slices of bread, trimmed of crusts and pulsed in a food processor)

1 small clove garlic, minced

One 1½-pound cod or haddock fillet, cut into 4 even portions

If you have the pesto already made and on hand—it keeps in the fridge for about three days and can be frozen as well—this dish comes together in minutes.

Make the pesto: Put the basil, pine nuts, parsley, garlic, ½ teaspoon kosher salt, and ⅛ teaspoon pepper in a food processor. With the machine on, slowly pour the olive oil into the feed tube and process, stopping to scrape down the bowl as needed, until the mixture is very finely chopped and pastelike. Season to taste with salt, if you like. Keep covered in the refrigerator for up to three days.

Cook the fish: Heat the oven to 450°F. Spread the tomato slices on a large plate and season with ¼ teaspoon kosher salt and a few grinds of black pepper. Heat a large sauté pan over medium heat for 1 minute. Pour in the olive oil, add the breadcrumbs, and season with ¼ teaspoon kosher salt. Cook, stirring, until the crumbs start to turn a light golden brown, about 4 minutes. Add the garlic and continue to cook, stirring, for another 1 minute.

Set the fish on a large rimmed baking sheet lined with aluminum foil. Season with salt and pepper. Divide the pesto evenly over the fish and top each with two or three tomato slices and the breadcrumbs. Roast until the fish is opaque on the sides and starts to flake, about 10 minutes. Serve immediately. *—Tony Rosenfeld*

Cod Stew with Chorizo, Leeks & Potatoes

Fish stew may not immediately come to mind when you're in the mood for a hearty winter meal. But when the stew features chorizo, a Spanish smoked pork sausage, it fits the bill perfectly. Best of all, this beautiful dish comes together very quickly so you can enjoy it any night of the week.

Trim off the root, the dark green, and most of the light green part of the leek. Chop into ½-inch pieces and rinse thoroughly to remove all the grit. Cut the chorizo in half lengthwise and slice into thin half-moons. Put the potatoes in a large saucepan and cover with cold water by 1 to 2 inches. Salt the water, cover partially, and bring to a boil. Reduce the heat as needed and cook at a steady boil until the potatoes are tender, 10 to 15 minutes; drain.

While the potatoes cook, heat the oil in a large pot (choose one that's wide enough to hold the fish in a single layer) over medium heat for 1 minute. Add the chorizo and leeks and cook, stirring occasionally, until the chorizo has browned slightly and the leeks are soft, about 6 minutes. Add the garlic and cook for 1 minute. Stir in the tomatoes and their juices, the wine, water, and ½ teaspoon kosher salt. Bring to a boil. Partially cover the pot, reduce the heat to medium, and simmer for 15 minutes. Add the potatoes and stir in half the parsley.

Season the cod with salt and pepper, set the fillets on top of the stew, cover, and simmer until just cooked through, 6 to 8 minutes. Using a wide metal spatula, carefully transfer the cod to shallow soup bowls (the fillets may break apart, which is fine). Taste the stew, adjust the salt and pepper, and spoon the stew over the cod. Serve immediately, garnished with the remaining chopped parsley. *—Eva Katz*

Serves four.

2 small or 1 large leek

6 ounces chorizo

1 pound red potatoes, cut into ¾-inch cubes

Kosher salt and freshly ground black pepper

1 tablespoon olive oil

3 cloves garlic, minced

One 28-ounce can diced tomatoes, with their juices

½ cup dry white wine

1½ cups water

¼ cup chopped fresh flat-leaf parsley

One 1-pound cod fillet, cut into 4 even portions

Flounder Fillets with Bacon, Red Onion & Citrus over Wilted Spinach

Serves four.

4 flounder fillets (6 to 7 ounces each)

2 oranges

2 grapefruit

8 slices lean bacon, cut into ¼-inch dice

½ teaspoon kosher salt

¼ teaspoon ground white pepper

1 large or 2 medium red onions, sliced as thinly as possible

1 tablespoon chopped fresh tarragon

1 to 1¼ pounds fresh spinach, washed well and drained

Serve the flounder with small boiled red potatoes, a salad, and good bread.

Trim the edges of the flounder to remove any traces of skin. Prepare the oranges and grapefruit by cutting away the rind and pith, then cutting the individual segments away from the membrane. Put into a bowl and set aside.

Sauté the bacon slowly in a heavy skillet until golden and crisp, stirring occasionally. Drain on paper towels and set aside. Pour all the bacon fat into a small bowl.

In the same heavy skillet, heat 2 tablespoons of the reserved bacon fat over high heat. Lightly season the fillets with salt and pepper and put them in the hot skillet. Sear well on one side, about 1 minute, then turn them. Sprinkle the sliced onion around the fish. Add the fruit segments and their juices, the bacon, and the tarragon. Cover with a tight-fitting lid. Remove from the heat and let steam for 5 to 6 minutes, depending on the thickness of the fillet.

Meanwhile, in another skillet, heat another 2 tablespoons of the bacon fat over medium high heat. (If you run out of bacon fat, supplement with vegetable oil.) Once the fat is hot, add the spinach. Toss with a spatula just until it's warm and has begun to wilt. Portion the spinach onto warm plates.

By this time, the flounder should be done. Lay the fillets on the spinach and arrange the fruit segments and onions over the fish. Spoon the bacon, tarragon, and pan juices over each portion and serve. *—Gary Coley*

Sautéed Tilapia over Swiss Chard with Tarragon Butter

This dish comes together in a flash. In fact, the most time-consuming step is washing and chopping the chard, which can be done in advance and refrigerated.

Heat the oil in a 10- to 12-inch nonstick skillet over medium high heat. Add the garlic and cook until fragrant, 30 to 45 seconds. Add a big handful of the Swiss chard and cook, tossing often, until it has collapsed enough to add more. Continue adding the chard in batches until it's all in the pan, then cook until tender, 2 to 3 minutes. Season to taste with salt and pepper, divide the chard between two dinner plates, and keep warm.

Wipe out the skillet and return it to medium high heat. Add 1 tablespoon of the butter and let melt. Sprinkle the tilapia with ¼ teaspoon kosher salt and a few grinds of pepper. Add the tilapia and cook, turning once halfway through cooking, until it's well browned and cooked through, 4 to 6 minutes. Top the chard with the tilapia and keep warm.

Add the shallot to the skillet and cook, stirring, until lightly browned and beginning to soften, 30 to 60 seconds. Add the lemon juice; it should evaporate almost instantly, but, if not, cook until nearly evaporated, about 30 seconds. Remove from the heat and add the 4 tablespoons of butter pieces and the tarragon, stirring constantly until the butter melts. Season to taste with salt and pepper. Pour the sauce over the fish and chard and serve immediately. —*David Bonom*

Serves two.

1 tablespoon extra-virgin olive oil

2 cloves garlic, minced

1 pound Swiss chard, fibrous stems and ribs discarded, leaves coarsely chopped, washed, and dried

Kosher salt and freshly ground black pepper

5 tablespoons unsalted butter (4 tablespoons of it cut into small pieces)

2 tilapia fillets (6 ounces each)

1 shallot, chopped

1 tablespoon fresh lemon juice

1½ tablespoons chopped fresh tarragon

Seared Tuna with Citrus, Tomato & Olive Sauce

Serves four.

2 medium plum tomatoes

Kosher salt and freshly ground black pepper

1 medium lemon

2 medium navel oranges

2 tablespoons coriander seeds

1 tablespoon black peppercorns

Four 1-inch-thick tuna steaks (6 to 7 ounces each)

5 tablespoons extra-virgin olive oil

2 anchovy fillets, rinsed and patted dry

1 large clove garlic, minced

½ cup pitted Kalamata olives, drained

Salting the tomatoes removes some of their water so they don't dilute the final dish. Serve with couscous and sautéed zucchini.

Cut each tomato into four wedges, cut out the cores, and remove the seeds and pulp, then slice lengthwise into ¼-inch-wide strips. In a colander, toss them with ¼ teaspoon kosher salt and let drain for 15 minutes.

Meanwhile, finely grate the zest of the lemon and place it in a medium bowl. Working over the bowl, segment the lemon and the oranges. In a spice grinder or with a mortar and pestle (or with a meat mallet; put the spices in a zip-top bag), coarsely grind the coriander and peppercorns together. Press them into both sides of the tuna steaks.

Gently heat 3 tablespoons of the oil in a 12-inch skillet over medium heat. Add the anchovies and mash them into the oil with the back of a spoon until nearly dissolved. Turn the heat to low, add the garlic, and cook until softened but not browned, 3 to 4 minutes. Remove from the heat. Add the drained tomato strips, the orange and lemon segments (with the zest and juice), and olives to the pan. Toss very gently to warm through, being careful not to break up the citrus segments. Season to taste with salt and pepper. Transfer to a serving bowl and keep warm.

Wipe out the skillet, set it over medium high heat, and pour in the remaining 2 tablespoons oil. Generously salt the tuna on both sides. Working in batches if necessary, sear the steaks, pressing on them while cooking to help a crust develop, until golden brown, 2 to 3 minutes. Flip and continue to cook until golden brown, another 2 to 3 minutes for medium rare to medium. Transfer the tuna to dinner plates and serve with the warm citrus sauce. *—Arlene Jacobs*

Prosciutto-Wrapped Halibut with Sage Butter Sauce

Make sure all your fillets are similar in size and thickness so they cook in the same amount of time. You could also use any firm white-fleshed fish.

Position a rack in the center of the oven and heat the oven to 400°F. Slicing crosswise, cut six ¼-inch-thick rounds from the center of one of the lemons. Repeat with the other lemon. Squeeze the juice from the ends of the lemons into a small bowl (you'll need 4 teaspoons) and set aside. Arrange the lemon rounds in slightly overlapping pairs on a heavy rimmed baking sheet.

Season the fish with salt and pepper. Set two sage leaves on top of each fillet, then wrap each fillet with a slice of prosciutto, leaving the fish exposed at either end. Lay one fillet on top of each pair of lemon slices. Bake until the fish is cooked through (it should flake and be opaque in the thickest part), 15 to 20 minutes, depending on the thickness of the fillets.

While the fish is cooking, melt the butter in a 10-inch skillet over medium low heat. Add the remaining sage and cook, turning once, until the leaves are crisp and the butter begins to brown, about 7 minutes. Add the lemon juice to the butter and season with ¼ teaspoon kosher salt or to taste.

Arrange each fillet (on its lemon slices) on each of six dinner plates. Pour any juices from the fish into the butter sauce in the skillet. Reheat the sauce if necessary. Spoon some of the sauce and a few sage leaves over each fillet and serve. *–Jennifer McLagan*

Serves six.

2 large lemons

Six 1-inch-thick halibut fillets (about 6 ounces each)

Kosher salt and freshly ground black pepper

36 medium fresh sage leaves

6 thin slices imported prosciutto

6 tablespoons unsalted butter

8 Vegetables

p270

p296

Slow-Cooked Broccoli
with Garlic & Pancetta
(recipe on page 285)

Braised Carrots, Red Onions & Bell Peppers with Ginger, Lime & Cilantro

¾ pound young carrots, preferably with the tops on

1 tablespoon fresh lime juice

1 teaspoon finely grated lime zest

1 teaspoon light brown sugar

2 tablespoons extra-virgin olive oil

1 tablespoon unsalted butter

Kosher salt

1 small yellow bell pepper, cored, seeded, and cut lengthwise into ½-inch-wide strips

1 small red onion, cut into ½-inch-wide strips

1 piece fresh ginger, 2x¾ inches, peeled and cut into thin matchsticks

½ small jalapeño, sliced crosswise into ¼-inch-thick thin circles (no need to remove the seeds

⅓ cup plus 2 tablespoons low-salt chicken broth

¼ cup loosely packed chopped fresh cilantro

The bright colors of this dish are matched only by its zesty flavor. The ginger and jalapeño add a touch of heat.

Trim the tops and tails from the carrots and peel them; you should have about 8 ounces trimmed carrots. Cut them in half crosswise, then cut the thicker end in half lengthwise to get pieces of about the same width, no more than ¾ inch (the length can vary). In a small bowl, combine the lime juice and zest and brown sugar; set aside.

Heat 1 tablespoon of the olive oil and 2 teaspoons of the butter in a 10-inch straight-sided sauté pan over medium-high heat. When the milk solids in the butter just begin to turn a nutty brown, add the carrots and ¼ teaspoon kosher salt. Toss well with tongs, then arrange the carrots in a single layer. Cook without stirring until the bottoms are nicely browned, 3 to 4 minutes. Toss and turn over, and cook for another 2 minutes to lightly brown another side. Transfer the carrots to a plate with tongs.

Heat the remaining 1 tablespoon olive oil in the pan. Add the bell pepper, onion, and a pinch of salt and sauté until browned, 3 to 5 minutes. Add the ginger and jalapeño, toss, and sauté for another 1 minute. Return the carrots to the pan, stir, and pour in the broth. Immediately cover the pan and simmer until the liquid is almost completely reduced, about 2 minutes.

Uncover the pan, remove it from the heat, and add the lime juice mixture, the remaining 1 teaspoon butter, and the cilantro. Toss to combine well, scraping any browned bits from the bottom of the pan with a heatproof spatula or a wooden spoon. Serve right away as individual servings or pour and scrape the contents of the pan onto a small platter and serve family style.

—*Susie Middleton*

Spicy Carrots with Jalapeño & Roasted Red Pepper

Serves eight as a side dish.

2 red bell peppers

1½ pounds medium carrots, peeled

5 tablespoons extra-virgin olive oil

1 cup thinly sliced yellow onion

6 cloves garlic, thinly sliced

Kosher salt

1 jalapeño, sliced crosswise into thin circles (no need to remove the seeds)

½ cup water

1 tablespoon coarsely chopped fresh oregano

1 tablespoon coarsely chopped fresh flat-leaf parsley

1 tablespoon fresh lime juice

Cayenne (optional)

Some jalapeños are very hot; others aren't. If, at the end, the dish isn't spicy enough for you, use cayenne to bump up the heat. Get a head start by prepping the ingredients in advance and refrigerating them (covered) up to four hours ahead.

Char the bell peppers over an open flame or in a pan under the broiler until the skins are blackened on all sides. Put them in a bowl and cover tightly with plastic to steam for about 15 minutes. Rub off the charred skins. Remove the stems and seeds and cut the flesh into long, thin strips.

Cut each of the carrots into six fairly evenly sized sticks by first cutting the carrots in half crosswise. Then quarter the thicker stem end lengthwise and cut the narrower root end in half lengthwise.

Pour 3 tablespoons of the olive oil into a large skillet or sauté pan with a lid. Add the onion, garlic, and a pinch of salt. Stir to coat everything with oil and cook, covered, over medium-low heat until softened, 6 to 8 minutes. Add the jalapeño, cover, and cook for 1 minute. Add the red pepper strips and another small pinch of salt and cook, covered, for another 3 minutes. Transfer to a bowl and let cool.

Heat the remaining 2 tablespoons olive oil in the pan over medium heat; add the carrots and season with a pinch of salt. Stir to coat and cook, covered, for 7 minutes.

Add the water and cook, uncovered, over medium-high heat, stirring occasionally, until the carrots are tender and most of the water has evaporated, 7 to 9 minutes. Add the red pepper mixture and cook for 1 to 2 minutes to warm through. Stir in the oregano, parsley, and lime juice. Season to taste with salt (and cayenne, if not hot enough). Serve immediately. *—Bill Telepan*

tip: Slicing the carrots into six even pieces not only makes for a more visually pleasing dish, but it also helps the carrots cook at the same rate.

Roasted Carrots with Herbs

Serves four as a side dish.

2 pounds carrots, peeled and
left whole if using baby
carrots, or cut into 1-inch
lengths

2 tablespoons extra-virgin
olive oil

1 teaspoon kosher salt

1 tablespoon chopped fresh
herbs, such as chives, flat-leaf
parsley, thyme, or a mix

Carrots are also wonderful roasted with their cousin, the parsnip, cut into pieces the same size as the carrot. If you can find baby carrots, they not only look prettier on the plate but will also taste sweeter.

Heat the oven to 450°F. In a large bowl, toss the carrots with the oil, salt, and herbs. Spread the carrots in a baking pan large enough to hold them in a single layer. Roast, shaking the pan once or twice, until the carrots are fork-tender, about half an hour. —*Seen Lippert*

Glazed Carrots with Marsala

These carrots go especially well with lamb. If you don't have Marsala, sweet sherry is a fine substitute.

Holding your knife at a sharp angle, cut each carrot into ¼-inch-thick oval slices. Melt the butter over medium heat in a 10- to 12-inch sauté pan. Add the carrots (they should be almost in a single layer), sugar, and salt and swirl the pan over medium heat until the sugar and salt dissolve and the carrots are evenly coated with butter. Add the Marsala, simmer for 3 minutes, then add enough water (about ⅓ cup) to come halfway up the sides of the carrots.

Increase the heat to medium high, bring to a boil, and cover the pan with the lid slightly askew. Cook at a steady boil, shaking the pan occasionally, until the carrots are tender but not soft (a paring knife should enter a carrot with just a little resistance), 6 to 8 minutes. Uncover and continue to boil until the liquid evaporates and forms a syrup. Shake the pan and roll the pieces around to evenly glaze the carrots. Toss the carrots with the parsley, if you like, and serve immediately. *—Tasha DeSerio*

Serves four to six as a side dish.

1½ pounds carrots (about 8), peeled

2 tablespoons unsalted butter

1 teaspoon granulated sugar

1 teaspoon kosher salt

⅓ cup sweet Marsala

1 tablespoon chopped fresh flat-leaf parsley (optional)

tip: Although carrots have good keeping qualities, they sacrifice sweetness and flavor to long storage. For that reason, aim to buy in quantities you'll use within a week or two rather than buying in bulk.

Roasted Carrots & Parsnips with Shallot & Herb Butter

Serves two to three as a side dish.

5 large carrots, peeled

4 large parsnips, peeled

3 tablespoons extra-virgin olive oil

1½ teaspoons kosher salt

½ teaspoon freshly ground black pepper

¼ cup unsalted butter, at room temperature

2 tablespoons minced shallot

2 tablespoons finely chopped fresh chives

1½ teaspoons finely chopped fresh rosemary

1½ teaspoons chopped fresh thyme

1 clove garlic, minced

Flavored butters, also called compound butters, should be a staple in every kitchen. You can swirl them into sauces, slather them on meats or toss them with rice. Here an assortment of fresh herbs brightens the earthy root vegetables, but you can also try curried butter or even maple butter. Compound butters keep well for several days in the refrigerator or several months in the freezer. Try making a double batch, shape the extra into logs, and slice off a pat whenever you need a quick boost of flavor.

Position a rack in the center of the oven and heat the oven to 450°F.

Cut the carrots and parsnips into 2x¼-inch matchsticks. Put them in a large bowl; toss with the oil. Sprinkle with the salt and pepper and toss again. Transfer to a 10x15-inch Pyrex dish and roast, stirring every 15 minutes, until nicely browned, 40 to 45 minutes.

Meanwhile, combine the butter, shallot, chives, rosemary, thyme, and garlic in a small bowl and stir well. Add the butter to the roasted vegetables and toss to coat. Serve immediately. —*Julianna Grimes Bottcher*

Three Steps to Customizing Your Own Roasted Vegetable Combinations

1 Choose veggies that cook at the same rate

If you want to improvise your own roasted vegetable dish, first choose vegetables that will all cook at about the same rate, and be sure to cut them into similar-size pieces.

Long cooking time
(30 minutes or longer):

potatoes
sweet potatoes
carrots
parsnips
rutabaga
winter squash
Brussels sprouts

Average cooking time
(about 20 to 30 minutes):

turnips
onions
cauliflower
broccoli
sugar snap peas
quartered shallots
fennel
whole garlic cloves

Quick cooking time
(under 20 minutes):

green beans
mushrooms
thinly sliced shallots or onions

2 Use a heavy pan and high heat

For roasting vegetables, use a heavy roasting pan or Pyrex baking dish, not a baking sheet. Because roasting pans and baking dishes are designed to withstand high heat, they help keep the vegetables from burning. Pick the right size pan for the job at hand. And don't be afraid to crank up the heat and let the vegetables sizzle. The heat blisters the vegetables' surfaces, and this is just what you're after—a pale-looking vegetable will have a pale flavor to match.

3 Add flavor after roasting with toss-ins

Nuts and seeds: toasted pecans, almonds, walnuts, pistachios, hazelnuts, pine nuts, pumpkin seeds, sesame seeds, shelled sunflower seeds

Cheeses: goat cheese, blue cheese, feta, shaved Parmigiano Reggiano

Sauces and dressings: vinaigrettes, curry pastes

Butter: flavored with herbs and zest

Juices: fresh lemon, lime, orange, or grapefruit

Zests: freshly grated lemon, lime, or orange

Delicate oils: truffle oil, walnut oil, avocado oil

Chopped fresh leafy herbs: basil, cilantro, parsley, mint, dill

Garlic: finely chopped (add according to vegetable cooking time)

Braised Asparagus & Cipolline Onions with Pancetta & Balsamic Butter Glaze

Serves three to four as a side dish.

1 pound medium or thick asparagus

2 teaspoons balsamic vinegar

2 teaspoons fresh lemon juice

1 teaspoon Dijon mustard

1 teaspoon honey

2 tablespoons extra-virgin olive oil

1½ ounces thinly sliced pancetta, cut into slivers

1 tablespoon plus 1 teaspoon unsalted butter

5 ounces small cipolline onions or large shallots, halved (quartered if very large) and peeled

Kosher salt

⅓ cup low-salt chicken broth

A sweet-and-sour glaze dresses up this quick braised dish. If you can't find cipolline onions, large shallots or even pearl onions will do fine.

Cut off the tough bottoms of the asparagus so that all the spears are 6 to 7 inches long. Combine the vinegar, lemon juice, Dijon, and honey in a small bowl; set aside.

Heat 1 tablespoon of the oil in a 10-inch straight-sided sauté pan over medium-high heat. Add the pancetta and cook, stirring frequently, until browned and crisp, 2 to 3 minutes (don't let them burn). Transfer the pancetta to a plate, leaving behind as much fat as possible.

Return the pan to medium-high heat, add 1 tablespoon of the butter to the fat and swirl to melt (there will be browned bits on the bottom of the pan). Add the onions and a pinch of salt and sauté until nicely browned on all sides and beginning to soften, 2 to 3 minutes. Take the pan off the heat and transfer the onions to another plate.

Return the pan to medium-high heat and add the remaining 1 tablespoon oil, the asparagus, and ¼ teaspoon kosher salt. Toss well. Cook without stirring until the bottoms of the spears are nicely browned, 3 to 4 minutes. Toss and turn over, and cook for 1 to 2 minutes to lightly brown another side. Return the onions to the pan, stir, and pour in the broth. Cover the pan and simmer until the liquid is almost completely reduced, about 3 minutes. Uncover, add the vinegar mixture, stir to coat thoroughly, and cook for a few seconds until it has a glazy consistency. Add the remaining 1 teaspoon butter and toss to melt and combine, scraping up any browned bits in the pan with a wooden spoon. Toss in the crisped pancetta. Serve right away.

–Susie Middleton

Sweet Onions in a Little Package

Cipolline (chip-oh-LEE-nee) onions, originally from Italy, have a sweet, delicate flavor. These petite flying-saucer shaped onions are a fun way to add oniony flavor to vegetable dishes, salads, stews, and more. They're also good baked until tender and sprinkled with a little Parmigiano-Reggiano, or blanched and threaded onto skewers and grilled.

Broiled Asparagus & Orange Slices with Olive Oil & Shallots

This pretty dish would go well with a grilled steak, especially one that's been treated to a spice rub. The cooked orange slices—skin and all—are not only edible but also delicious and tender but with a snappy zing. Feel free to substitute lemon in place of the orange.

Position a rack as close to the broiling element as possible. Heat the broiler on high. In a bowl, toss the asparagus spears with the olive oil to coat and season with salt and pepper. Arrange the shallot rings in a thin layer on one side of a rimmed baking sheet or jellyroll pan. Put the asparagus in a single layer on top of them. Toss the orange slices with the leftover oil, salt, and pepper in the bowl you used for the asparagus. Arrange the slices in a single layer alongside the asparagus. Broil until the asparagus and oranges just start to char, 5 to 8 minutes.

Remove from the oven and sprinkle the asparagus with the orange zest. Arrange the asparagus, shallots, and oranges on a serving dish. Serve hot, warm, or at room temperature. —*Pam Anderson*

Serves four as a side dish or three as a first course.

1 pound asparagus, woody stem ends snapped off and discarded

2 tablespoons extra-virgin olive oil

Kosher salt and freshly ground black pepper

1 shallot, thinly sliced and separated into rings

4 very thin orange slices, quartered

¼ teaspoon finely grated orange zest

Baby Spinach with Scallions & Lemon

Serves six as a side dish.

2½ pounds baby spinach

3 tablespoons olive oil

4 scallions, trimmed and sliced, white and green parts separated

Kosher salt and freshly ground black pepper

1 tablespoon lightly packed finely grated lemon zest (from about 1 large lemon)

⅛ teaspoon freshly grated nutmeg

This dish is very forgiving and keeps just fine while sitting in the pan on the stove until you're ready to reheat it and serve.

Rinse and drain the spinach. (You needn't dry it completely; clinging droplets of water are fine.) Heat the olive oil in a large, deep Dutch oven or wok over medium heat. Add the scallion whites and cook, stirring, until they start to soften, about 1 minute. Pile in the spinach and cook, turning with tongs so it gets evenly heated. (You'll need to add the spinach in stages; as it heats, it will shrink.) Once all the spinach is in the pan, cover and cook, stirring occasionally, until all the leaves have wilted and released their liquid, about 2 minutes. Uncover the pan, increase the heat to high, and cook, stirring occasionally, until the spinach is very soft, about 5 minutes. Remove from the heat and season with salt and pepper to taste. Just before serving, reheat gently, adding the scallion greens, lemon zest, and grated nutmeg. Drain briefly in a colander before serving. —*Randall Price*

Mushrooms & Spinach with Soppressata Crisps

What's nice about this dish is that the vegetables don't need to be cooked separately. Instead, they're added to the pan in succession, according to the amount of time each needs to cook.

Put the soppressata in a 12-inch skillet over medium heat. Cook until crisp, 5 to 7 minutes. Transfer to a small plate lined with paper towels.

Increase the heat to medium high and let the pan heat up for 1 minute. Pour in the oil and swirl to coat the pan. As soon as the oil is shimmering—but not smoking—add the mushrooms in an even layer. Season with salt and pepper and let cook undisturbed until they begin to brown, about 3 minutes. Add the scallions and sauté, stirring as needed, until the mushrooms are golden brown and tender and the scallions lightly browned in places and softened, another 6 to 7 minutes. If the vegetables seem to be cooking too fast or the pan bottom is starting to burn, lower the heat to medium. (Or, if using an electric stovetop, take the pan off the heat momentarily to let the pan cool.) Stir in the garlic and cook for another 30 seconds. Turn off the heat and add the spinach and crisped soppressata, flipping and stirring to blend and to wilt the spinach. Season to taste with salt and pepper, drizzle with a little olive oil, and serve immediately.—*Maryellen Driscoll*

Serves four to five as a side dish.

1 ounce very thinly sliced hot soppressata or other spicy dried sausage, slices quartered

2 tablespoons extra-virgin olive oil; more for drizzling

1 pound cremini mushrooms, halved if small or quartered or cut into sixths if very large

Kosher salt and freshly ground black pepper

5 medium scallions (white and green parts), cut into 1-inch pieces

2 medium cloves garlic, minced

5 ounces baby spinach

Black Kale with Ham, Garlic & Onion

Serves eight as a side dish.

3 pounds kale, preferably black Tuscan cavolo nero, also known as lacinato kale

Kosher salt and freshly ground black pepper

6 tablespoons unsalted butter

One 6-ounce slice smoked ham, cut into ¼-inch dice (about 1 cup)

1½ cups thinly sliced yellow onion

6 cloves garlic, thinly sliced

1½ cups low-salt chicken or vegetable broth

Red-wine vinegar (optional)

You can use any variety of kale for this dish; I'm partial to the spicy flavor of black kale. This recipe can be made completely up to a day ahead.

Remove the tough stems from the kale leaves by slicing a narrow "V" up into each leaf to remove the entire stem. Wash the leaves well in cold water and drain in a colander. Stuff into large zip-top bags and put in the freezer for at least 2 hours or up to a month.

Fill an 8-quart pot with 2 inches of water and bring it to a boil. Add a good pinch of salt and add the frozen kale. Cover with the lid slightly askew and cook on high heat, turning occasionally, until tender, about 20 minutes. The kale should still have a little bite but shouldn't be stringy or tough. Drain in a colander and press with the back of a large spoon to squeeze out as much liquid as possible. When cool enough to touch, chop it into small pieces.

Melt 3 tablespoons of the butter in the 8-quart pot over medium-high heat. Add the ham and cook until it starts to brown a little, about 3 minutes. Reduce the heat to medium. Add the onion and garlic and a pinch of salt; cook covered, stirring occasionally, until softened, about 5 minutes. If the onion or garlic start to brown, lower the heat. Add the broth, bring to a boil, reduce the heat to maintain a gentle simmer, and cook for 5 minutes. Return the kale to the pot, stir in the remaining 3 tablespoons butter, season generously with pepper, and cook gently until the flavors are well blended, about 7 minutes. Taste and adjust the seasonings as necessary. Transfer to a serving bowl and serve immediately with a slotted spoon. Offer red-wine vinegar for sprinkling on individual portions, if you like. *—Bill Telepan*

How to Trim Kale

Unlike spinach and chard, kale leaves take a while to cook to a tender texture, and kale stems are nearly impervious to tenderizing. That's why the first step in preparing kale is trimming the stems. The aim is not just to trim the stems below the leaves, but also to remove most of the stem from the center of the leaf, where it acts like a supporting rib. To do this, lay a leaf upside down on a cutting board and use a paring knife to cut a V shape along both sides of the rib, cutting it free from the leaf.

The kale shown here is black kale, a.k.a. Tuscan kale, lacinato kale, cavolo nero, or dinosaur kale.

Broccoli & Cauliflower Sauté with Garlic & Ginger

Serves four as a main course; six as a side dish.

1 pound broccoli

1 small head cauliflower

9 tablespoons extra-virgin olive oil; more as needed

Kosher salt

¾ cup water

1 small red onion, thinly sliced

Large pinch red pepper flakes; more to taste

Pinch saffron threads, crumbled

½ teaspoon yellow mustard seeds

½ teaspoon brown or black mustard seeds

4 medium cloves garlic, finely chopped

1 tablespoon peeled and finely chopped fresh ginger

⅓ cup chopped fresh cilantro

1 lime, cut into wedges

This makes a tasty vegetarian meal when served with rice and a yogurt sauce, but it's also superb as a side dish for grilled lamb chops.

Tear off any broccoli leaves and trim the bottoms of the stems. Cut the florets just above where they join the large stem, then cut each floret through its stem (but not the buds) so that each piece is about ¼ inch thick at the stem end. Using a vegetable peeler or paring knife, peel the tough outer skin from the large stem, removing as little flesh as possible. Cut the stem into baton-shaped pieces about ¼ inch wide and 2 inches long. Cut the core out of the cauliflower to separate the florets, then cut each floret through its stem so it's about ¼ inch thick at the stem end. Discard the core.

Set a 12-inch skillet over high heat. Pour in 3 tablespoons of the olive oil, then add the broccoli florets and stem pieces. Season with salt and carefully add the water. Reduce the heat to medium high and cook, stirring occasionally, until the broccoli is tender and browned in spots, 8 to 10 minutes. (If the pan begins to scorch before the broccoli is cooked, add another 1 tablespoon olive oil and reduce the heat a little. If the pan does scorch, rinse and dry the pan before cooking the cauliflower.) Transfer the broccoli to a large bowl. Wipe out the pan and cook the cauliflower the same way. Add the cooked cauliflower to the bowl with the broccoli.

Wipe out the pan (if it's scorched, rinse and dry it) and return it to the stovetop over medium heat. Add 2 tablespoons of the olive oil, the onion, red pepper flakes, and saffron; season with salt. Sauté, stirring frequently, until the onion is golden brown and tender, about 8 minutes. Push the onion to one side and add 1 tablespoon of the olive oil and all the mustard seeds. Let them sizzle for 1 minute, then add the garlic and ginger. Cook, stirring, for 1 minute more—be careful not to let them burn.

Return the broccoli and cauliflower to the pan, stir to combine, and cook until hot, about 2 minutes. Taste and add salt if necessary. Transfer to a platter, sprinkle the cilantro on top, and serve the lime wedges on the side.

—Tasha DeSerio

Roasted Broccoli with Lemon & Pecorino

Serves four as a side dish.

1½ pounds broccoli

¼ cup plus 2 tablespoons
extra-virgin olive oil

1 teaspoon kosher salt

2 tablespoons fresh lemon
juice; more to taste

⅓ cup freshly grated Pecorino
Romano cheese

Roasting brings out broccoli's sweeter side. A delicious accompaniment to roast chicken or pork, this dish can be cooked in the already hot oven while the meat rests before carving.

Position a rack in the center of the oven and heat the oven to 450°F.

Tear off any broccoli leaves and trim the bottoms of the stems. Cut the florets just above where they join the large stem, then cut each floret through its stem (but not the buds) so each piece is about ¼ inch thick at the stem end. Using a vegetable peeler or paring knife, peel the tough outer skin from the large stem, removing as little flesh as possible. Cut the stem into baton-shaped pieces about ¼ inch wide and 2 inches long.

Put the florets and stem pieces on a rimmed baking sheet, drizzle with the olive oil, sprinkle with the salt, and toss well to combine. Spread into an even layer and roast until tender and golden brown, 15 to 20 minutes. Transfer the broccoli to a serving platter and toss with the lemon juice to taste and grated Pecorino. —*Tasha DeSerio*

Slow-Cooked Broccoli with Garlic & Pancetta

This dish can be served warm or at room temperature. It's delicious on its own, or serve it on grilled bread rubbed with garlic.

Tear off any broccoli leaves and trim the bottoms of the stems. Cut the florets just above where they join the large stem, then cut each floret through its stem (but not the buds) so that each piece is about ¼ inch thick at the stem end. Using a vegetable peeler or paring knife, peel the tough outer skin from the large stem, removing as little flesh as possible. Cut the stem into baton-shaped pieces about ¼ inch wide and 2 inches long.

Heat the oil in a 12-inch skillet over medium heat. Add the pancetta and cook until translucent and just starting to render its fat, about 2 minutes. Add the broccoli, garlic, salt, and red pepper flakes; stir to combine. Reduce the heat to medium low and cook uncovered, stirring every 5 to 10 minutes, until the broccoli is tender and slightly browned, about 45 minutes total. Taste and add more salt, if necessary. Let cool briefly and serve. *–Tasha DeSerio*

Serves four as a side dish.

1¼ to 1½ pounds broccoli

¼ cup extra-virgin olive oil

3 ounces pancetta, sliced ¼ inch thick and cut crosswise into ¼-inch-wide pieces

8 medium cloves garlic, thinly sliced

¾ teaspoon kosher salt; more to taste

¼ teaspoon red pepper flakes

Getting Broccoli Ready for Cooking

1 Snap off any leaves and cut the florets just above where they join the main stem. Use a vegetable peeler to remove the tough outer layer of the stem. (A paring knife works as well, but be careful not to remove too much flesh.)

2 Cut the florets into the size you need, but don't cut through the buds—instead, use a small knife to cut lengthwise through the stem. This method lets the florets separate easily but keeps the buds intact. You get fewer "bud crumbs" (which can burn easily) in the pan, and the florets will retain their tree-like form.

3 You'll end up with intact florets, some of which will have a flatter surface area on the stems; this helps them brown easier. Cut the large broccoli stem into baton-shaped pieces.

Broccoli with Black Olives, Garlic & Lemon

Serves six as a side dish.

1½ pounds broccoli crowns

⅓ cup extra-virgin olive oil

⅓ cup pitted Kalamata olives, drained

1 small to medium clove garlic, finely chopped

½ teaspoon kosher salt

½ teaspoon crumbled dried oregano

1 medium lemon

Freshly ground black pepper

1½ tablespoons chopped fresh oregano

Olives with pits tend to have more flavor, plus there's more variety to choose from. If buying pitted olives, make sure they are high-quality, or pit your own by crushing them with the flat side of a chef's knife and removing the pit.

In a large pot (one that accommodates your steamer), bring about 2 inches of water to a boil.

Meanwhile, trim and cut the broccoli into 2- to 3-inch florets. When the water is boiling, steam the broccoli in a steamer basket until it's just cooked, 7 to 9 minutes.

While the broccoli steams, heat the oil in a small saucepan over medium-low heat. Add the olives, garlic, salt, and dried oregano. Cook until the garlic is lightly colored, 3 to 5 minutes. Remove the pan from the heat. Finely grate the zest from the lemon; set aside. Squeeze 4 teaspoons juice from the lemon and add the juice to the oil. Season with pepper.

Spread the broccoli on a warmed serving platter. Reheat the dressing until it begins to bubble, then pour it over the broccoli. Sprinkle with the lemon zest and fresh oregano. Serve immediately. —*Jennifer McLagan*

Garlic-Roasted Green Beans & Shallots with Hazelnuts

Chopped hazelnuts are a fine flavor match for green beans—and a refreshing departure from the more expected almonds.

Position a rack in the center of the oven and heat the oven to 450°F.

Slice each shallot lengthwise into ¼-inch-thick slices. Put the shallots, green beans, and garlic in a large bowl; toss with the oil. Sprinkle the salt and pepper over the vegetables and toss again. Transfer to a 10x15-inch Pyrex dish and roast until they're tender and very lightly browned, stirring once, 18 to 20 minutes.

Meanwhile, combine the parsley, hazelnuts, and lemon zest in a small bowl. Sprinkle this mixture over the roasted vegetables and toss to coat. Serve immediately. —*Julianna Grimes Bottcher*

Serves four as a side dish.

6 medium shallots, peeled

1 pound green beans, trimmed

5 medium cloves garlic, coarsely chopped

3 tablespoons extra-virgin olive oil

1 teaspoon kosher salt

½ teaspoon freshly ground black pepper

¼ cup finely chopped fresh flat-leaf parsley

¼ cup coarsely chopped toasted hazelnuts

1 teaspoon finely grated lemon zest

Brown-Butter Green Beans with Pine Nuts

Serves four to six as a side dish.

1 pound green beans, trimmed

3 tablespoons unsalted butter

½ cup pine nuts, coarsely chopped

Kosher salt

2 teaspoons fresh lemon juice

Freshly ground black pepper

Nutty browned butter and toasted pine nuts provide a slight twist on green beans amandine. This recipe would be delicious made with yellow wax beans, or even sugar snap peas. You can boil the green beans ahead of time, but you'll need to rewarm them a bit longer in the brown butter, covered, over low heat.

Bring a 4- to 6-quart pot (like a Dutch oven) of generously salted water to a boil. Add the green beans and cook until tender to the bite, 5 to 7 minutes. Drain them in a colander. Return the pot to the stove over low heat and melt the butter in the pot. Add the pine nuts and ¼ teaspoon kosher salt, turn the heat to medium, and cook, stirring constantly, until the butter browns and the pine nuts turn mostly golden, 3 to 5 minutes. Turn off the heat (or remove the pot from the stove) and add the green beans and ½ teaspoon kosher salt. Toss to combine thoroughly, sprinkle with the lemon juice, and toss again. Taste and add salt and pepper if necessary. Serve warm. *–Susie Middleton*

Slightly Spicy Sugar Snap Peas with Mint & Lime

Serves two to three as a side dish.

2 tablespoons unsalted butter

¼ teaspoon Thai red curry paste

¾ pound sugar snap peas, trimmed

⅓ cup water

2 tablespoons thinly sliced fresh mint

2 teaspoons fresh lime juice

Kosher salt

Rather than letting an opened jar of curry paste languish in the fridge, try this unconventional approach of using the paste like a condiment for pan-steamed snap peas. The peas have a mild, slow-burning heat, but if you like things hotter, try doubling the amount of curry paste. This treatment is also good with green beans or broccoli, though you may want to leave out the mint.

Heat 1 tablespoon of the butter in a medium saucepan over medium heat. As soon as the butter melts, add the curry paste and mash it around with the back of a fork until it's mostly broken up and distributed through the butter. Add the peas and toss with tongs to coat in the butter. Add the water, cover with the lid slightly askew, raise the heat to medium high, and steam until the peas are almost tender, about 5 minutes. Remove the lid and let any remaining liquid boil off. Stir in the remaining 1 tablespoon butter, the mint, and the lime juice. Season to taste with salt and serve immediately. *—Jennifer Armentrout*

Thai Curry Paste

Intensely flavored curry pastes are a staple of Thai cuisine. These moist, concentrated blends of chiles, spices, and aromatics like lemongrass, lime leaves, shrimp paste, shallots, ginger, garlic, and cilantro are stirred into coconut milk or broth to make the sauce for all sorts of curry dishes.

Thai curry pastes are classified according to their color. Green curry pastes get their color mainly from fresh hot green chiles; they tend to be the hottest curry pastes. Red curry pastes are made with dried red chiles; they're pretty fiery, too. Yellow curry pastes are colored by turmeric and Indian-style curry powder; their spice level is relatively mild.

Tightly wrapped or sealed, curry paste lasts about a month in the refrigerator and up to three months in the freezer.

Green　　　　**Red**　　　　**Yellow**

Sweet Corn Relish with Avocado, Jalapeño & Cilantro

Spoon a generous amount of this relish on top of grilled fish or chicken breasts, or just serve it as a side salad. To add more volume, add some halved cherry tomatoes or diced red bell pepper.

Bring a small pot of water to a boil. Add the corn kernels and blanch for 1 minute. Drain and set aside.

In a medium bowl, combine the onion, jalapeño, lime juice, vinegar, and a generous pinch of salt.

Dice the avocado: Use a paring knife to carefully make ¼-inch-thick slices through the flesh without piercing the skin. Rotate the avocado 90 degrees and slice again, to create ¼-inch squares. With the avocado in the palm of your hand, slide a large metal spoon between the skin and flesh and gently scoop out the squares.

Add the avocado, corn, and cilantro to the onion mixture. Add the olive oil and another pinch of salt and stir gently. Season to taste, adding more salt or lime juice as needed. *–Tasha DeSerio*

Serves four as a side dish.

Kernels cut from 3 large ears corn (about 2½ cups)

1 small red onion, cut into ⅛-inch dice

½ jalapeño, cored, seeded, and minced

3 tablespoons fresh lime juice; more to taste

1 teaspoon Champagne vinegar or white-wine vinegar

Kosher salt

½ ripe avocado

⅓ cup chopped fresh cilantro

3 tablespoons olive oil

Southwestern Squash Sauté

Serves four to six as a side dish.

3 tablespoons olive oil

1 medium onion, diced

Kosher salt

1 medium red bell pepper, cored, seeded, and diced

3 small or 2 medium zucchini or summer squash, cut into ⅓-inch dice

Kernels from 1 large ear fresh corn

2 cloves garlic, minced

1 large or 2 small fresh hot chiles (such as serrano or jalapeño), seeded and minced, or 1 mild green chile (such as poblano or Anaheim), roasted, peeled, seeded, and diced

Freshly ground black pepper

½ teaspoon ground cumin

¼ teaspoon chili powder (optional)

1 to 2 tablespoons roughly chopped fresh cilantro, to taste

½ lime

This sauté is an especially good partner to grilled fish, chicken, or pork. With the addition of some cheese and a sliver of ripe avocado, you get a wonderful filling for quesadillas and soft tacos.

Set a large skillet over medium-high heat. When hot, add 2 tablespoons of the oil and let it heat. Add the onion, season with a little salt, and sauté until translucent, about 2 minutes. Add the bell pepper and a little more salt and sauté for another 1 to 2 minutes. Transfer the pepper and onion to a bowl or plate.

Turn the heat to high and add the remaining 1 tablespoon oil and the squash. Season with salt and sauté for 3 or 4 minutes, stirring only occasionally, so that it begins to brown lightly and the flesh turns slightly translucent and is pleasantly tender (don't overcook; it should still be toothy, not mushy). Return the pepper and onion to the pan, add the corn, garlic, and chiles, season again with salt, and sauté for another few minutes. Season with a few grinds of pepper, the cumin, and chili powder (if using). Toss in the cilantro, squeeze the lime over all, toss, and serve immediately. —*Ruth Lively*

Sautéed Zucchini with Sun-Dried Tomatoes & Basil

Two quick and easy steps give you the best-tasting, best-textured zucchini ever: Salting it well for about 10 minutes before cooking draws out some of the water and cooking it over very high heat caramelizes the flesh before it has a chance to steam and get soggy.

Wash the zucchini well to remove any grit and dry with paper towels; trim off the ends. Quarter each lengthwise. Slice off the top ¼ to ½ inch of the soft seed core by running a sharp knife down the length of each quarter; it's fine if some of the seeds remain. Arrange the zucchini, cut side up, on a baking sheet lined with paper towels. Sprinkle with salt (about ½ teaspoon per pound of zucchini) and set aside for 10 minutes, then blot the quarters dry with paper towels and cut each on the diagonal into ¾-inch-thick diamonds.

Heat a 12-inch skillet over medium-high heat for 1 minute. Pour in 2 tablespoons of the oil. When hot, add the zucchini and garlic and sauté, stirring occasionally, until the zucchini browns and softens enough that you can cut through it with the side of a fork, about 5 minutes. Take the pan off the heat, toss in the tomatoes and basil, and season generously with salt and pepper. Drizzle with the lemon juice and the remaining 1 tablespoon oil and serve immediately. —*Tony Rosenfeld*

Serves four as a side dish.

3 small or 2 medium zucchini

Kosher salt

3 tablespoons extra-virgin olive oil

2 cloves garlic, smashed and peeled

2 oil-packed sun-dried tomatoes, finely diced

6 fresh basil leaves, torn into large pieces

Freshly ground black pepper

1 teaspoon fresh lemon juice

Farmhouse Ragoût with Pesto

Serves four.

For the ragoût:

3 tablespoons extra-virgin olive oil

2 bay leaves

2 medium onions, cut into large chunks

7 plump cloves garlic, halved

3 sprigs fresh thyme

6 fresh sage leaves

¾ pound carrots, peeled and cut into 2-inch lengths

¾ pound small new potatoes, scrubbed

Kosher salt and freshly ground black pepper

½ pound yellow or green wax beans (or a mix), trimmed and halved crosswise

1 yellow bell pepper, cored, seeded, and cut into 1-inch pieces

1 pound summer squash, cut into 1-inch-thick rounds

5 plum tomatoes, peeled, seeded, and cut into large chunks

1 pound fresh shell beans, husked, or one 15-ounce can top-quality white beans, rinsed and drained

For the pesto:

1 cup packed fresh basil leaves

2 cloves garlic, peeled

6 tablespoons olive oil

3 tablespoons water; more or less as needed

Pinch kosher salt

½ cup freshly grated Parmigiano-Reggiano cheese (optional)

This humble braise more or less cooks itself as you layer on the vegetables. You'll probably end up with a little extra pesto, but it's great on other vegetables and, of course, on pasta.

Make the ragout: In a large, flameproof casserole or Dutch oven with a snug-fitting lid, heat the oil with the bay leaves over low heat. When fragrant, add the onions, 6 of the garlic cloves (if using canned beans instead of fresh, add all 7 cloves), 2 of the thyme sprigs (if using canned beans, add all 3 sprigs), and the sage, stirring to coat everything thoroughly with oil. Cover and cook over low heat for 2 minutes, then add the carrots. If the potatoes are the size of large marbles, leave them whole, but quarter larger ones or cut fingerlings in half lengthwise. Add the potatoes to the pot in a single layer; season with salt and pepper. Add the wax beans, bell pepper, and squash to the pot in layers, seasoning each layer with a little salt and pepper as you go. Add the tomatoes, sprinkling their juices over all. Cover and cook over low heat until the vegetables are tender, 40 to 65 minutes. If tightly covered, the vegetables will produce plenty of flavorful juices. There's no need to stir, but if the pot seems dry, add a few tablespoons water or dry white wine, if you like.

Make the pesto: Process the basil, garlic, and oil together in a blender, adding a little water to loosen if needed. Add the salt and the cheese, if using. Taste and adjust the seasonings if needed.

Cook the shell beans: If you're using fresh shell beans, put them in a saucepan with enough water to total 3 cups, beans included. Add the remaining garlic clove, thyme sprig, and a little olive oil. Simmer, uncovered, until tender, 30 to 45 minutes. Season with salt and pepper.

Add the beans and their cooking liquid to the pot (if using canned beans, add a bit of water or broth). Discard the bay leaves. Ladle into soup plates, drizzle some pesto over each dish, and serve. —*Deborah Madison*

Balsamic-Glazed Brussels Sprouts with Pancetta

Serves two to three as a side dish.

One 2-ounce slice pancetta, cut into ¼-inch dice (about ½ cup)

1 to 2 tablespoons extra-virgin olive oil

⅓ cup water; more as needed

10 ounces Brussels sprouts, ends trimmed and halved through the core

¼ cup balsamic vinegar

Freshly ground black pepper

2 tablespoons unsalted butter

Kosher salt

This simple one-pan preparation is long on flavor, thanks to the pancetta and balsamic vinegar. If pancetta is hard to come by, substitute two thick slices of bacon.

In a heavy 10-inch straight-sided sauté pan set over medium-low heat, slowly cook the pancetta in 1 tablespoon of the oil until golden and crisp all over, 10 to 15 minutes. With a slotted spoon, transfer the pancetta to a plate lined with paper towels, leaving the fat behind. You should have about 2 tablespoons of fat in the pan; if not, add the remaining 1 tablespoon oil.

Put the pan over medium-high heat and arrange the sprouts cut side down in a single layer. Cook undisturbed until nicely browned, 2 to 3 minutes. When the sprouts are browned, add the water to the pan, cover immediately, and simmer until the sprouts are tender when poked with a fork or skewer, about 3 minutes. (If the water evaporates before the sprouts get tender, add more water, ¼ cup at a time.) With a slotted spoon, transfer the sprouts to a plate.

Return the pan to medium-high heat and, if any water remains, let it boil off. Add the vinegar and a few grinds of pepper and boil until it's reduced to about 2 tablespoons and looks lightly syrupy, about 2 minutes. Reduce the heat to low, add the butter, and stir until melted. Return the sprouts and pancetta to the pan and swirl and shake the pan to evenly coat the sprouts with the sauce. Season to taste with salt and more pepper and serve immediately.

—Ruth Lively

Sweet-Sour Red Cabbage

This classic side dish pairs brilliantly with pork because of its slight sweetness. The smoky bacon and the vinegar keep the flavor complex.

In a 5- or 6-quart Dutch oven, heat the oil over high heat, add the bacon, and cook, stirring occasionally, until its fat is rendered and the bacon is crisp, 3 to 4 minutes. Add the onion and cook, stirring frequently, until softened and lightly colored, about 3 minutes. Add the cabbage and cook, stirring, until just wilted, about 5 minutes. Add the brown sugar and vinegar, stir well, and let cook until the cabbage is wilted but still has a bit of crunch left to it, about 5 minutes. Season with ¾ teaspoon kosher salt and several grinds of pepper. Adjust the acidity or sweetness with a touch more vinegar or sugar if you like, and add more salt and pepper if needed. The cabbage will hold well, in the covered pot, for several hours. —*Ris Lacoste*

Serves six as a side dish.

1 tablespoon olive oil

6 ounces sliced applewood-smoked bacon (about 7 slices), cut crosswise into julienne

1 large yellow onion, thinly sliced

1 small head red cabbage, cored, cut into eighths, and thinly sliced crosswise

1 cup packed dark brown sugar

¼ cup red-wine vinegar

Kosher salt and freshly ground black pepper

Wild Mushroom Ragoût

Serves four to six as a side dish.

1 ounce mixed dried mushrooms (such as chanterelles, porcini, morels, and oyster; about 1¼ cups)

½ ounce dried shiitakes (about 5 medium caps)

2 tablespoons unsalted butter

2 large shallots, minced

Kosher salt and freshly ground black pepper

2 tablespoons Cognac or brandy

1 tablespoon soy sauce

1 teaspoon chopped fresh thyme

¼ cup thinly sliced fresh chives

1 tablespoon heavy cream or unsalted butter

Fresh lemon juice to taste (optional)

Keep a batch of this tasty little ragoût on hand because it's great as a side dish, garnish, or mix-in. Stored in an airtight container in the refrigerator, it will keep for four to five days.

Soak the mushrooms in hot water to cover until softened. Drain (reserving the liquid) and remove and discard the woody stems from the shiitakes. Chop the mushrooms and strain the soaking liquid; reserve.

Heat the butter in a 10- or 12-inch nonstick skillet over medium heat until it melts and begins to foam. Add the shallots, sprinkle with a pinch of salt, and cook, stirring, until softened and translucent, 2 to 3 minutes. Add the mushrooms and cook, stirring occasionally, until they start to brown in places, about 5 minutes. Add the Cognac and cook, stirring, for 1 minute. Add the mushroom soaking liquid, soy sauce, and thyme and cook until the liquid reduces by about half, 5 to 7 minutes.

If using right away, stir in the chives and cream. Season to taste with salt, pepper, and lemon juice, if using.

If making ahead, let cool and refrigerate. Reheat over low heat, adding a couple of tablespoons of water, if necessary, to keep the sauce moist. Add the chives and cream and season to taste with salt and pepper and lemon juice, if using. *—Tony Rosenfeld*

Dried Mushrooms

How to Soak Dried Mushrooms

Put the mushrooms in a medium heatproof bowl. Pour in enough boiling water to completely submerge them and weight down the mushrooms with a small plate so they are submerged. Soak until they're plumped and softened, about 20 minutes (some varieties might take longer). Use a slotted spoon to transfer the mushrooms to a cutting board, squeezing any excess liquid from them back into the soaking liquid. Let cool. Remove and discard any tough stems. Coarsely chop the mushrooms. Strain the soaking liquid through a coffee filter or paper towel set in a sieve. Set aside the mushroom "broth" for use in your dish or freeze for another time.

Shiitakes

Versatile, affordable dried shiitakes are a "go-to" mushroom. Its meaty texture and smoky flavor are great alone or paired with other varieties. Shiitakes are an obvious choice for Asian dishes, filling out soy-based braises or stews or perking up quick stir-fries.

Look for shiitakes with thick brown caps ridged with white. The stems can be woody, so trim them off and discard after soaking.

Porcini

Chewy, succulent, and intensely flavorful, dried porcini (also called cèpes) have a deep, earthy essence that complements Italian seasonings and is delicious with pork and chicken.

Porcini (pronounced pour-CHEE-nee) have thick stems and broad caps and are generally sliced before they're dried. After rehydrating them, you can use them just as you would fresh mushrooms.

Chanterelles

The golden, apricot hue of chanterelles befits their bright, fruity flavor. Their size can vary from tiny blossom-like specimens to impressive 5-inch trumpets and, in the dried form, they can be quite pricey. When rehydrated, their texture is pleasantly chewy; the stems, however, can be woody, so, after soaking, trim off tough stems and discard them. Pair chanterelles with eggs and cream sauces.

Morels

Nutty, buttery, and somewhat smoky, dried morels go beautifully with spring ingredients like asparagus and spring onions. The hollow, honeycombed caps of wild morels can harbor sandy grit. With cultivated varieties this isn't as much of a problem, but to be on the safe side, it's a good idea to rinse morels with water before soaking them.

Mushroom Sauté

Serves four as a side dish.

1 tablespoon olive oil

1 tablespoon unsalted butter

1 pound mixed fresh mushrooms, washed, trimmed, and sliced ¼ inch thick, to yield 5½ to 6 cups

2 cloves garlic, minced

½ teaspoon kosher salt

2 tablespoons chopped fresh flat-leaf parsley

Freshly ground black pepper

2 to 3 tablespoons heavy cream, broth, or lemon juice (optional)

Additional chopped herbs, such as thyme, sage, and chives (optional)

A blend of shiitake, cremini, and white button mushrooms works well in this recipe, and those varieties don't cost too much and are easy to find at most grocery stores.

Heat the oil and butter in a 12-inch sauté pan or skillet over medium heat until the butter foams. Add the mushrooms and garlic. Like sponges, the mushrooms will immediately absorb all the fat in the pan. Sprinkle with the salt and stir with a wooden spoon until the mushrooms start to release their moisture and begin to shrink, 2 to 3 minutes. Increase the heat to medium high so that you hear a steady sizzle; stir occasionally. In about 5 minutes, when the liquid evaporates and the mushrooms start to brown, give just an occasional sweep with the spoon (about once a minute) to allow the mushrooms to brown nicely, cooking them another 2 to 4 minutes. Resist the inclination to stir too often. Turn off the heat and toss the mushrooms with the parsley and pepper to taste, adding more salt if needed. Be prudent with salt if you're using the sauté in another recipe. If serving as a side dish, stir in a few tablespoons cream, broth, or lemon juice to moisten the mushrooms and to deglaze the pan, scraping the browned bits off the bottom of the pan into the mushroom mixture. Add other chopped herbs if you like. *—Lynne Sampson*

Maximum Mushroom Flavor

1 Cook out the moisture

Concentrate the flavor by allowing enough time for the mushrooms to release all of their water.

2 Brown for deep flavor

Crank up the heat to brown them, and resist the inclination to stir too much.

Quick-Braised Vegetables

Browning the vegetables before braising adds depth of flavor and color to the finished dish.

Peel the carrots and cut them into sticks no more than ¾-inch thick (the length can vary). Trim or snap off the tough woody ends of the asparagus, and trim the ends of the green beans, cutting away any brown spots.

Heat the olive oil and 2 teaspoons of the butter in a 10-inch straight-sided sauté pan over medium-high heat. Be sure your pan you has a lid. When the milk solids in the butter are just beginning to turn a nutty brown, add the vegetables and salt and toss well with tongs. Arrange the vegetables in a single layer (or as many as possible in one layer); they should cover the bottom of the pan with a minimum of overlapping. Cook without stirring until the bottoms are nicely browned, 3 to 4 minutes. Toss and turn over, and cook for another 2 minutes to lightly brown another side. Pour in the broth, immediately cover the pan, and simmer until the liquid has almost completely evaporated, 2 to 3 minutes. Remove from the heat, add the lemon juice, Dijon, and remaining 1 teaspoon butter, and toss to combine well, scraping any browned bits from the bottom of the pan with a heatproof spatula or wooden spoon. Serve right away as individual servings or pour and scrape the contents of the pan onto a small platter and serve family style. *—Susie Middleton*

Serves two to three as a side dish.

- 1 pound fresh vegetables (choose from: 1 pound medium or thick asparagus; 1 pound carrots; ¾ pound green beans; or a mix)
- 1 tablespoon extra-virgin olive oil
- 1 tablespoon unsalted butter
- Scant ½ teaspoon kosher salt
- ⅓ cup low-salt chicken broth
- 1 to 2 teaspoons fresh lemon juice
- 1 teaspoon Dijon mustard

Moroccan Vegetable Ragoût

Serves three to four.

1 tablespoon extra-virgin
   olive oil

1 medium yellow onion,
   thinly sliced

One 3- to 4-inch-long cinnamon
   stick

1½ teaspoons ground cumin

2 cups peeled and medium
   diced (½-inch) sweet potatoes

One 14- to 16-ounce can
   chickpeas, drained and rinsed

One 14.5-ounce can diced
   tomatoes, with their juices

½ cup pitted green Greek or
   Italian olives, drained

6 tablespoons orange juice,
   preferably fresh

1½ teaspoons honey

1 cup water

2 cups lightly packed very
   coarsely chopped kale leaves

Kosher salt and freshly ground
   black pepper

Piquant olives and bitter kale temper the sweetness of this easy to prepare, slow-simmered stew. To make a complete meal from it, serve with a green salad and couscous studded with toasted almonds.

Heat the oil in a 5- to 6-quart Dutch oven or other heavy pot over medium-high heat. Add the onion and cook, stirring frequently, until soft and lightly browned, about 5 minutes. Add the cinnamon stick and cumin and cook until very fragrant, about 1 minute. Add the sweet potatoes, chickpeas, tomatoes and their juices, olives, orange juice, honey, and water; bring to a boil. Reduce the heat to medium low and simmer, covered, stirring occasionally, until the sweet potatoes are barely tender, about 15 minutes. Stir in the kale. Cover and continue cooking until wilted and softened, about another 10 minutes. Season with salt and pepper to taste. *—Kate Hays*

How to Pit Olives

If you've got an olive pitter, great, but it's probably just as easy to use a more ordinary kitchen tool, such as a chef's knife or a small skillet or saucepan. Apply pressure with the bottom of the pan or the side of the knife blade until the olive splits, exposing the pit enough that it can be plucked away by hand.

9
Potatoes Every Day

p316

p324

Red Potato Slices
Roasted with Lemon
& Olives
(recipe on page 318)

Smashed Red Potatoes with Basil & Parmesan

Serves four as a side dish.

2 pounds medium or large red potatoes, scrubbed and cut into 1½- to 2-inch chunks

Kosher salt and freshly ground black pepper

¼ cup olive oil

2 cloves garlic, minced

¼ cup finely chopped fresh basil

¾ cup freshly grated Parmigiano-Reggiano cheese

This rustic mash packs plenty of flavor without relying on gobs of butter and cream—a little olive oil and Parmigiano cheese do the trick. You can adjust the texture so the potatoes are perfectly "smashed" by adding a few spoonfuls of the cooking water.

Put the potatoes and 1 teaspoon kosher salt in a large saucepan and fill with enough cold water to cover the potatoes by about 1 inch. Bring to a boil, then reduce the heat to maintain a steady simmer, cover the pot partially, and cook until the potatoes are quite tender when tested with a fork, 15 to 20 minutes. Reserve some of the cooking water, then drain the potatoes. Dump them back in the pot, set over medium heat, and dry the potatoes by shaking the pan and stirring until most of the moisture has steamed off, about 2 minutes. Remove from the heat.

Using the side of a large metal spoon, cut through the skins and flesh of the potatoes, reducing the chunks to a very coarse mash. Stir in the olive oil and garlic. Add up to a couple of tablespoons of the cooking water to loosen the mash if necessary. Stir in the basil and cheese. Season to taste with salt and pepper and serve immediately. *—Eva Katz*

High-starch potatoes

Potatoes such as russets, Idahoes, and Russet Burbanks are high in starch and lower in moisture. They have thick skins, so they bake to perfection and make the fluffiest mashed potatoes. As they cook, their cells tend to separate and absorb lots of moisture, which creates their characteristic mealy, fluffy texture. When you eat these potatoes, you can sense their abundance of starch, as they feel granular and dry on your tongue.

The moisture-absorbing quality of high-starch potatoes also makes them good thickeners in soups. As chunks of high-starch potatoes cook in a soup, they fall apart, releasing starch granules into the broth, where they sop up liquid and thicken the soup. But that same quality prevents these potatoes from holding together during cooking, so they're not ideal for any dish where you want the potato to retain its shape: scalloped potatoes, whole roasted, or hash browns.

High-starch potatoes are your best bet for frying. Picture a freshly cut fry as it hits hot fat. Starch granules on the outside immediately swell in the heat and start pulling moisture from the interior of the potato. As the outside cooks and browns, the surface seals, preventing the french fry from absorbing lots of cooking fat. What you get is a french fry with a crisp, golden exterior and a dry, fluffy interior.

Medium-starch potatoes

Yukon Golds, with their slightly nutty flavor, and Yellow Finns, with their golden skin and flesh, have less starch and a creamier texture than high-starch potatoes. You can mash medium-starch potatoes if you like (and a lot of people do), but expect the result to be creamy rather than light and fluffy. Some cooks also prefer the in-between starch content of these potatoes for pan-fried potatoes and potato salads.

Low-starch potatoes

Red-skinned potatoes and round whites are considered "waxy." When you slice into one of these high-moisture, low-starch potatoes, the flesh looks translucent and firm.

The cells of low-starch potatoes adhere to one another and swell little during cooking, so they hold their shape and don't fall apart easily when handled. They also contain more sugar, which turns deliciously brown during cooking. These qualities make them suited equally well for boiling, roasting, or sautéing. Because the flesh contains less starch and more sugar, it remains moist and toothsome even while the outside becomes crisp and brown.

We love little waxy potatoes boiled and served whole with butter and parsley. Waxy potatoes are also ideal for scalloped potatoes because their slices retain a pretty shape and appealing texture during cooking, instead of disintegrating into the surrounding sauce. Because of their low starch content, these varieties only lightly absorb salad dressing, so use them if you like a potato salad that's chunky, rather than creamy.

Smashed Parslied Potatoes

Serves six as a side dish.

2 pounds Yukon Gold potatoes, peeled

Kosher salt

1 bay leaf

3 medium cloves garlic, thinly sliced

½ cup whole milk

2 tablespoons chopped fresh flat-leaf parsley

6 tablespoons extra-virgin olive oil

Freshly ground black pepper

Yukon Golds have a richer flavor and a firmer texture than starchy russets. Be gentle when adding ingredients to the mashed potatoes— overworking can make the potatoes gluey.

Cut the potatoes into 1½-inch chunks and put them in a large saucepan. Add 1 tablespoon kosher salt, the bay leaf, garlic, and enough water to cover the potatoes by 1 inch. Bring to a boil, then reduce the heat to a simmer, and cook until the potatoes are completely tender when pierced with a fork, 15 to 18 minutes.

Drain the potatoes and garlic in a colander. Discard the bay leaf. Return the potatoes and garlic to the pan over medium heat and stir occasionally until they're no longer steaming profusely (a little steam is fine) and dry out, about 3 minutes. Mash with a potato masher (the mash should be somewhat coarse).

Heat the milk in a small saucepan (or the microwave on high for 1 minute). Add 1 teaspoon kosher salt to the milk, stir to dissolve, and, using a spatula, slowly stir it into the potatoes. Stir in the parsley and olive oil. Season with several grinds of pepper and more salt to taste if needed.

If you're not serving the potatoes immediately, keep them warm in a metal bowl covered with a saucepan lid. Put the bowl over a saucepan filled with an inch of simmering water and set over low heat. —*Jennifer McLagan*

Creamy Mashed Potatoes with Warm Spices

With its yellow split peas and curry spices, these mashed potatoes are a nod to Indian dals—purées of spiced lentils, beans, or peas. They would make an exciting partner to simply grilled or roasted meats.

Put the potatoes in a large saucepan, add cold water to cover by at least an inch, add 1 teaspoon kosher salt, and bring to a boil. Cover the pan, reduce the heat to medium to maintain a steady (not raging) boil, and cook until the potatoes are tender all the way through but don't fall apart when pierced with a fork, about 20 minutes.

Meanwhile, heat the oil in a medium saucepan over medium-high heat. Add the split peas and cook just until they start to turn golden brown (watch carefully: split peas can quickly go from golden brown to dark brown to burned), about 3 minutes. Add the cumin seeds and cook, stirring, for 30 seconds. Add the butter, onion, and turmeric and cook until the onion is transparent, 4 to 5 minutes.

In a small bowl, whisk the honey and mustard powder until smooth. Stir in the milk and cream, then add this to the onions and spices. Reduce the heat to low and simmer for 5 minutes. Cover the pan and remove from the heat.

When the potatoes are tender, drain and return them to their pan, set over medium heat. Dry the potatoes, shaking the pan and stirring with a rubber spatula, until they look floury and leave a light film on the bottom of the pan. Put the dry potatoes through a ricer or food mill, or mash them with a hand masher until they're lump-free. Pour the hot, creamy onion mixture into the mashed potatoes. Stir slowly with a wooden spoon to thoroughly combine. If the potatoes seem dry, moisten with a little more milk. Transfer the spiced mashed potatoes to a serving bowl. Season with salt and pepper to taste. Serve at once. *—Floyd Cardoz*

Serves six to eight as a side dish.

2½ to 3 pounds Yukon Gold potatoes, peeled and quartered

Kosher salt

1 tablespoon corn oil

1½ teaspoons yellow split peas

1 teaspoon cumin seeds

2 tablespoons unsalted butter

1 large white onion, cut into ¼-inch dice

¼ teaspoon turmeric

2 teaspoons honey

1 teaspoon Colman's® mustard powder

¾ cup whole milk; more if needed

2 tablespoons heavy cream

Freshly ground black pepper

Keeping Mashed Potatoes Warm

You can't hold mashed potatoes directly over a burner, because they'll dry and scorch. The secret to keeping them hot is to hold them in a covered double boiler or in a metal bowl covered with a lid or aluminum foil set over a pan of barely simmering water. This way, the mash stays soft and moist. Check the water occasionally to be sure it's not boiling or has fully evaporated.

Gratinéed Red Potatoes with Chives

Serves four as a side dish.

1 pound small new red
  potatoes, scrubbed

Kosher salt and freshly ground
  black pepper

3 tablespoons olive oil

½ cup freshly grated
  Parmigiano-Reggiano cheese

1 tablespoon thinly sliced
  fresh chives

Like a simpler version of twice-baked potatoes, whole small potatoes are boiled until tender before being topped with cheese and roasted until crisp.

Position a rack in the center of the oven and heat the oven to 425°F.

Put the potatoes in a saucepan and add enough cold water to cover by 1 inch. Add 1 teaspoon kosher salt. Bring to a boil, then reduce the heat to maintain a gentle simmer. Cook until the potatoes are tender when pierced with a fork, 15 to 20 minutes. Drain the potatoes and let them cool slightly.

Oil the bottom of an 8-inch-square baking pan with 1 tablespoon of the oil. Put the potatoes in the pan. Pierce each one with the tines of a fork, twisting the fork slightly to break the skin a bit. Then gently squeeze the sides of each potato to make it pop open slightly (as you would for a baked potato). Season the potatoes generously with salt and pepper. Drizzle the remaining 2 tablespoons oil over the potatoes and sprinkle with the cheese. Roast until the potatoes are golden brown and crisp, 25 to 30 minutes. Sprinkle with the chives and serve immediately. *–Eva Katz*

Red Potato & Tomato Gratin with Leeks, Gruyère & Rosemary

This dish has it all. It's absolutely delicious, tastes better for being made ahead, and looks pretty, too. Try it with Yukon Gold potatoes or substitute some of the red tomatoes with yellow, orange, or even green tomatoes.

Cook the leeks: Heat the olive oil in a medium skillet (preferably nonstick) over medium heat. Add the leeks and sauté, stirring frequently, until limp and lightly browned, about 15 minutes. Spread the leeks evenly in the bottom of an oiled 2-quart shallow gratin dish (preferably oval). Let cool.

Cook the potatoes: In a medium saucepan, cover the potato slices with generously salted water and bring to a boil. Reduce the heat to a gentle boil and cook for 5 minutes, until the potatoes are just barely tender. Drain and rinse under cold running water until cool. Pat dry. Toss the potatoes with the olive oil, rosemary, and ½ teaspoon kosher salt.

Assemble and cook the gratin: Heat the oven to 375°F. Sprinkle ½ teaspoon of the chopped rosemary over the leeks. Starting at one end of the baking dish, lay a row of slightly overlapping tomato slices across the width of the dish. Prop the tomatoes against the dish at a 60-degree angle. Cover the row of tomatoes with a generous sprinkling of Gruyère. Next, arrange a row of potato slices over the tomatoes. Sprinkle again with Gruyère. Repeat with alternating rows of tomatoes and potatoes, sprinkling each with cheese, until the gratin is full. Sprinkle about ½ teaspoon kosher salt and the remaining ½ teaspoon rosemary over all and season with pepper. Drizzle with the olive oil. Mix any remaining Gruyère with the breadcrumb mixture and spread this over the whole gratin. Cook until the gratin is well browned all over and the juices have bubbled for a while and reduced considerably, 60 to 65 minutes. Let cool for at least 15 minutes before serving. You can make this a day ahead and reheat it; the flavors will be even more concentrated and delicious.
—Susie Middleton

Serves six to eight as a side dish; four as a main dish.

For the leeks:
1½ tablespoons olive oil

3 cups sliced leeks (about 3 large, white and pale green parts only), washed thoroughly

For the potatoes:
1¼ pounds red potatoes, left unpeeled, cut into ¼-inch-thick slices

1½ tablespoons olive oil

2 teaspoons chopped fresh rosemary

Kosher salt

For the gratin:
1 teaspoon chopped fresh rosemary

1¼ pounds ripe tomatoes, cored and cut into ¼-inch-thick slices

1¾ cups grated Gruyère cheese

Kosher salt and freshly ground black pepper

1½ tablespoons olive oil

⅔ cup fresh breadcrumbs mixed with 2 teaspoons olive oil

Potato, Thyme & Olive Oil Gratin

Serves six to eight as a side dish.

5 tablespoons extra-virgin olive oil

3 pounds Yukon Gold potatoes

1 teaspoon chopped fresh thyme

Kosher salt and freshly ground black pepper

½ cup low-salt chicken broth

The recipe can be made completely up to 4 hours ahead; let the dish sit on the counter and, 20 minutes before serving time, reheat it in the oven until warmed through.

Position a rack in the center of the oven and heat the oven to 375°F. Coat the inside of a 9-inch-square or equivalent baking dish with 1 tablespoon of the olive oil. Peel the potatoes, slice them into ⅛-inch-thick rounds, and put them in a bowl. Add the thyme, 1½ teaspoons kosher salt, and a few grinds of pepper and toss to coat everything evenly, making sure that you separate all the sticking potatoes. Pour the potatoes into the baking dish and arrange them in an even layer.

Bring the broth to a simmer in a small saucepan. Whisk the remaining 4 tablespoons oil into the broth and pour the mixture over the potatoes. Press down on the potatoes with the back of a spatula to distribute the liquid. Cover the baking dish with aluminum foil and bake for 30 minutes. Remove from the oven and remove the foil. Press down on the potatoes with a spatula to get the juices to bubble up over the edges of the potatoes. Return the pan to the oven, uncovered, and cook for another 15 minutes. Repeat this process of pressing on the potatoes every 15 minutes two more times for a total cooking time of 1 hour and 15 minutes. When done, the gratin will be lightly brown on top and the potatoes tender when pierced with the tip of a small knife. If the top of the gratin isn't browned after this amount of time, press on the potatoes again with the spatula and return the pan to the oven for up to another 10 minutes.

Remove the dish from the oven. Press one last time with the spatula, then let the dish rest on a cooling rack for 30 minutes before serving. —*Bill Telepan*

tip: For a tender texture and golden brown top keep the potatoes moist and flavorful by pressing down on the gratin with a spatula several times during baking to redistribute the liquid.

Mustard & Rosemary Roasted Potatoes

Serves four to six as a side dish.

⅓ cup plus 1 tablespoon Dijon mustard

¼ cup olive oil

1 tablespoon dry vermouth or other dry white wine

2 cloves garlic, minced

1 tablespoon chopped fresh rosemary

1 teaspoon kosher salt

Freshly ground black pepper

2 pounds red potatoes, cut into ¾- to 1-inch dice

These potatoes start out looking very wet, but the mixture cooks down to leave the potatoes crisp, crusty, and tangy. They are especially delicious with deeply flavored red-wine braises and stews.

Heat the oven to 400°F. In a large bowl, whisk the mustard, olive oil, vermouth, garlic, rosemary, salt, and pepper. Add the potatoes and toss to coat. Dump the potatoes onto a large rimmed baking sheet and spread them in a single layer. Roast, tossing with a metal spatula a few times, until the potatoes are crusty on the outside and tender throughout, 50 to 55 minutes. Serve hot. *–Molly Stevens*

Skillet-Roasted Rosemary Potatoes

These potatoes take some time in the oven, but their preparation is very quick, meaning you can go ahead and get the rest of the meal together while the potatoes cook up deliciously crisp and nicely browned. The best kind of pan for roasting these is an old-fashioned cast-iron skillet. A 10-inch skillet will hold about 8 potatoes (16 halves), while a 12-inch skillet can fit ten (20 halves). Using smallish potatoes—2 or 3 inches in diameter—cut just in half keeps the interiors moist and creamy. Sea salt's large crystals give a nice crunch without oversalting the potatoes, but kosher salt works nicely, too.

Position an oven rack at the bottom of the oven and heat the oven to 425°F. Pour enough of the oil into a large, heavy skillet, preferably cast-iron, tilting it to cover the bottom. Strip the leaves from the rosemary sprig and scatter them in the pan. Sprinkle the salt over the rosemary. Set the potatoes, cut side down, on the rosemary and salt. Roast until the potatoes are tender and the bottoms are crisp and well browned, 30 to 40 minutes. —*Ruth Lively*

Serves three to four as a side dish.

2 to 3 tablespoons olive oil

One 8-inch sprig fresh rosemary; more to taste

¾ teaspoon sea salt or kosher salt

8 to 10 small red or other waxy potatoes, scrubbed and halved

Red Potato Slices Roasted with Lemon & Olives

Serves six as a side dish.

2 pounds medium or large red potatoes, scrubbed and sliced ¼ inch thick

3 tablespoons olive oil; more for the pan

1 lemon, very thinly sliced (discard the ends and seeds)

2 cloves garlic, minced

¼ cup chopped fresh flat-leaf parsley

1½ teaspoons kosher salt

¼ teaspoon freshly ground black pepper

⅓ cup pitted oil-cured olives (optional), drained

This dish gets a bright burst of flavor from thinly sliced lemons that caramelize during cooking. You can vary the flavors by adding other Mediterranean herbs, such as rosemary, thyme, or lavender.

Position a rack in the center of the oven and heat the oven to 425°F. Generously oil a large baking dish (9x13-inch works well, or use an oval gratin dish). In a large bowl, combine the potatoes, oil, lemon slices, garlic, parsley, salt, and pepper; toss well. Spread the mixture in the baking dish so the potatoes are evenly layered (it can be rustic looking). Roast, turning the potatoes with a metal spatula every 20 minutes, until most are crisp and golden and the lemon skins are shriveled and caramelized, about 1 hour. Scatter the olives, if using, over the potatoes for the last 3 to 5 minutes of cooking. *—Eva Katz*

Little Potatoes Roasted with Onions, Thyme & Sherry Vinegar

Simple elements add up to a flavorful accompaniment to anything from roast chicken to pan-seared fish. Aim for potatoes that are all the same size; if you have some larger ones, cut them in thirds or quarters. You can try varying the vinegar and herbs to create new flavor profiles.

Position a rack in the center of the oven. Heat the oven to 425°F.

Trim the root ends of the onions, leaving enough of the core intact to hold the onion wedges together. Trim the other end of the onions and cut the onions in half vertically. Cut each half into four wedges, about 1 inch wide.

In a medium bowl, combine the onions, potatoes, olive oil, and vinegar and season with salt and pepper. Toss to coat well. Spread the vegetables and any liquid in the bowl on a large heavy rimmed baking sheet in a single layer, making sure the potatoes are all cut side down. Roast until the cut sides of the potatoes are crusty and golden brown, about 35 minutes. Turn the potatoes and onions using a metal spatula. Sprinkle the thyme over the potatoes, return the pan to the oven, and roast until the potatoes are tender and the onions very brown, about another 5 minutes. Taste and season with more salt if needed. *—Eva Katz*

Serves six as a side dish.

2 small red onions

2 pounds very small red potatoes, scrubbed and halved

3 tablespoons olive oil

3 tablespoons sherry vinegar

Kosher salt and freshly ground back pepper

3 tablespoons fresh thyme leaves (from about 1 bunch)

Twice-Baked Potatoes with Crème Fraîche & Chives

Serves eight as a side dish.

4 medium russet potatoes, scrubbed

3½ tablespoons unsalted butter, at room temperature

½ cup crème fraîche or sour cream, at room temperature

¼ cup half-and-half, whole milk, or buttermilk, warmed

¾ teaspoon kosher salt

Freshly ground white pepper

2 tablespoons snipped fresh chives or finely chopped scallions (white and green parts)

The richness and flavor of mashed potatoes are presented here in individual little packages, all of which is edible, if you like the skins. Make sure to leave enough flesh lining the potato skins so they'll hold up during the second round of baking.

Position a rack in the center of the oven and heat the oven to 350°F. Set the potatoes directly on the oven rack and bake until tender all the way through, 1 to 1¼ hours. Transfer the potatoes to a work surface and let them cool for 10 to 15 minutes.

Examine each potato to see if there's one way to halve it to give you two shallow, wide halves rather than narrower, taller ones. With a large chef's knife, slice each potato in half lengthwise, cutting cleanly rather than sawing so as not to tear the skin. Using a dishtowel or oven mitt to protect your hand from the heat, hold a potato half in one hand and gently scoop out the flesh with a spoon, leaving the shells ¼ to ⅛ inch thick. Repeat with the remaining halves. Force all the flesh through a potato ricer or mash it with a potato masher; transfer it to a mixing bowl.

With a wooden spoon, stir in 3 tablespoons of the butter, then the crème fraîche, and finally the half-and-half. Season with the salt, pepper to taste, and the chives. Taste and adjust the seasonings.

Scoop the filling into the potato skins, compacting it lightly. For a rough-textured surface, mark it with the tines of a fork. Top each with bits of the remaining ½ tablespoon butter.

Heat the oven to 400°F. Arrange the potatoes on a baking sheet or in a large baking dish. Bake until heated through and beginning to brown in spots on top, 25 to 30 minutes (or 35 to 40 minutes if made ahead and refrigerated). Let sit for about 10 minutes before serving. *—Molly Stevens*

Making Baked Potatoes Twice as Good

1 Scoop out the flesh, leaving a thin layer in the shell so it doesn't fall apart.

2 Use a light hand when mixing in the filling ingredients so the potatoes remain light and fluffy.

3 Spoon the filling back into the shell, pressing just enough so it holds together.

Steamed Baby Potatoes with Mellow Garlic & Basil Vinaigrette

Serves four as a side dish; yields about ½ cup vinaigrette.

3 small garlic cloves, smashed and peeled

6 tablespoons good-quality extra-virgin olive oil

14 fresh basil leaves

1 pound baby new potatoes, very small ones left whole, larger ones halved

2 tablespoons white-wine vinegar

1 teaspoon packed finely grated lemon zest

½ teaspoon Dijon mustard

¼ teaspoon kosher salt

⅛ teaspoon freshly ground black pepper

Cooking the garlic allows its great flavor to permeate the dressing without the harshness raw garlic can add. The vinaigrette, which keeps well refrigerated, would also be delicious drizzled over green beans or even a piece of fish.

Put the garlic and oil in a small saucepan and heat over medium low, so the cloves are just barely sizzling but not browning. Simmer for 10 minutes, remove from the heat, and add 10 of the basil leaves. Let sit for about another 15 to 20 minutes, then remove the garlic and basil.

While the basil is steeping, steam the potatoes over boiling water. Cover and cook until just tender when pierced with a paring knife, about 15 minutes. (Alternatively, boil the potatoes in generously salted water until tender. Drain, return them to the pot, and set over low heat for a few seconds to dry them.) Transfer the cooked potatoes to a medium bowl.

In a small bowl, whisk the vinegar, lemon zest, mustard, salt, and pepper. Slowly whisk in the flavored oil until the dressing is creamy and blended. Roll the remaining basil leaves into a tight roll and slice across to make thin shreds. Stir into the dressing. Taste and adjust the seasonings. (The dressing can be made ahead; it will keep for up to a week in the refrigerator.)

Pour enough of the dressing over the steamed potatoes to coat them well. Serve the potatoes immediately while still quite hot, or serve warm or at room temperature. If serving at room temperature, taste and add a little more of the vinaigrette if most of it has been absorbed. —*Martha Holmberg*

Potato Salad with Green Beans, Artichokes, Red Peppers & Olives

Serves four as a light lunch or six as a side dish.

2 tablespoons red-wine vinegar

½ teaspoon dried oregano

Kosher salt and freshly ground black pepper

⅓ cup extra-virgin olive oil

½ teaspoon green beans, trimmed and cut into 2-inch lengths

1½ pounds red potatoes, cut into ¾-inch pieces

4 to 5 scallions, finely chopped, white and green parts separated

One 14-ounce can water-packed artichoke hearts or bottoms, drained and quartered

½ cup roasted red pepper strips, cut into 2-inch pieces

½ cup pitted Kalamata olives, drained and halved

½ cup crumbled goat cheese

You can speed up preparation time by making the vinaigrette and blanching the green beans a day in advance. For a dressier presentation, make the potato salad with only the scallions, olives, and feta. Then dress the beans, artichokes, and peppers individually (you'll need a double batch of dressing). Line each plate with a few leaves of bibb lettuce drizzled with dressing and arrange all the elements artfully on top. If you like, add a bit of canned tuna or cooked chicken.

Combine the vinegar and oregano in a small bowl; season with salt and pepper. Whisk in the olive oil and taste for seasoning.

Bring a large saucepan of generously salted water to a boil. Add the beans and boil until just tender, about 4 minutes. Using a strainer, scoop out the beans and rinse under cold running water.

Let the water in the saucepan come back to a boil. Add the potatoes and simmer, adjusting the heat as necessary, until they are tender, 10 to 15 minutes. Drain and transfer the potatoes to a large bowl; add the scallion whites, drizzle on a few teaspoons of the dressing, and toss to coat. Season with salt and pepper to taste. Set aside to cool slightly.

When ready to serve, add the scallion greens, the green beans, artichokes, red peppers, olives, and goat cheese to the potatoes. Pour over the remaining dressing and toss to combine. Season to taste with salt and pepper and serve. *—Molly Stevens*

Potato Cakes with Chives & Sour Cream

Yields four potato cakes.

1 pound Yukon Gold potatoes, peeled

Kosher salt

¼ cup packed finely grated Asiago cheese

5 tablespoons extra-virgin olive oil

3 tablespoons sour cream; more for serving

¼ teaspoon freshly ground black pepper

¼ cup thinly sliced fresh chives; more for serving

These are essentially seasoned mashed potatoes shaped into cakes and pan-fried until they've developed a delicious crusty exterior. They can be shaped into patties up to a day before frying. Serve with bacon and eggs or alongside roasted meats. Of course, you can skip the frying and just serve the chive mashed potatoes as is.

Put the potatoes and 1 teaspoon kosher salt in a medium saucepan and add water to cover by about ½ inch. Cover and bring to a boil. Uncover, reduce the heat to prevent a boilover, and boil until the potatoes are tender when pierced with a fork, 20 to 25 minutes.

Drain the potatoes and pass them through a ricer or food mill back into the saucepan (or mash them as smoothly as possible with a hand masher). Add the cheese, 3 tablespoons of the olive oil, the sour cream, pepper, and ½ teaspoon kosher salt; mix thoroughly. Add the chives and stir until well mixed. Taste and add more salt and pepper, if necessary. Divide the potato mixture into quarters and shape each into a squat patty about ¾ inch thick. (If making ahead, put the patties on a plate or tray in a single layer, cover with plastic, and refrigerate.)

Heat the remaining 2 tablespoons oil in a 10-inch nonstick pan over medium-high heat. When the oil is hot, set the cakes in the pan so they aren't touching. Cook until a deep brown crust forms, 2 to 3 minutes, then turn and brown the other side, another 2 to 3 minutes (the cooking time will be a bit longer if the patties were chilled). Serve immediately, topped with a dab of sour cream and a sprinkle of chives. *—Ruth Lively*

Pan-Fried Potatoes with Pancetta & Rosemary

Searing the potatoes creates a crispy crust, then the heat is lowered and the pan is covered, allowing them to steam into tenderness. If you can't find pancetta (Italian bacon), use regular bacon, though the dish will have a smoky flavor that the unsmoked pancetta doesn't bring.

Put the pancetta and oil in a 12-inch heavy skillet over medium heat and cook, stirring frequently, until the pancetta is crisp, 6 to 8 minutes. With tongs, transfer the pancetta to a plate. Add the potatoes to the skillet and spread them into a single layer so a cut side faces down. Cook until golden brown on the bottom (the pan should sizzle but not smoke; adjust the heat if necessary), 5 to 8 minutes. Turn the potatoes with tongs so the other cut side faces down. Cook until that side is deep golden brown, another 5 to 8 minutes. Reduce the heat to medium low and cover tightly with a lid. Cook, tossing occasionally, until the potatoes are tender when pierced with a fork, 10 to 15 minutes more. If the potatoes are browning too much, reduce the heat to low.

While the potatoes cook, combine the garlic, lemon juice, and rosemary in a small bowl. When the potatoes are tender, add the garlic mixture, stirring to distribute it gently. Cook, uncovered, until the garlic mixture is heated through and fragrant, about 1 minute. Crumble the pancetta over the potatoes. Season to taste with salt and pepper and serve immediately. *—Eva Katz*

Serves four as a side dish.

3 ounces thinly sliced pancetta

2 tablespoons olive oil

1 pound medium to large low-starch potatoes, scrubbed and cut into 1-inch wedges (measured at the widest point)

2 medium cloves garlic, minced

1 tablespoon fresh lemon juice

2 teaspoons minced fresh rosemary

Kosher salt and freshly ground black pepper

Oven Fries

Serves four as a side dish.

2 large russet potatoes, peeled
and cut lengthwise into ¼- to
½-inch-thick sticks

Kosher salt

2 tablespoons extra-virgin
olive oil

Fleur de sel or other coarse salt,
or Lemon-Fennel Salt (recipe
follows)

This recipe is easily doubled; just use a second baking sheet so you don't crowd the fries.

Rinse the potatoes: Choose a pot large enough to hold the potatoes without crowding (4 to 5 quarts) and fill it with cold water. Drop the potato sticks into the water to rinse off the starch. You can immediately drain them and proceed to the next step. Or, if you want to prep the potato sticks in advance and roast them later in the day, you can leave them in the water. If you plan to wait more than 2 hours before roasting the fries, however, put the pot in the refrigerator.

Parboil the potatoes: Drain the potatoes, rinse well, and return them to the pot with enough cold water to cover by 1½ inches. Add 1 teaspoon kosher salt. Partially cover the pot and bring to a boil. As soon as the water boils, reduce the heat to a calm boil and boil for 3 minutes. Gently drain the potatoes in a large colander, then spread on paper towels to dry. (The potatoes can sit for up to an hour before roasting.)

Roast the fries: When you're ready to roast the fries, put a baking sheet on the center oven rack and heat the oven to 450°F. Put the potatoes in a large bowl, add the olive oil, and toss to coat, being careful not to break the sticks.

Remove the hot baking sheet from the oven and arrange the potatoes on it, leaving at least ½ inch between each. Roast, turning the fries over and rotating the baking sheet once after 15 minutes and then again every 6 to 8 minutes, until the fries are nicely browned and crisp, a total of about 30 minutes. Sprinkle with fleur de sel or lemon-fennel salt, toss gently, and serve immediately. *—Molly Stevens*

Lemon-Fennel Salt

Yields about 1 tablespoon.

The flavor of freshly toasted and ground spices is vastly superior to the preground variety.

½ teaspoon fennel seeds

½ teaspoon coriander seeds

¼ heaping teaspoon white peppercorns

1 teaspoon finely grated lemon zest

½ teaspoon kosher salt

Toast the fennel, coriander, and peppercorns in a small, dry skillet over medium heat until fragrant, about 2 minutes. Pour into a mortar or spice grinder and grind to a fine powder. In a small dish, combine the lemon zest and salt with the spices. (This salt will keep in the refrigerator for up to three days.)

Great Oven Fries Begin with Russet Potatoes and a Ruler

To get the most satisfying ratio of crunchy, salty exterior to fluffy, potatoey interior, choose high-starch baking potatoes, like russets, and cut them lengthwise into ½-inch square sticks or batons (a little thinner is fine, but don't go wider). It helps to shop for long, evenly shaped russets, but don't worry if each fry isn't perfect; a little variation in the size of the fries is nice.

1 Rinse

Rinsing the sliced potatoes in cold water washes away surface sugars and helps the fries form a crisp (rather than leathery) exterior.

2 Parboil

A quick boil in salted water before roasting ensures that the potatoes will cook all the way through by the time the outsides are handsomely golden. This step also fluffs up the starches, making the fries soggy. Once the potatoes are parboiled, they can sit for up to an hour on paper towels.

3 Roast

Thoroughly heating the oven and the baking sheet provides an initial blast of heat that helps the fries crisp evenly. Be sure to leave space between the fries so they get crisp on all sides.

10
Cakes, Cookies & Other Sweet Endings

p353

p360

**Triple Strawberry
Ice Cream Sundaes
(recipe on page 362)**

Sweet Wine & Honey Roasted Pears

Serves four.

1 tablespoon unsalted butter, softened

4 firm-ripe pears (any variety), peeled, halved, and cored

2 tablespoons plus 2 teaspoons honey

½ cup sweet dessert wine, such as a late-harvest Muscat or a Viognier

⅓ to ½ cup heavy cream, at room temperature, for serving

If you want to get fancy, you can top the pears with ice cream, Devon cream, crème fraîche, or mascarpone, but plain old heavy cream is awfully good, and has the virtue of simplicity. A scattering of toasted almonds would also be welcome.

Position a rack in the center of the oven and heat the oven to 375°F. Smear the butter over the bottom of a 9x13-inch baking dish or small roasting pan. Set the pear halves cut side down in the dish. Drizzle 1 teaspoon of honey over each pear half. Pour in the wine. Roast for 40 minutes. Remove the dish from the oven and, using pot holders, tilt the dish so the juices pool in one corner. With a spoon, baste each pear with the juices. Continue to roast until the juices cook down to a glazy consistency and the pears are very tender and take on a light toasted color, another 15 to 20 minutes. Lift up the cut side of a pear; it should look nicely caramelized. Turn off the oven and leave in the oven to keep warm until serving time (the liquid will continue to thicken and the pears will brown a bit more).

If the juices have completely evaporated add a tablespoon or two of hot water to the pan and swirl to recreate a syrupy glaze. Drizzle the glaze over each pear. Serve warm and pass a pitcher of heavy cream to pour over. Leftovers are good at room temperature or warmed gently. *—Ruth Lively*

Pears from September to June
Though most of the year, you'll find several varieties of pears at the market, each with different colors and textures.

Bartlett
A ripe Red Bartlett is bright red; a ripe Bartlett is bright yellow. Aromatic and sweet, this pear is perfect eaten raw. It's the first pear to appear in late August.

Comice
This very sweet, very juicy pear is wonderful raw. Its season starts in early September and lasts into December.

Forelle
The slightly crunchy texture of this pear, which appears in September, means it holds up well when cooked, but it's also delicious raw and in salads.

Seckel

The smallest of pears, it has extremely sweet, very dense, crisp flesh, and it's lovely poached or roasted. Its season is September through December.

Bosc

It comes into season in September and can be available well into spring. Its dense, grainy flesh has an elegant, aromatic flavor that's perfect for cooking.

Anjou

Juicy and very sweet, it becomes creamy when ripe. It appears in October and is available well into the early summer.

Fresh Oranges with Caramel & Ginger

Serves four to six.

5 seedless oranges, such as navel, including some blood oranges if possible

2 tablespoons chopped crystallized ginger

⅓ cup granulated sugar

8 to 10 mint leaves, very thinly sliced

If you serve this pretty dessert soon after assembling it, you'll get bits of crunchy caramel with the orange slices. If you let it sit for a couple of hours, the caramel will dissolve and blend with the orange juices to make a toasty syrup. Both ways are very appealing.

Finely grate the zest (use a rasp-style grater if you have one) from one of the oranges to get 2 teaspoons zest. Cut the tops and bottoms off of each orange, being sure to cut into some of the flesh; reserve the tops and bottoms. Cut the peel off the sides, exposing the flesh by cutting under the pithy membrane. Discard the peels cut from the sides. Cut each orange in half vertically, trim out the pithy core, and then slice each piece crosswise into ¼-inch half-moons. Arrange the slices on a large, shallow serving dish or deep platter.

Combine the zest and crystallized ginger on a cutting board and chop them together until they're well mixed. Scatter the ginger and zest evenly over the oranges.

Put 2 tablespoons water in a small, heavy saucepan and pour the sugar on top. Bring to a boil over high heat, lower the heat to medium high, and boil without stirring until the syrup has turned a deep medium brown, 5 to 8 minutes. Watch the pan carefully during the last few minutes, as the caramel goes quickly from brown to burnt. Using a heavy potholder to hold the pan, immediately drizzle the caramel over the oranges, getting a bit of caramel on each slice. Scatter the mint over the oranges. Squeeze the juice from the reserved ends of the oranges over all. *—Ruth Lively*

Apricots with Moscato & Thyme Syrup

Moscato can be expensive, but there are delicious, affordable examples, such as Sutter Home Moscato, that work well in this recipe. A pluot is a cross between a plum and apricot.

In a small saucepan, bring 2 cups of the wine to a boil. Remove from the heat and add the dried apricots. Cover the pan and let them macerate for at least 8 hours or overnight.

Strain the wine from the macerated fruit into a measuring cup. You'll need a total of 1 cup wine; if you have less, supplement with more wine from the bottle. If you have more, discard the extra. Combine the 1 cup wine and sugar in a small saucepan. Bring to a simmer over medium heat, stirring occasionally until the sugar dissolves. Add the thyme and reduce the heat to low. Cook for 7 minutes to let the thyme infuse the syrup. Strain through a fine sieve, let cool, and refrigerate until completely chilled.

Just before serving, cut the plumped dried apricots into quarters, slicing them lengthwise. Cut the fresh apricots in half, pit them, and slice each half into ½-inch-wide wedges. Put all the fruit in a large serving bowl. Pour on just enough of the Moscato syrup to lightly coat the fruit, about ⅓ cup. Garnish with fresh sprigs of thyme, if you like. *−Irit Ishai*

*Serves four to six; yields
1 cup syrup.*

2 to 3 cups Moscato or Moscato d'Asti (or any dessert wine made from Muscat grapes)

5 ounces dried apricots (15 to 20)

5 tablespoons granulated sugar

4 sprigs fresh thyme; more for garnish

2 pounds fresh apricots or pluots

Apricot-Raspberry Buckle

Serves eight to ten.

For the streusel:

⅓ cup minus 1 tablespoon
  unbleached all-purpose flour

¼ cup granulated sugar

1 teaspoon ground cinnamon

Pinch table salt

¼ cup cold unsalted butter, cut
  into small pieces

For the cake:

1⅓ cups unbleached all-
  purpose flour

1½ teaspoons baking powder

½ teaspoon table salt

¾ cup unsalted butter, at room
  temperature

1 cup granulated sugar

1½ teaspoons pure vanilla
  extract

¼ teaspoon pure almond
  extract

3 large eggs

¾ pound firm, fresh apricots,
  halved, pitted, and cut into
  ¾-inch pieces (to yield
  2 cups)

2 cups fresh raspberries

A buckle is a tender yellow cake with a fruit and streusel topping. This version features fresh apricots and raspberries both in the cake and on top.

Position a rack in the lower third of the oven and heat the oven to 375°F. Butter a 9-inch-square baking pan.

Make the streusel: In a medium bowl, combine the flour, sugar, cinnamon, and salt. Add the cold butter and cut it in with a pastry blender or two table knives until the butter pieces resemble small peas. Refrigerate until needed.

Make the cake: Sift the flour, baking powder, and salt into a small bowl. With a hand or electric stand mixer (use the paddle attachment) beat the butter on medium speed until smooth, about 1 minute. Add ¼ cup of the sugar and the extracts. Beat for 1 minute. Gradually add the remaining ¾ cup sugar while beating on medium speed. Stop and use a rubber spatula to scrape the bowl and beater. Beat on medium-high speed until pale and slightly fluffy (the sugar will not be dissolved), about 3 minutes. Reduce the speed to medium and add the eggs, one at a time, mixing until the batter is smooth each time. Stop and scrape the bowl and the beater. On low speed, add the flour mixture and beat only until incorporated. The batter will be thick. Add half the apricots and half the raspberries to the batter and fold them in gently with a large rubber spatula. Some of the raspberries will break; when baked, the pinkish cast will disappear. Spread the batter into the prepared pan and distribute the remaining fruit evenly on top. Sprinkle the streusel over the fruit. Bake until the cake springs back in the center when lightly pressed and a toothpick comes out clean, 45 to 50 minutes.

Let the cake cool in its pan on a rack. Serve warm or at room temperature.

—Greg Patent

Italian Plum Cobbler

Italian plums are great for cooking because they don't fall apart the way juicier ones usually do. If you can't find them, bigger Empress plums work well, as do apricots. You can also use a combination of plums and apricots.

Make the cobbler dough: In a food processor or electric mixer (use the paddle attachment) combine the flour, granulated sugar, baking powder, and salt. Pulse or mix to combine. Add the butter, then pulse or mix until the mixture resembles fine crumbs. Add ⅔ cup of the cream and pulse until the dough just comes together, scraping the paddle and bowl if necessary. Turn onto a lightly floured surface and gently pat it together. Shape the dough into eight 2-inch balls. Set each ball on a baking sheet and flatten slightly. Refrigerate for at least 20 minutes but no longer than 2 hours.

Make the filling: Heat the oven to 350°F. In a large bowl, combine the plums, cinnamon, cardamom, and sugar; toss well. Spoon the fruit into a 2-quart gratin or other shallow casserole dish (don't use a metal dish). Arrange the flattened dough balls on top of the fruit, leaving about 1 inch of space around each biscuit. Brush them with the remaining 1 tablespoon cream and sprinkle with the turbinado sugar. Bake on a baking sheet until the fruit is bubbling and the top is lightly browned, 40 to 45 minutes. Serve hot or warm, topped with crème fraîche or ice cream, if you like. —*Claudia Fleming*

Serves six to eight.

For the cobbler dough:

1⅔ cups unbleached all-purpose flour

3½ tablespoons granulated sugar

1½ tablespoons baking powder

⅛ teaspoon table salt

6 tablespoons cold unsalted butter, cut into ½-inch cubes

⅔ cup plus 1 tablespoon heavy cream

1 teaspoon turbinado (raw) sugar

For the filling:

2¼ pounds Italian prune plums, pitted and quartered (to yield 6 cups)

¼ teaspoon ground cinnamon

¼ teaspoon ground cardamom

¼ cup granulated sugar

Crème fraîche or vanilla ice cream for serving (optional)

Lemon Pudding Cakes

Yields eight individual cakes.

Softened butter for the ramekins

¼ cup unsalted butter, melted and cooled slightly

1 cup granulated sugar

3 large eggs, separated, at room temperature

¼ cup unbleached all-purpose flour

¼ plus ⅛ teaspoon table salt

1¼ cups whole milk, at room temperature

⅓ cup fresh lemon juice, at room temperature

1 tablespoon finely grated lemon zest

Lightly sweetened whipped cream for serving (optional)

Yes, this is the pudding cake of your childhood, and yes, it's still delicious, especially when you dollop on a bit of real whipped cream.

Position a rack in the center of the oven; heat the oven to 350°F. Butter eight 6-ounce ceramic ovenproof ramekins or Pyrex custard cups and arrange them in a baking dish or roasting pan (a 10x15-inch Pyrex dishes works well).

In a large bowl, whisk the melted butter with ⅔ cup of the sugar and the egg yolks until smooth and light, about 1 minute. Add the flour and salt and pour in just enough milk to whisk the flour smoothly into the egg yolk mixture. Then whisk in the remaining milk and the lemon juice until smooth. The mixture will be very fluid.

Put the egg whites in a large bowl. Beat with a hand or stand mixer (use the whisk attachment) on medium speed until the whites begin to foam, 30 to 60 seconds. Increase the speed to high and beat just until the whites hold soft peaks; another 1 to 2 minutes. Reduce the speed to medium. With the mixer running, very slowly sprinkle in the remaining ⅓ cup sugar; this should take about a minute. Stop and scrape the bowl. Beat on high speed until the whites hold medium-firm peaks; about another 30 seconds.

Scrape one-third of the egg whites onto the egg yolk mixture, sprinkle the lemon zest on top, and whisk until combined. Gently incorporate the remaining whites into the batter, using the whisk in a folding/stirring motion. The batter will still be thin. Portion the mixture evenly among the ramekins, filling them to within ⅛ inch of the top. Pull out the oven rack and put the baking dish full of ramekins on the rack. Pour warm water into the dish to reach halfway up the sides of the ramekins. Bake until the tops of the cakes are light golden and slightly puffed; they should feel spongy and spring back a bit but hold a shallow indentation, 25 to 30 minutes. Using tongs, carefully transfer the ramekins to a rack. Let cool to room temperature, then refrigerate for at least 2 hours and up to 24 hours. Serve with whipped cream if you like. *—Nicole Rees*

The Path to Perfect Pudding Cakes

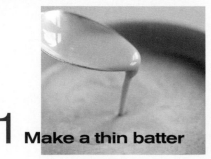

1 Make a thin batter

After you mix the melted butter, sugar, egg yolks, flour, milk, and flavorings, you'll have a very thin batter that flows off a spoon like liquid. Don't worry. A liquid batter lets pudding cakes separate into two layers as they bake.

2 Whip the egg whites to medium firm peaks

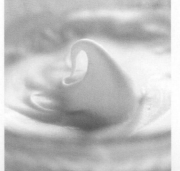

The peaks should curl over slightly, then hold their shape when the whip is pulled away from the whites.

3 Whisk the whipped whites into the batter

Use a stirring motion to incorporate one-third of the whites. Then, still using the whisk, quickly but gently fold in the rest. The batter will still be thin.

Creamy Lemon Parfaits

Yields four parfaits.

Two 3-ounce packages cream cheese, softened

¾ cup confectioners' sugar, sifted

Pinch salt

1 cup heavy cream, chilled

1½ tablespoons fresh lemon juice

1 teaspoon finely grated lemon zest

1 tablespoon finely chopped fresh mint (optional); plus 4 sprigs for garnish

4 cups fresh berries (a mix of raspberries, strawberries, and blueberries is nice), rinsed and drained well

This bright and beautiful finale is endlessly adaptable. Try layering the parfait with crushed cookies, crumbled biscotti, or even slices of cake. You can also use the lemon cream, with or without the fruit, as a topping for pound cake or angel food cake.

Combine the cream cheese, confectioners' sugar, and salt in a medium bowl. Using a hand mixer, beat on low speed until the cream cheese is smooth and the sugar incorporated. Add the heavy cream and beat on low speed until smooth, stopping to scrape down the sides of the bowl as needed. Increase the speed to medium high and beat until the cream is billowy and holds medium-firm peaks, 30 to 60 seconds. Add the lemon juice and zest and chopped mint, if using. Stir briefly to blend.

Line up four parfait glasses or stemmed wineglasses. Beginning and ending with the berries, evenly layer all the berries and all but about ⅔ cup of the cream into the glasses. Top with a dollop of the remaining cream and garnish with a mint sprig. The parfaits can be made an hour or two ahead of serving. *—Abigail Johnson Dodge*

Mocha Pudding Cakes

Yields eight individual cakes.

Softened butter for the ramekins

¼ cup unsalted butter, melted and cooled slightly

1 cup granulated sugar

3 large eggs, separated, at room temperature

⅓ cup unsweetened Dutch-processed cocoa

2 tablespoons unbleached all-purpose flour

¼ plus ⅛ teaspoon table salt

1¼ cups strong brewed coffee, at room temperature

⅓ cup whole milk, at room temperature

1 teaspoon pure vanilla extract

Lightly sweetened whipped cream for serving (optional)

tip: Wrap rubber bands around the ends of your tongs to get a better grip when lifting the ramekins out of the water bath.

If you don't have what you need to actually brew some strong coffee, you can use an instant espresso powder, found in the coffee section of most grocery stores.

Position a rack in the center of the oven and heat the oven to 350°F. Butter eight 6-ounce ovenproof ceramic ramekins or Pyrex custard cups and arrange them in a baking dish or roasting pan (a 10x15-inch or two 8-inch-square Pyrex dishes work well).

In a large bowl, whisk the melted butter with ⅔ cup of the sugar and the egg yolks until smooth and light, about 1 minute. Add the cocoa, flour, and salt and pour in just enough coffee to whisk the flour smoothly into the egg yolk mixture. Then whisk in the remaining coffee, the milk, and vanilla until smooth. The mixture will be very fluid.

Put the egg whites in a large bowl. Beat with a hand or stand mixer (use the whisk attachment) set at medium speed until the whites begin to foam, 30 to 60 seconds. Increase the speed to high and beat just until the egg whites hold soft peaks; another 1 to 2 minutes. Reduce the speed to medium. With the mixer running, very slowly sprinkle in the remaining ⅓ cup sugar; this should take about a minute. Stop the mixer and scrape the bowl. Beat on high speed until the whites hold medium-firm peaks; about another 30 seconds.

Scrape one-third of the egg whites onto the egg yolk mixture and whisk until combined. Gently incorporate the remaining egg whites evenly into the batter, using the whisk in a folding/stirring motion. The batter will still be thin.

Portion the mixture evenly among the ramekins; the cakes don't rise much, so you can fill the ramekins to within ⅛ inch of the top. Pull out the oven rack and put the baking dish full of ramekins on the rack. Pour warm water into the dish to reach halfway up the sides of the ramekins. Bake until the tops of the cakes are slightly puffed and, when touched with a finger, they feel spongy and spring back a bit but hold a very shallow indentation, 25 to 30 minutes. Using tongs, carefully transfer the ramekins to a rack. Let cool to room temperature and then refrigerate for at least 2 hours and up to 24 hours. Serve with whipped cream, if you like. *—Nicole Rees*

No-Cook Chocolate Pudding

To make mixing easier, microwave the cream in an 8-cup Pyrex measuring cup and use that vessel as the mixing bowl—the pour spout is extremely useful.

Have ready six 4- to 6-ounce ramekins or teacups. Heat the heavy cream in a small saucepan or microwave until just boiling. Remove from the heat and whisk in the cocoa until smooth. Add the chocolate, butter, sugar, vanilla, and salt, and whisk until the chocolate and butter are melted and the mixture is smooth. Pour into the ramekins or cups. Depending on their size, they'll be filled about two-thirds to three-quarters of the way. Cover with plastic (not touching the surface of the puddings) and refrigerate until chilled and thickened, at least 6 hours or up to three days.

Serve with a dollop of sweetened whipped cream and a few chocolate shavings, if you like. *—Abigail Johnson Dodge*

Serves six.

1¾ cups heavy cream

2 tablespoons unsweetened cocoa powder, preferably Dutch-processed

½ pound bittersweet chocolate, finely chopped (1½ cups)

¼ cup unsalted butter, cut into four pieces

2 tablespoons granulated sugar

1 teaspoon pure vanilla extract

Pinch salt

Sweetened whipped cream and chocolate shavings for garnish (optional)

Chocolate Mousse

Serves six; yields about 6½ cups.

10 ounces best-quality bittersweet chocolate, chopped (Lindt® is a good option)

¼ cup strong brewed coffee

¾ cup whole milk

4 large egg yolks

2 tablespoons granulated sugar

Pinch kosher salt

2 cups cold heavy cream; plus another ½ cup for garnish

3 tablespoons dark chocolate shavings for garnish (optional)

This mousse is lightened with whipped cream only (no egg whites), so the chocolate flavor remains intense and creamy. It's essential to use the best-quality dark chocolate you can find.

Put the chocolate and coffee in a heavy saucepan. Heat gently over low heat until the chocolate starts to melt; set aside. In a medium saucepan, heat the milk until bubbles begin to form around the edge; don't let it boil. In a small mixing bowl, whisk the egg yolks with the sugar and a pinch of salt just until well blended.

Whisk half of the hot milk into the egg yolks. Return the yolk mixture to the milk in the saucepan. Cook slowly over low heat, stirring continuously with a wooden spoon, until the custard thickens slightly and coats the back of the spoon (enough so that a finger run through the sauce will leave a clean trail). The time it takes for this thickening to occur will vary. It may take as little as a few minutes or as many as 20, but once the thickening begins, it happens quickly; watch carefully or the eggs will coagulate. Check with a thermometer; don't let the temperature exceed 160°F. Immediately pour the custard through a strainer over the partially melted chocolate. Whisk until smooth. Transfer to a large mixing bowl and let cool, stirring occasionally, until the mixture is about 96°F; if you dab a bit on your lip, it should feel just slightly cooler than your lip. Don't let the mixture set or the mousse won't be smooth. (If it cools too far, set it over a pan of hot water briefly and whisk until smooth.)

Beat 2 cups of the heavy cream until it holds soft peaks. With a rubber spatula, gently fold half of the whipped cream into the chocolate mixture until no white streaks remain. Gently fold in the remaining whipped cream. Spoon the mousse into six goblets or one large bowl. Cover and chill for at least 3 hours or up to two days.

To serve, beat the remaining ½ cup heavy cream until it holds soft peaks. Dollop a little on each serving and scatter with the chocolate shavings, if using.

This mousse is lightened with whipped cream only (no egg whites), so the chocolate flavor remains intense and creamy.
—Randall Price

Flourless Chocolate Cake with Chocolate Glaze

Bittersweet chocolate isn't the same as unsweetened, so don't use the little squares that you'd use for making brownies. Get the best quality you can find; if all you find is semi-sweet, go ahead and use that.

Make the cake: Position a rack in the center of the oven and heat the oven to 300°F. Lightly butter the bottom of a 9x2-inch round cake pan and line it with a round of parchment. Lightly butter the parchment and sides of the pan and dust with cocoa powder. Tap out any excess.

Melt the chocolate and butter in the microwave or in a medium metal bowl set in a skillet of barely simmering water, stirring with a rubber spatula until smooth. Remove the bowl from the water bath and set aside to cool slightly. In the bowl of a stand mixer fitted with the whisk attachment, combine the eggs, sugar, vanilla, salt, and water. Beat on medium-high speed until the mixture is very foamy, pale in color, and doubled in volume, 2 minutes. Reduce the speed to low and gradually pour in the chocolate mixture. Increase the speed to medium high and beat until well blended, about 30 seconds. Add the cocoa and mix on medium low just until blended, about 30 seconds.

Pour the batter into the prepared pan. Bake until a pick inserted in the center comes out looking wet with small gooey clumps, 40 to 45 minutes. Don't overbake. Let cool in the pan on a rack for 30 minutes. If necessary, gently push the edges down with your fingertips until the layer is even. Run a small knife around the pan to loosen the cake, cover the pan with a wire rack, and invert. Remove the pan and parchment and let the cake cool completely. Transfer to a cake plate. Cover and refrigerate the cake until it's very cold, 6 hours or overnight.

Glaze the cake: Melt the chocolate and butter in the microwave or in a medium metal bowl set in a skillet of barely simmering water, stirring with a rubber spatula until smooth. Pour the warm glaze over the chilled cake and, using an offset spatula, spread it evenly to within ¼ inch of the edge. Refrigerate the cake until the glaze is set, 20 to 40 minutes. Before serving, remove the cake from the refrigerator and let it come to room temperature, 20 to 30 minutes. To serve, cut the cake into small, if not tiny, slices using a hot knife. *—Abigail Johnson Dodge*

Yields one 9-inch cake; serves twelve generously.

For the cake:
- ¾ pound bittersweet chocolate, coarsely chopped
- ¾ cup unsalted butter, cut into six pieces; more for the pan
- 5 large eggs
- 1 cup granulated sugar
- 1½ teaspoons pure vanilla extract
- ¼ teaspoon salt
- 2 tablespoons water
- ¼ cup unsweetened natural cocoa powder, sifted if lumpy; more for the pan

For the glaze:
- ¼ pound bittersweet chocolate, coarsely chopped
- 3 tablespoons unsalted butter

Classic Vanilla Layer Cake with Vanilla Mascarpone Frosting & Raspberries

Yields one 9-inch cake; serves twelve.

For the cake layers:

1 cup unsalted butter, at room temperature; more for the pan

All-purpose flour for the pan

3 cups cake flour

1 tablespoon plus 1 teaspoon baking powder

¾ teaspoon table salt

1¾ cups granulated sugar

Seeds scraped from ¾ vanilla bean, or 2 teaspoons pure vanilla extract

1 cup whole milk

6 large egg whites, at room temperature

For the frosting:

1 pound mascarpone cheese, at room temperature

2 cups heavy cream

⅔ cup granulated sugar

Seeds scraped from 1 vanilla bean, or 2 teaspoons pure vanilla extract

Pinch salt

2 pints raspberries, rinsed and patted dry

Vanilla beans and their tiny seeds give an intense flavor and heavenly aroma to any dessert, but feel free to use pure vanilla extract instead.

Make the cake: Position a rack in the center of the oven; heat the oven to 350°F. Butter two 9-inch round cake pans. Line the bottoms with parchment and lightly flour the sides of the pans, tapping out any excess. Sift the cake flour, baking powder, and salt together. In a large bowl, beat the butter with a hand or stand mixer (use the paddle attachment) on medium speed until smooth, 1 minute. Add 1½ cups of the sugar and the vanilla seeds. Beat until well combined and fluffy, 2 minutes. Scrape the bowl as needed. On low speed, add one-third of the dry ingredients at a time, alternating with ½ cup of the milk at a time. After the last addition, scrape the bowl and mix for about 30 seconds.

In a medium bowl, beat the egg whites with a hand or stand mixer (use the whisk attachment) on medium-high speed until soft peaks form. Increase the speed to high and gradually add the remaining ¼ cup sugar. Continue beating until the whites form medium-firm peaks. Using a rubber spatula, scoop up one-quarter of the whites and stir them gently into the cake batter to lighten it. Gently fold in the remaining whites until just blended. Scrape the batter evenly into the prepared pans. Bake until the tops are light brown and a toothpick inserted in the center comes out clean, about 30 minutes. Let cool on a rack for about 15 minutes. Run a knife around each cake to loosen it. Invert the layers onto a rack, lift off the pans, and peel away the parchment. Let cool completely.

Make the frosting: In a medium bowl, beat the mascarpone, cream, sugar, vanilla seeds, and salt with an electric mixer on low speed until almost smooth, 30 to 60 seconds. Increase the speed to medium high and beat until it's thick and holds firm peaks, another 30 to 60 seconds. Don't overbeat.

Assemble the cake: Set one cake layer, top side down, on a flat serving plate. Using a metal spatula or the back edge of a table knife, spread about 2 cups of the frosting evenly over the layer. Arrange about half the berries in a single layer on the frosting but leave a ½-inch border uncovered. Place the second cake layer, top side down, on top of the frosting; press gently. Apply a very thin layer of frosting over the entire cake. Refrigerate for 5 minutes. Spread the remaining frosting over the top and sides of the cake. Garnish with the remaining berries. Refrigerate the cake for 4 hours or up to two days (cover loosely with plastic after it has chilled for 1 hour).

—Abigail Johnson Dodge

Berry Buttermilk Cake with Vanilla-Scented Crème Fraîche

Serves twelve to sixteen.

For the crumb topping:

½ cup unbleached all-purpose flour

⅓ cup firmly packed light brown sugar

¼ teaspoon kosher salt

¼ cup unsalted butter, chilled

For the cake:

2 cups fresh blueberries, raspberries, or a mix

3 cups unbleached all-purpose flour; more for the pan and for the berries

4 teaspoons baking powder

1 teaspoon baking soda

¾ teaspoon kosher salt

¾ cup unsalted butter, at room temperature; more for the pan

1½ cups granulated sugar

3 large eggs

2 teaspoons pure vanilla extract

1½ cups buttermilk

For the vanilla crème fraîche:

1 pound (2 cups) crème fraîche

1 teaspoon pure vanilla extract

1 tablespoon granulated sugar

For the best flavor, make both this deliciously moist Bundt® cake and its crème fraiche topping one day in advance. Any leftovers make a great breakfast treat for houseguests.

Make the crumb topping: Mix the flour, brown sugar, and salt in a medium bowl. Cut the butter into chunks and add to the dry mixture. Rub the flour and butter between your fingers until the mixture just comes together and has a nice crumbly texture. (This can be made ahead and stored, tightly covered, in the refrigerator for up to a week.)

Make the cake: Rinse the berries well in a colander under running water and spread on paper towels. Let air-dry for at least 15 minutes. Meanwhile, position a rack in the center of the oven and heat the oven to 350°F. Generously butter and flour a 12-cup Bundt pan or tube pan. In a medium bowl, mix the flour, baking powder, baking soda, and salt.

With a hand or stand mixer fitted with a paddle attachment, in a large bowl whip the butter and sugar together on medium-high speed until light and fluffy, about 3 minutes. Add the eggs one at a time, beating well for 15 seconds after each. Scrape the bowl, add the vanilla, and continue whipping until the mixture is light and fluffy, 1 to 2 minutes. On low speed, add the dry ingredients one-third at a time, alternating with the buttermilk ½ cup at a time. After the last addition of buttermilk, scrape the bowl, increase the speed to medium, and beat for about 15 seconds to mix fully.

Transfer the berries to a medium bowl and toss gently with 2 teaspoons flour. Gently fold the berries into the cake batter with a rubber spatula to avoid crushing the berries too much. Scrape the batter into the prepared pan with the spatula, level the batter, and sprinkle with the crumb topping.

Bake until a toothpick or wooden skewer comes out clean when inserted into the middle of the cake, 45 to 55 minutes. Let the cake rest for 10 minutes before turning it out onto a rack. Flip the cake back over so that the crumb topping is upright. Let cool completely and wrap tightly. Store at room temperature overnight before slicing.

Make the vanilla crème fraîche: With a hand or stand mixer fitted with a whisk attachment, in a medium bowl whip the crème fraîche, vanilla extract, and sugar together until soft peaks form, about 2 minutes. Cover and refrigerate until ready to use.

To serve: Slice the cake and serve each slice with a dollop of the crème fraîche. *—Maria Helm Sinskey*

Carrot Cake with Orange Cream Cheese Frosting

Serves twelve to fourteen.

For the cake:

Olive oil for the pans

1 cup granulated sugar

1 cup firmly packed light brown sugar

¾ cup olive oil

2 cups unbleached all-purpose flour, sifted

2 teaspoons ground cinnamon

1 teaspoon grated nutmeg, preferably freshly grated

2 tablespoons baking powder

½ teaspoon table salt

1½ pounds carrots, peeled and cut into 1-inch chunks

4 large eggs, at room temperature

2 teaspoons pure vanilla extract

1 cup pecans, lightly toasted, cooled, and finely chopped by pulsing in a food processor

¼ cup dark rum

For the frosting:

1 pound cream cheese, somewhat softened

½ cup honey

1 tablespoon grated orange zest

½ cup heavy cream

Use a mild olive oil for this recipe; you won't taste the "olive" flavor per se, just the rich fruitiness of it. This cake really comes into its own on its second day, when the flavors have mellowed to perfection.

Make the cake: Position a rack in the center of the oven and heat the oven to 350°F. Oil two 9x2-inch cake pans with olive oil, line the bottoms with parchment or waxed paper, and oil the paper.

Put the granulated sugar, brown sugar, and olive oil in a large bowl and set aside. In a medium bowl, combine the flour, cinnamon, nutmeg, baking powder, and salt; mix well and set aside. In a food processor fitted with the metal blade, process the carrots until in tiny pieces, scraping down the sides of the bowl, about 25 seconds. Measure 3 cups of carrots and set aside. In a small bowl, lightly beat the eggs with a fork, stir in the vanilla, and set aside.

Beat the sugar mixture on low with a hand or stand mixer until well combined, scraping down the sides of the bowl once, 2 to 3 minutes (it will look like wet sand). Continuing on low speed, gradually mix in half the dry ingredients. Add the remaining dry ingredients in three or four additions, alternating with the egg mixture, and ending with the dry; scrape the bowl once or twice. Stir in the carrots, pecans, and rum, scraping the bowl once. Let the batter sit for 15 minutes.

Divide the batter between the cake pans (if you have a scale, weigh them to see if they're even) and bake until a toothpick inserted in the center of each comes out clean, 35 to 40 minutes. Let cool in the pans on a rack for 15 minutes. Run a paring knife around the inside edge to release the cakes. With the help of a second rack, turn each pan over so the bottom faces up, remove the pan, and carefully peel off and discard the paper liner. Using the racks again, flip each layer over so the top faces up again. Let cool completely.

Make the frosting: Put the cream cheese, honey, and orange zest in a medium bowl and, with a hand or stand mixer, whip on high until smooth and light, 1 to 2 minutes, scraping the bowl. Add the cream and whip on medium, scraping the bowl, just until you see tracks from the beaters, 1 to 2 minutes.

Frost the cake: Set one cake layer on a cardboard base or other support (like a removable tart pan bottom) and spread it evenly with about one-third of the frosting. Set the second layer on top and cover the top smoothly (or with little swirls) with about one-third more of the frosting. Coat the sides evenly with a very thin layer of frosting, then use what remains to finish the sides with a second coat. Refrigerate the cake for several hours—this firms up the frosting and mellows the flavors—but give it some time at room temperature before serving to take off the chill. *—Leslie Revsin*

Strawberry Crisp

Serves eight.

3 pints small, ripe strawberries, hulled and halved

2½ cups coarse fresh white breadcrumbs

½ cup confectioners' sugar

½ teaspoon finely grated lemon zest

¼ teaspoon table salt

½ cup coarsely chopped hazelnuts

¼ cup unsalted butter, melted

3 tablespoons granulated sugar

Heavy cream or vanilla ice cream for serving (optional)

This comforting crisp is like the best buttered toast and strawberry jam. For the breadcrumbs, use firm-textured white bread or a white sourdough, removing the crusts and pulsing cubes of the bread in a food processor until you have large, irregular, coarse crumbs.

Position a rack in the center of the oven and heat the oven to 375°F.

In a bowl, toss the strawberries with 1 cup of the breadcrumbs, the confectioner's sugar, lemon zest, and salt; scrape into an 8-inch-square Pyrex baking dish. In another bowl, toss the remaining 1½ cups breadcrumbs with the hazelnuts, melted butter, and granulated sugar; sprinkle evenly over the berries. Bake until the berries are bubbling, about 40 minutes. Let cool on a wire rack for about 10 minutes.

Spoon the warm crisp into bowls and top with a drizzle of heavy cream or a scoop of ice cream, if you like. —*Lori Longbotham*

Chocolate French Toast

Serves two to four.

⅔ cup granulated sugar

⅓ cup unsweetened cocoa powder

⅛ teaspoon baking powder

¼ teaspoon table salt

1 cup whole milk

4 large eggs

1 teaspoon pure vanilla extract

Four 1-inch-thick slices challah bread (stale is fine)

¼ cup unsalted butter

Confectioners' sugar, for garnish (optional)

Fresh raspberries, strawberries, or sliced bananas, for garnish (optional)

This recipe calls for challah bread, which isn't a conventional baking staple but is convenient to have on hand. Keep thick slices of this braided egg bread in the freezer so you can turn out this snack at any time.

In a medium bowl, combine the granulated sugar, cocoa, baking powder, and salt. Whisk until well blended and no cocoa lumps remain. Pour in about half of the milk and whisk until the mixture is a lump-free paste. Add the remaining milk, the eggs, and vanilla. Whisk until well blended.

Arrange the bread in a single layer in a 9x13-inch baking dish and pour the cocoa mixture over it. Turn the bread once to get both sides nicely coated. Poke each slice repeatedly with a fork to encourage the bread to absorb the batter. Let soak, turning every 10 minutes, until the bread is well saturated, 20 to 30 minutes.

Set a griddle or large nonstick skillet over medium heat. When the pan is hot, add the butter and spread to cover the pan. (If using a skillet, you'll need to cook in two batches, using 2 tablespoons butter for each batch.) Using your fingers and a large rubber spatula, carefully transfer the bread slices, one at a time, from the batter to the griddle. Cook until the underside looks browned and lightly crisp, 3 to 4 minutes. (Reduce the temperature if the slices are browning too fast.) Flip and cook until the slices are slightly puffed in the center and bouncy to the touch, another 3 to 4 minutes. Transfer to plates and serve immediately, dusted with confectioners' sugar and fruit if you like. *—Abigail Johnson Dodge*

Roasted Strawberry Shortcakes with Vanilla Biscuits

Serves six.

1¾ cups unbleached all-purpose flour

½ cup plus 3 tablespoons granulated sugar; more for sprinkling

1 tablespoon baking powder

¼ teaspoon table salt

1½ cups chilled heavy cream; more for brushing

2 teaspoons pure vanilla extract

1 quart small, ripe strawberries, hulled

½ cup sour cream

2 tablespoons confectioners' sugar

These vanilla biscuits are best fresh from the oven, so, if you can, bake them about an hour before you plan to serve the shortcakes. The whipped cream in the biscuit dough is a bit unusual, and the results are out of this world.

Position a rack in the center of the oven and heat the oven to 425°F. Grease a large baking sheet.

In a large bowl, whisk the flour, 3 tablespoons of the granulated sugar, the baking powder, and salt. In another large bowl, beat 1 cup of the cream with an electric mixer on medium high just until the cream holds soft peaks when the beaters are lifted. Beat in the vanilla.

Make a well in the center of the flour mixture, add the whipped cream, and stir with a fork just until the mixture begins to hold together as dough. Turn the dough out onto a lightly floured surface and knead just until well combined, about six times. Pat the dough until it's about ½ inch thick. Cut out a total of six rounds with a 3-inch crinkle- or smooth-edged biscuit cutter, gathering the scraps and reshaping as needed. Lightly brush the tops of the rounds with cream and sprinkle with granulated sugar. Arrange the biscuits on the baking sheet. Bake until golden brown, 12 to 15 minutes. Transfer with a metal spatula to a rack and let cool.

Increase the oven temperature to 450°F. Meanwhile, toss the strawberries in a bowl with the remaining ½ cup granulated sugar. Transfer to a rimmed baking sheet. When the oven is ready, roast the berries, stirring every 5 minutes, until they're soft and fragrant, about 15 minutes total.

To serve, whip the remaining ½ cup cream with the sour cream and confectioners' sugar until it holds soft peaks when the beaters are lifted. Split each biscuit horizontally with a fork, lay a bottom half on each of six serving plates, and spoon over a portion of the warm roasted berries. Garnish with a dollop of cream, add the biscuit top, drizzle with the syrup from the roasted berries, and serve immediately.

—*Lori Longbotham*

A New Secret for Tender Biscuits

The cream is first whipped, then folded into the dry ingredients with a fork to give the biscuits an ethereal texture.

Individual Apple Charlottes

Serves eight.

For the filling:

1 lemon, rinsed

3 pounds Braeburn or Golden Delicious apples, peeled, cored, and cut into ¼-inch dice

1 vanilla bean, split lengthwise, seeds scraped (reserve the seeds and pod)

⅓ cup dark raisins

⅓ cup golden raisins

5 tablespoons unsalted butter

¼ cup granulated sugar

1 tablespoon Calvados (or other apple brandy)

For the crust:

1 loaf sliced white bread (Pepperidge Farm Classic White works well; you may want to buy an extra loaf just in case)

1 cup unsalted butter

¾ cup granulated sugar

Crème fraîche or vanilla ice cream for serving

These can be prepared a day ahead, covered (still in the molds) with plastic, and refrigerated. To reheat, let them sit at room temperature while you heat the oven to 350°F. Bake until hot, about 12 minutes, and unmold.

Make the filling: Using a vegetable peeler, peel the zest off half the lemon in long strips, avoiding the bitter white pith. In a large bowl, toss the apples, lemon zest, vanilla seeds and spent pod, and raisins. In a 12-inch skillet, melt the butter over medium-high heat, then stir in the sugar. Add the apple mixture and cook, stirring, until the apples look soft on the outside (they'll still be a little crunchy inside), about 7 minutes. Set aside to cool slightly, then add the Calvados.

Prepare the crust: Position a rack in the center of the oven; heat the oven to 475°F. Trim the bread crusts. Cut eight rounds to fit the bottoms of eight 8-ounce ramekins. Cut enough rectangles to line the sides. (The bread should come to within at least ¾ inch of the ramekin's rim, if not the top.) Melt the butter in a medium skillet and put the sugar in a shallow dish. Brush the insides of the ramekins with butter. Generously dip both sides of each piece of bread in butter, followed by sugar on one side. Lay one round in each ramekin, sugared side down. Nestle the rectangles, sugared side facing outward toward the ramekin, so they line the sides of each one.

Assemble and bake: Pick the lemon zest and vanilla bean halves out of the filling. Fill each ramekin generously, pressing to get rid of air pockets. Set the ramekins on a rimmed baking sheet and cover snugly with a sheet of foil. Bake for 40 minutes. To see if they are done, run a paring knife around the side and invert a ramekin onto a plate; the bottom should be nicely caramelized and will

Assembling the Apple Charlottes

Trace around the ramekin

Trace around the ramekin bottom with a paring knife to cut a round of bread to line each ramekin.

2 Cut strips of bread to line the sides.

The bread needn't come all the way up the sides of the ramekin, but it should be close to the rim.

have caramelized more than the sides. (If they are not done, bake for a few more minutes). Unmold and serve with a spoonful of crème fraîche or a scoop of vanilla ice cream on the side. —*Ris Lacoste*

3 Add the apple mixture

Add the apple mixture to the bread-lined ramekins, packing it firmly.

Triple Chocolate Ice Cream Pie

Serves eight to twelve.

6 ounces (about 30) chocolate wafer cookies

5 tablespoons unsalted butter, melted; more for greasing the pan

2 pints chocolate ice cream, slightly softened

Quick Hot Fudge Sauce (recipe follows), at room temperature

1 pint coffee ice cream, slightly softened

1 pint vanilla ice cream, slightly softened

This pie features a chocolate crust, chocolate ice cream, and chocolate sauce, with a few scoops of coffee and vanilla added for contrast.

Position a rack in the center of the oven and heat the oven to 350°F. Butter a 9-inch Pyrex or metal pie plate.

Put the cookies in a zip-top bag and crush them with a rolling pin (or process in a food processor) until you have fine crumbs. Measure 1½ cups of crumbs (crush more cookies, if necessary) and put them in a bowl. Add the melted butter and stir until the crumbs are evenly moistened. Transfer to the pie plate and, using your fingers, press the mixture evenly into the bottom and sides (but not on the rim). Bake for 10 minutes. Let cool completely on a wire rack.

Scoop 1 pint of the chocolate ice cream into the cooled crust and spread it evenly with a rubber spatula. Place in the freezer to firm up for about 30 minutes. Remove the pie from the freezer and, working quickly, drizzle ½ cup of the room-temperature fudge sauce over the ice cream. Using a small ice cream, scoop round balls of the chocolate, coffee, and vanilla ice creams and arrange them over the fudge sauce layer (you may not need all of the ice cream). Drizzle with about ¼ cup of the remaining fudge sauce, using a squirt bottle if you have one. Freeze until the ice cream is firm, about 2 hours. If not serving right away, loosely cover the pie with waxed paper, then wrap with aluminum foil. Freeze for up to two weeks.

To serve, let the pie soften in the refrigerator for 15 to 30 minutes (premium ice cream brands need more time to soften). Meanwhile, gently reheat the remaining fudge sauce in a small saucepan over medium-low heat. Pry the pie out of the pan with a thin metal spatula. (If the pie doesn't pop out, set the pan in a shallow pan of hot water for a minute or two to help the crust release.) Set the pie on a board, cut into wedges, and serve drizzled with more hot fudge sauce, if you like. *—Lori Longbotham*

Quick Hot Fudge Sauce

Yields 1½ cups.

This sauce will keep for at least two weeks in the refrigerator and for several months in the freezer.

1 cup heavy cream

2 tablespoons light corn syrup

Pinch salt

½ pound bittersweet chocolate, finely chopped

Bring the cream, corn syrup, and salt just to a boil in a medium heavy saucepan over medium-high heat, whisking until combined. Remove from the heat, add the chocolate, and whisk until smooth. Let cool to a bit warmer than room temperature before using in the ice cream pie. The sauce thickens as it cools; you want it warm enough to drizzle but not so warm that it melts the ice cream.

Triple Strawberry Ice Cream Sundaes

Serves four to six.

1 quart small ripe fresh
strawberries, hulled

½ cup granulated sugar

1 quart vanilla ice cream

Strawberry Whipped Cream
(recipe follows) or lightly
sweetened whipped cream

¼ cup sliced almonds, toasted

4 to 6 Chocolate-Dipped
Strawberries (recipe follows)

Strawberry sauce, strawberry whipped cream, vanilla ice cream, and chocolate-covered strawberries. Yum, yum, yum, and yum.

Position a rack in the center of the oven and heat the oven to 450°F. Toss the strawberries in a bowl with the sugar. Transfer to a rimmed baking sheet. When the oven is hot, roast the strawberries, giving them a stir every 5 minutes, until they're soft and fragrant, about 15 minutes total. Transfer the sheet to a rack to cool for 5 minutes, then scrape the berries with their sauce into a small bowl. Chill in the refrigerator until cold, about 2 hours, or up to a day.

To make the sundaes, in tall glasses, layer scoops of the ice cream with the roasted strawberries. Top with a dollop of the whipped cream, a scattering of almonds, and a chocolate-dipped strawberry. Serve immediately.

–Lori Longbotham

Strawberry Whipped Cream

Yields 2 cups.

For a uniform pale pink cream, be sure all the strawberry purée is folded in.

10 small, ripe strawberries, hulled

¾ cup heavy cream

2 tablespoons confectioners' sugar

Pinch salt

Purée the strawberries in a food processor until smooth. Pour through a fine sieve set over a bowl, pressing hard on the solids. (You should have about ¼ cup purée.) Discard the solids. Refrigerate the purée until very cold, about 15 minutes.

In a deep bowl, beat the cream with an electric mixer on medium high just until the cream begins to thicken. Add the sugar and beat just until soft peaks form when the beaters are lifted. Slowly beat in half of the strawberry purée and the salt. Beat just to stiff peaks. Drizzle the remaining purée over the cream and gently fold it in with a rubber spatula. Serve immediately, or refrigerate, covered, for a few hours, whisking lightly to recombine before serving.

Chocolate-Dipped Strawberries

Yields about 1 dozen.

Use the best strawberries and chocolate you can, and be sure your strawberries are bone-dry before you dip them into the melted chocolate or the chocolate will seize into a mass.

3 ounces bittersweet chocolate, chopped into almond-size pieces

2 teaspoons neutral vegetable oil, such as grapeseed or canola

1 pint medium, ripe strawberries (preferably with stems), rinsed and dried

Melt the chocolate with the oil in a small, deep heatproof bowl set in a skillet holding about 1 inch of barely simmering water, whisking occasionally until smooth. Remove the bowl from the heat.

Line a small rimmed baking sheet with waxed paper. Tilt the bowl to pool the chocolate on one side. Dip each strawberry into the chocolate to cover about two-thirds of the berry, until the chocolate reaches the strawberry's shoulders. Turn the berry to coat it evenly, lift it out of the chocolate, and gently shake off any excess. Carefully lay it on the waxed paper. If the dipping chocolate begins to cool and thicken, return the bowl to the water bath to heat it briefly.

Let the berries stand at room temperature for 15 minutes, then refrigerate until the chocolate is set, 20 to 30 minutes. Carefully remove the berries from the paper. Serve immediately or refrigerate for up to 8 hours before serving.

Bourbon Pumpkin Tart with Walnut Streusel

Yields one 10-inch tart; serves eight to ten.

For the tart crust:

2 cups unbleached all-purpose flour

⅓ cup granulated sugar

1 teaspoon finely grated orange zest

½ teaspoon table salt

11 tablespoons cold unsalted butter, cut into ½-inch cubes

1 large egg, lightly beaten

¼ cup heavy cream; more if needed

For the pumpkin filling:

One 15-ounce can pure solid-pack pumpkin

3 large eggs

½ cup granulated sugar

¼ cup packed dark brown sugar

2 tablespoons unbleached all-purpose flour

1 teaspoon ground ginger

1 teaspoon ground cinnamon

¼ teaspoon ground cloves

¼ teaspoon table salt

½ cup heavy cream

¼ cup bourbon

For the streusel topping:

¾ cup unbleached all-purpose flour

⅓ cup granulated sugar

⅓ cup packed dark brown sugar

½ teaspoon ground cinnamon

½ teaspoon table salt

½ cup cold unsalted butter, cut into ½-inch cubes

¾ cup walnut halves, toasted and coarsely chopped

¼ cup chopped crystallized ginger

Lightly sweetened whipped cream for garnish (optional)

This tart makes an elegant change from classic pumpkin pie, with a fragrant orange-scented crust and a crunchy walnut streusel top. It's actually a little easier to make than a regular pie, and it's much easier to cut evenly for serving.

Make the tart crust: Using a hand or stand mixer fitted with a paddle attachment, mix the flour, sugar, orange zest, and salt in a large bowl on low speed for about 30 seconds. Add the butter and combine on low speed until the mixture looks crumbly, with pieces of butter about the size of dried peas, about 3 minutes. Add the egg and cream, mixing on low speed until the dough is just combined. If the dough is too dry to come together, add more cream, a tablespoon at a time. Gently mold the dough into a 1-inch-thick disk and wrap in plastic wrap. Refrigerate for at least 1 hour or for up to a week; the dough can also be frozen for up to a month.

Make the pumpkin filling: Spoon the pumpkin into a large bowl. Whisk in the eggs, one at a time, until thoroughly incorporated. Add both sugars and the flour, ginger, cinnamon, cloves, and salt. Whisk about 30 seconds. Whisk in the heavy cream and bourbon.

Make the streusel topping: Combine the flour, both sugars, cinnamon, and salt in a food processor fitted with a metal blade. Pulse briefly to mix. Add the butter and pulse until it has blended into the dry ingredients and the mixture is crumbly. Remove the blade and stir in the walnuts and crystallized ginger.

Assemble the tart: Position a rack in the center of the oven and heat the oven to 350°F. Take the tart dough from the refrigerator and let it warm up until pliable, 5 to 15 minutes. Unwrap and set it on a lightly floured surface. With as few passes of the rolling pin as possible, roll the disk into a 13-inch round, about 3/16 inch thick. Drape the round into an 11-inch fluted tart pan with a removable bottom, gently fitting it into the contours of the pan. Fold the excess dough into the sides of the pan and press to create an edge that's flush with the top of the pan and about ½ inch thick. Pour the pumpkin mixture into the unbaked tart crust. Scatter the streusel topping evenly over the top.

Bake until the topping is evenly cooked and no longer looks wet in the center, 50 to 65 minutes. Let the tart cool on a rack for at least 2 hours before serving (or wrap it in plastic and refrigerate overnight; before serving, let it sit at room temperature for 1 to 2 hours). Serve warm, at room temperature, or slightly chilled, with lightly sweetened whipped cream, if you like.

—Rebecca Rather

New York Style Cheesecake with Cranberry-Cointreau Sauce

Yields one 9-inch cake; serves twelve to sixteen.

For the cheesecake:

Four 8-ounce packages cream cheese

4 large eggs

¾ cup sour cream

1⅓ cups granulated sugar

1 tablespoon all-purpose flour

2 tablespoons fresh lemon juice

1 teaspoon pure vanilla extract

For the graham cracker crust:

1½ packed cups finely ground graham cracker crumbs (about 10 cracker rectangles)

¼ cup granulated sugar

5 tablespoons unsalted butter, melted; plus 1 teaspoon melted butter for the pan

Cranberry-Cointreau Sauce (recipe follows)

Cranberry-Cointreau Sauce

1¼ cups granulated sugar

½ cup honey

¾ cup water

12 ounces fresh cranberries, rinsed and picked over

2 tablespoons Cointreau

In a medium saucepan, bring the sugar, honey, and water to a boil, stirring until the sugar dissolves. Reduce the heat to medium and stir in the cranberries. Cook, stirring occasionally, until the foam turns fuchsia and many berries have popped, about 5 minutes. Remove from the heat; stir in the Cointreau. Refrigerate until cold, about 3 hours, but preferably overnight. The sauce can be made 2 days ahead and refrigerated.

Cheesecakes aren't hard to make, but you can't always prevent the top from cracking, which can ruin the look. This beauty avoids that problem altogether with its brilliant jewel-like topping.

At least 4 hours before you begin, set the cream cheese, eggs, and sour cream on the counter; it's essential that they be at room temperature.

Meanwhile, make the crust. Position a rack in the center of the oven; heat the oven to 350°F. In a medium bowl, mix the graham cracker crumbs and sugar. Stir in the melted butter until the crumbs are evenly moistened. Dump the crumbs into a 9-inch springform pan that's about 2½ inches deep and press firmly into the bottom and about halfway up the side. Bake until the crust is fragrant and warm to the touch, 5 to 7 minutes; it shouldn't brown too much. Let cool on a rack while you prepare the batter.

With a hand or stand mixer (use the paddle attachment), beat the cream cheese with the sugar at medium-low speed until smooth and somewhat fluffy, about 2 minutes. On low speed, beat in the flour. One at a time, beat in the eggs on low speed, mixing only 15 to 20 seconds after each egg, scraping the bowl each time. Don't overbeat. Add the sour cream, lemon juice, and vanilla. Beat at low speed until well combined and smooth, about 30 seconds.

Wrap the outside of the springform pan tightly with two sheets of extra-wide heavy-duty aluminum foil to make the pan waterproof. Brush the inside rim with the remaining 1 teaspoon melted butter, taking care not to disturb the crust. Pour the batter into the prepared crust; it should come to within about ½ inch of the pan's rim. Put the springform in a roasting pan and pour hot water into the roasting pan to reach halfway up the sides of the springform. Bake at 350°F, 70 to 75 minutes without opening the oven door for the first hour, until the top is golden brown and doesn't wobble in the middle when the pan is nudged (a little jiggle is fine). It will be gooey in the middle; it will set as it cools.

Remove the pan from the water bath, remove the foil wrapping, and set the pan on a wire rack. Run a thin knife around the inside rim. Let cool on the rack until barely warm. Refrigerate, uncovered, for at least 8 hours or overnight. It will firm up during chilling.

Run a thin knife around the rim. Unclasp and remove the side of the pan, then use a wide spatula to transfer the cake to a serving plate. Right before serving, use a slotted spoon to scoop the cranberries out of the syrup. Let them drain briefly and spoon them onto the cake. Use a warmed, thin knife to slice. *—Nicole Rees*

Double Ginger Crackles

Yields about four dozen cookies.

2¼ cups unbleached all-purpose flour

2¾ teaspoons ground ginger

1 teaspoon baking soda

¼ teaspoon table salt

¾ cup unsalted butter, at room temperature

1⅓ cups granulated sugar

1 large egg, at room temperature

¼ cup molasses

3 tablespoons finely chopped crystallized ginger

The double hit of ginger here comes from both ground and crystallized ginger. Ginger flavor intensifies with time, making these cookies excellent candidates for long keeping. When stored in an airtight container, the cookies remain impressively delicious for up to five days after baking, and up to several weeks in the freezer.

Position racks in the upper and lower thirds of the oven; heat the oven to 350°F. Line two large cookie sheets with parchment.

In a medium bowl, whisk the flour, ground ginger, baking soda, and salt. In a large bowl, beat the butter and 1 cup of the sugar with a hand or stand mixer (use the paddle attachment) on medium-high speed until well blended. Add the egg, molasses, and crystallized ginger; beat well. Add the dry ingredients and mix on low speed until well blended.

Pour the remaining ⅓ cup sugar into a shallow bowl. Using a small ice cream scoop, a 1-tablespoon cookie scoop, or two tablespoons, shape the dough into 1-inch balls. Roll each ball in the sugar to coat and set 1½ to 2 inches apart on the prepared cookie sheets.

Bake, rotating the sheets halfway through baking, until the cookies are puffed and the bottoms lightly browned, 12 to 14 minutes. If you touch a cookie, it should feel dry on the surface but soft inside; the surface cracks will look a bit wet. Let the cookies sit on the sheet for 5 minutes, then transfer them to a rack to cool completely. When cool, store in airtight containers.

−Abigail Johnson Dodge

Shopping for and Storing Ginger

Fresh
Look for unblemished, firm roots; avoid the older, wrinkly ones. Fresh ginger keeps in the fridge for two weeks or so. To use, gently scrape away the thin layer of skin from a portion of the root with a spoon. For finely grated fresh ginger, use a rasp-style grater.

Dried or ground
Like all dried spices, ground ginger's intensity diminishes over time, so buy in small quantities and use it up within six months. If you're not sure if your ground ginger is still fresh, smell it: It should have an assertive, spicy, gingery aroma.

Crystallized
This soft, candied form of ginger is sold in many sizes, all of which are found in natural-foods or gourmet stores, Asian markets, and, increasingly, supermarket spice sections. Whether you buy ¼-inch-thick quarter-size rounds or chopped or diced crystallized ginger, be sure it's moist, pliable, and visibly coated with sugar granules.

Jumbo Dried Cherry Oatmeal Jumbles

Yields 16 to 18 big, chewy cookies.

¾ cup unsalted butter, at room temperature

½ cup granulated sugar

½ cup packed light brown sugar

1 large egg, at room temperature

1 tablespoon light corn syrup

1 teaspoon pure vanilla extract

1½ cups unbleached all-purpose flour

¼ cup cake flour

1 teaspoon baking soda

½ teaspoon table salt

½ cup sweetened dried cherries

½ cup rolled oats (old-fashioned, not quick-cooking)

½ cup pecan pieces or coarsely chopped pecan halves, lightly toasted

½ cup sweetened coconut flakes, lightly toasted

3½ ounces good-quality white chocolate, coarsely chopped

If you're not a fan of white chocolate, you can omit it from this recipe and double the amount of dried cherries instead.

Position two racks near the center of the oven and heat the oven to 325°F. Line three baking sheets with parchment.

In a large bowl, with a hand or stand mixer (use the paddle attachment) beat the butter and both sugars at medium speed until light and fluffy, about 2 minutes. Scrape the bowl. Add the egg, corn syrup, and vanilla; beat for 1 minute on medium speed. Mix in half the all-purpose flour on low speed until thoroughly combined, 30 to 60 seconds. Scrape the bowl. Briefly mix in the remaining half of the all-purpose flour. Sprinkle over the cake flour, baking soda, and salt and beat on low speed until well blended, 30 to 60 seconds. With a wooden spoon or a rubber spatula, stir in the cherries, oats, pecans, coconut, and chocolate.

Using your fingertips, shape 2-ounce pieces of dough (about a scant ¼ cup) into 2-inch-diameter disks that are ½ inch thick. Space them at least 2 inches apart on the prepared sheets. Bake until the edges and bottoms are golden and the centers feel dry on the surface but still soft inside, 15 to 16 minutes. When baking two pans of cookies at once, switch the position of the pans after 8 minutes for even browning. Let the cookies cool on the baking sheets for at least 1 minute before transferring them to a wire rack to cool completely. They will keep for three or four days at room temperature or for several weeks in the freezer. —*Nicole Rees*

Double Chocolate Chunk Fudge Brownies

If you use a metal pan, the edges of these brownies will be flat and the texture even. If you use Pyrex, your brownies will have puffier, drier edges, but it will be easier to get them out of the pan.

Position a rack in the center of the oven and heat the oven to 350°F. Generously butter the bottom and sides of an 8-inch-square baking pan.

Melt the butter in a medium saucepan over medium heat, stirring occasionally. Off the heat, add the cocoa. Whisk until smooth. Add the sugar and salt and whisk until blended. Add 1 egg and whisk until just blended. Whisk in the vanilla and the second egg until just blended. Sprinkle the flour over the mixture and stir with a rubber spatula until just blended. Add the chopped chocolate and stir until combined.

Scrape the batter into the prepared baking pan and spread evenly. Scatter the nuts evenly over the batter, if using. Bake until a toothpick inserted in the center comes out with small, gooey clumps of brownie sticking to it, 33 to 38 minutes. Don't overbake or the brownies won't be fudgy. Transfer the pan to a rack and let cool completely.

Run a knife around the edges of the brownie, then pry it from the pan in one piece. Using a sharp knife, cut the cooled brownie into three equal strips and cut each strip into four equal pieces. Or, use a bench scraper to cut the brownie in the pan, then use a metal spatula to lift out the cut brownies. The cooler the brownie is, the cleaner the cutting will be, but these fudgy brownies will always leave some sticky crumbs on the knife. –*Abigail Johnson Dodge*

Yields 12 brownies.

- ¾ cup unsalted butter, cut into 6 pieces; more for the pan
- ⅔ cup unsweetened cocoa powder
- 1⅔ cups granulated sugar
- ¼ teaspoon table salt
- 2 large eggs
- 1 teaspoon pure vanilla extract
- 1 cup unbleached all-purpose flour
- ¼ pound semisweet or bittersweet chocolate very coarsely chopped
- ½ cup coarsely chopped walnuts or pecans (optional)

Mexican-Style Pecan-Chocolate Squares

Yields sixteen 2½-inch squares.

For the cookie base:

¾ cup cold unsalted butter, cut into ½-inch pieces

2 cups unbleached all-purpose flour

½ cup packed light brown sugar

2 teaspoons ground cinnamon

½ teaspoon table salt

2 ounces bittersweet chocolate, finely grated

For the pecan topping:

10 ounces (3 cups) pecans, toasted

½ cup unsalted butter

1 cup packed dark brown sugar

⅓ cup honey

2 tablespoons heavy cream

½ teaspoon table salt

A pinch of cinnamon and ample salt in the dough make the cookie base for these squares good enough to eat on its own. But go ahead and top it off with the bittersweet chocolate (use semisweet, if that's all you can find) and the chewy pecan layer for a killer treat. The squares are wonderful as a full-fledged dessert when served with a scoop of vanilla ice cream.

Make the cookie base: Position a rack in the center of the oven and heat the oven to 350°F.

Put the butter in a food processor, along with the flour, brown sugar, cinnamon, and salt. Pulse until well combined (about 20 pulses). Scatter the dough into a 9-inch-square baking pan and press it evenly over the bottom. (Wipe out the processor bowl but don't bother washing it.) Bake the base until firm and lightly browned, about 25 minutes. When it comes out of the oven, sprinkle the grated chocolate evenly over the top. (Don't turn off the oven.) Set the pan aside.

Make the pecan topping: As the cookie base bakes, pulse the pecans in the food processor until coarsely chopped. In a medium, heavy saucepan, melt the butter. Stir in the brown sugar, honey, cream, and salt. Simmer for 1 minute, stirring occasionally. Stir in the pecans. Pour the mixture over the chocolate-sprinkled cookie base, spreading evenly. Bake until much of the filling is bubbling (not just the edges), 16 to 18 minutes.

Let cool completely in the pan. When ready to serve, cut into 16 squares. Tightly covered, these bars will keep for about five days (though they never last that long). *—David Norman and Paula Disbrowe*

Honey Caramels, with Honey-Nut and Vanilla-Tangerine Variations

Yields about a hundred
¾-inch-square caramels.

1⅔ cups heavy cream

1 teaspoon pure vanilla extract

1½ cups granulated sugar

¼ cup plus 3 tablespoons honey

3 tablespoons unsalted butter,
  at room temperature; more
  for the pan

½ teaspoon table salt

For the Honey-Nut version:

1 to 1¼ cups salted mixed
  whole nuts (don't use a
  mixture containing peanuts–
  they'll overwhelm the flavor
  of the other nuts), very lightly
  toasted to refresh the flavors

For the Vanilla-Tangerine version:

Finely grated zest of
  2 tangerines (about
  2 tablespoons plus
  1 teaspoon)

Caramels are one of the few candies that are worth making yourself. They're easy (if you follow the recipe precisely) and make wonderful gifts. The honey adds its own flavor but also helps to prevent the sugar mixture from crystallizing.

Butter an 8-inch-square baking pan, line the bottom with parchment, and butter the parchment. Don't worry if the parchment pops up a bit, the weight of the caramel will press it back down.

If making honey-nut caramels, scatter the nuts evenly over the bottom of the pan.

In a small saucepan, heat the cream with the vanilla over medium heat until it comes to a simmer. Reduce the heat to very low and keep the cream hot.

Heat the sugar with the honey in a 4-quart or larger saucepan over medium-high heat, stirring occasionally with a long-handled wooden spoon, until the sugar is mostly dissolved and it starts to boil, 4 to 5 minutes. Stop stirring and brush down the sides of the pot with a clean pastry brush dipped in water to dissolve any clinging sugar crystals. Clip a candy thermometer to the pot and let the mixture boil, without disturbing the bubbling sugar, until it reaches 305°F, 2 to 5 minutes. Rinse any clinging sugar off your spoon and dry it with a towel.

Add the 3 tablespoons butter and the salt. Slowly stir in the warm cream. The mixture will boil furiously and bubble up considerably as soon as you begin adding things: Just keep slowly and steadily pouring in the cream and stirring. By the time all the cream is added, the temperature of the mixture will have started to drop. Continue stirring, watching the thermometer closely, until the temperature is back up to 250°F. Take the pan off the heat.

If making vanilla tangerine caramels, stir in the tangerine zest now.

Immediately pour the hot caramel into the prepared pan. Do not scrape the pot. What sticks to the pot should stay in the pot. If making honey-nut caramels, be sure to keep the pot moving back and forth as you pour so that the nuts don't float away and congregate around the edge of the pan.

Set the pan on a rack in a cool part of your kitchen and don't disturb until the caramel is fully cool and set, at least 5 hours, but preferably overnight.

Run a table knife around the edges of the pan and turn the caramel out onto an oiled cutting board. Peel off the parchment. With a chef's knife, cut into 100 squares (about ¾ inch each) and wrap each one snugly in cellophane or other candy wrappers. Once cut, the caramels will slowly lose their shape, so it's important to wrap them right away. The wrapped caramels will keep for about four weeks if stored in an airtight container at room temperature.

—Jennifer Davis

Tips for Caramel-Making Success

Caramels aren't difficult; you just need to be attentive. You'll get excellent results if you simply take extra care at a few crucial points in the process.

Start by buttering the pan (and parchment) so the caramels will release easily later.

Brush the sides of the pot with a wet pastry brush to dissolve stray sugar crystals and to prevent the caramel from recrystallizing.

As you stir in the cream, the caramel will boil furiously, so stir with care.

Don't scrape the pot when you pour the caramel into the buttered pan or you could cause the caramel to recrystallize.

Contributors

Fine Cooking would like to thank all the talented and generous contributors who have shared their recipes with our readers.

Bruce Aidells is the founder of the Aidells Sausage Company and one of the country's foremost authorities on meat; his most recent book is *Bruce Aidells's Complete Book of Pork*.

Pam Anderson, a contributing editor to *Fine Cooking*, is the author of many cookbooks, including *The Perfect Recipe*. She is the food columnist for *USA Weekend* magazine.

Jennifer Armentrout, a graduate of the Culinary Institute of America, is the Test Kitchen Manager for *Fine Cooking* magazine.

John Ash teaches wine training and cooking classes around the world. His latest book is *Cooking One on One: Private Lessons from a Master Teacher*. John's previous book, *From the Earth to the Table*, received IACP awards for Cookbook of the Year and Best American Cookbook and was nominated for the James Beard Foundation's Best American Cookbook.

Nancy Verde Barr is the author of *We Called It Macaroni* and *Make It Italian*, among other cookbooks. She teaches cooking classes and has served as executive chef to Julia Child.

David Bonom is a New Jersey-based food writer.

Julianna Grimes Bottcher is a freelance food writer and recipe developer. In 2004, she started her own food consulting business, Flavor Matters, Inc.

Floyd Cardoz is the executive chef at Tabla restaurant in New York City, which serves modern American cuisine infused with the sensual flavors and spices of Floyd's native India.

Gary Coley is a private chef in Atlanta. He trained at Dumas Père school for chefs and apprenticed at the Ritz-Carlton in Chicago.

Amanda Cushman is a Los Angeles-based private chef and caterer; she also teaches private cooking classes.

Derrin Davis is one half of a brother-sister food writing team in the Pacific Northwest. He graduated from Johnson & Wales University and is now a chef at Bay House restaurant in Lincoln City, on the Oregon coast.

Jennifer Davis owns Samaki Chocolates in Lethbridge, Alberta.

Erica De Mane is a cookbook author and food writer specializing in Italian cooking.

Tasha DeSerio was a cook at Chez Panisse Restaurant & Café for five years. She currently teaches and writes about cooking and is the proprietor of Berkeley, California's Olive Green Catering.

Paula Disbrowe is a former food editor and a food writer who has cooked in France and Italy; her cookbook, *Cowgirl Cuisine*, will be published next spring.

Abigail Johnson Dodge is a contributing editor to *Fine Cooking* and a cookbook author; her book *The Weekend Baker* was nominated for a 2005 IACP award. Abby was the founding director of *Fine Cooking's* test kitchen.

Beth Dooley is a food and garden writer based in Minneapolis; she is the co-author with Lucia Watson of *Savoring The Seasons Of The Northern Heartland*.

Maryellen Driscoll is a freelance writer, editor, and recipe developer; she is *Fine Cooking's* editor at large.

Ali Edwards is one of the founding farmers of Dirty Girl Produce and runs The Green Table, an organic catering company, both in Santa Cruz, California.

Allison Ehri is *Fine Cooking's* test kitchen associate and food stylist.

Eve Felder is Associate Dean for Curriculum and Instruction for Culinary Arts at the Culinary Institute of American in Hyde Park, New York.

Claudia Fleming is a pastry chef in New York City. She is the recipient of the 2000 James Beard Award for Outstanding Pastry Chef.

Nathan Fong is a food writer and television host in Vancouver, British Columbia. He is also a food stylist for film and for print advertising.

Gordon Hamersley is the chef-owner of Hamersley's Bistro in Boston. Gordon is the recipient of many culinary awards and the author of the award-winning *Bistro Cooking at Home*.

Kate Hays is the chef-owner of Dish catering, based in Shelburne, Vermont, where she also does recipe testing, development, and food styling.

Peter Hoffman is chef-owner of Savoy restaurant in New York City. He is chair of the Chefs Collaborative and an active force in New York City's Greenmarkets.

Martha Holmberg is the food editor of *The Oregonian* newspaper in Portland, Oregon. She is the former editor and publisher of *Fine Cooking* magazine.

Jill Silverman Hough spent her first career as an advertising copywriter before becoming a food writer, recipe developer, and a cooking instructor at Copia, the American Center for Wine, Food and the Arts in Napa, California.

Irit Ishai is the pastry chef and owner of Sugar Butter Flour bakery in Santa Clara, California.

Raghavan Iyer was named cooking teacher of the year in 2004 by the IACP. He has written two award-winning cookbooks and is hard at work on a third. He also leads food and cultural tours to India.

Arlene Jacobs is a chef and cooking teacher in New York City; for many years, she worked with acclaimed chef Jean-Georges Vongerichten.

Sarah Jay is a former daily newspaper reporter, and is now the executive editor of *Fine Cooking*.

Elizabeth Karmel is one of America's top grilling experts. Her most recent cookbook is *Taming the Flame: Secrets to Hot and Quick Grilling* and *Low-and-Slow BBQ*.

Eva Katz has worked as a chef, caterer, teacher, recipe developer and tester, food stylist, and food writer. Eva is on the advisory board of the Cambridge School of Culinary Arts.

Ris Lacoste is the former award-winning executive chef of 1789 Restaurant in Washington, D.C. A member of the National Board of Directors for the American Institute of Wine and Food, Ris also serves on the board of and as a mentor for the Marriott Hospitality Public Charter High School.

Seen Lippert is a former cook at Chez Panisse and chef at several New York restaurants. She's now a member of Yale University's Sustainable Food Project.

Ruth Lively writes the In Season column for *Fine Cooking* magazine. She is the former senior editor of *Fine Gardening* magazine.

Lori Longbotham is a food writer and the author of several cookbooks, including most recently, *The Scoop: How to Change Store-Bought Ice Cream into Fabulous Desserts*. She has worked as a chef, caterer, recipe tester and developer, and food editor.

Deborah Madison is the author of several award-winning vegetarian cookbooks. A former cook at Chez Panisse, she is also active in the Slow Food movement, Seed Savers Exchange, and the Center for Sustainable Environments.

Waldy Malouf is the chef-owner of Beacon Restaurant in New York City, where he focuses on open-fire cooking. He has also written two cookbooks, most recently *High Heat*.

Luke Mangan is the owner of Salt Restaurant, Bistro Lulu, and Moorish in Sydney, Australia.

Domenica Marchetti is a former newspaper reporter who covered crime and other topics before it dawned on her that what she really wanted to write about was food. Her first cookbook is *Four Seasons of Italian Soups & Stews*.

Jennifer Martinkus is one half of a brother-sister food writing team. Jennifer worked as a caterer and private cook before becoming the food editor for *Delicious Living*. She's now a freelance food writer in Yakima, Washington.

Joanne McAllister Smart is a former *Fine Cooking* editor and the co-author of chef Scott Conant's *New Italian Cooking*. She is also the co-author of *Bistro Cooking at Home* and editor of *Fine Cooking's Cooking New American*, both IACP award winners.

Nancie McDermott is a food writer and cooking teacher specializing in the cuisines of Southeast Asia.

Jennifer McLagan is a Toronto-based food writer and stylist and the author of the IACP award-winning cookbook *Bones*. She has worked as a chef in her native Australia as well as London and Paris.

Umberto Menghi owns three popular restaurants in Vancouver, British Columbia, two in Whistler, and a restored 16th-century villa in the heart of rural Tuscany.

Susie Middleton is *Fine Cooking's* editor and a blue-ribbon graduate of the Institute of Culinary Education (formerly Peter Kump's New York Cooking School).

David Norman was the head bread baker at Bouley Bakery and Danube in Manhattan, and has been an instructor at the French Culinary Institute and the San Francisco Baking Institute.

Greg Patent is an award-winning cookbook author and baking expert. His book *Baking in America* won a 2003 James Beard award.

Brian Patterson is Hospitality Manager for the American Medical Association and an instructor at L'Academie de Cuisine cooking school in Bethesda, Maryland.

Frank Pellegrino is a co-owner of Rao's restaurant and the author of *Rao's Cookbook* and *Rao's Recipes from the Neighborhood*. Frank is also an actor who has appeared in films and television shows, including *The Sopranos*.

Scott Phillips graduated from Rochester Institute of Technology with a BFA in professional photographic illustration. He's the photography manager for all of The Taunton Press and photographs the majority of recipes in every issue of *Fine Cooking*.

Randall Price is a private chef with clients in Paris and Auvergne; he is the former chef to the American ambassador to Hungary.

Rebecca Rather is the owner of Rather Sweet Bakery in the Texas Hill Country town of Fredericksburg. Her first cookbook is *The Pastry Queen*.

Nicole Rees co-wrote the revised edition of *Understanding Baking*, a book on the science and technique of baking, as well as its companion recipe book, *The Baker's Manual*. She works as a baker, food writer, and food technologist in Portland, Oregon.

Leslie Revsin was a cookbook author and cooking teacher. She was the first woman chef at New York's Waldorf-Astoria hotel.

Tony Rosenfeld, a contributing editor to *Fine Cooking*, lives in Boston, where he also works as a food writer and restaurant consultant. His first cookbook is *150 Things to Make with Roast Chicken (and 50 Ways to Roast It)*.

Lynne Sampson is a former chef at The Herbfarm restaurant near Seattle and is now a food writer, editor, and recipe tester. She now teaches cooking classes in eastern Oregon's Wallowa Mountains.

Tania Segal is the chef-owner of Tania's Table, a catering company in Miami.

Maria Helm Sinskey is the former chef of San Francisco's PlumpJack Cafe and the author *In The Vineyard Kitchen: Menus Inspired by the Seasons*. She now oversees the culinary programs at Napa Valley's Robert Sinskey Vineyards, which she owns with her husband.

Bob Sloan teaches theater at The Dalton School in Manhattan. He is the author of six cookbooks, including *The Tailgating Cookbook*.

Stu Stein is the chef at Rivers restaurant in Portland, Oregon. Stu wrote *The Sustainable Kitchen: Passionate Cooking Inspired by Farms, Forests, and Oceans*.

Molly Stevens, a cooking teacher, cookbook author, and contributing editor to *Fine Cooking*, is the author of *Williams-Sonoma's New England*, and co-wrote *One Potato, Two Potato*. For her latest book, *All About Braising: The Art of Uncomplicated Cooking*, Molly nabbed both a James Beard and an IACP cookbook award.

Bill Telepan graduated from the Culinary Institute of America, trained in top restaurants in New York and France and was the executive chef at Manhattan's Judson Grill. He now has his his own restaurant, Telepan, on Manhattan's Upper West side.

Rori Trovato is an author and food stylist who has been developing recipes for leading food magazines for several years. She is the author of *Dishing with Style*. Rori teaches cooking in Provence in summer and lives in Santa Barbara, California.

Robb Walsh is a former editor in chief of *Chile Pepper* magazine. A two-time James Beard award winner and the restaurant critic of the *Houston Press*, Robb is also the author of *The Tex-Mex Cookbook: A History in Recipes and Photos*.

Lucia Watson is the chef-owner of Lucia's restaurant in Minneapolis. She frequently partners with writer Beth Dooley on projects, including their cookbook *Savoring The Seasons of the Northern Heartland*.

Joanne Weir has written seven cookbooks, including the recently re-released *From Tapas to Meze* and *Weir Cooking in the City*, which is a companion to her PBS television series of the same name. Joanne cooked for five years at Chez Panisse and is a frequent contributor to *Fine Cooking*.

Laura Werlin is a leading expert on American cheeses. She's the author of several cookbooks, including the award-winning *The New American Cheese*. Laura is on the board of the American Cheese Society.

Index